Running for Women

Jason R. Karp, PhD

Carolyn S. Smith, MD

Human Kinetics

Library of Congress Cataloging-in-Publication Data

Karp, Jason.
  Running for women / Jason R. Karp, Carolyn S. Smith.
    p. cm.
  Includes index.
  ISBN-13: 978-1-4504-0467-9 (soft cover)
  ISBN-10: 1-4504-0467-7 (soft cover)
  1. Running for women. I. Smith, Carolyn S., 1965- II. Title.
  GV1061.18.W66K37 2012
  796.42082--dc23
                              2012003780

ISBN-10: 1-4504-0467-7 (print)
ISBN-13: 978-1-4504-0467-9 (print)

This publication is written and published to provide accurate and authoritative information relevant to the subject matter presented. It is published and sold with the understanding that the author and publisher are not engaged in rendering legal, medical, or other professional services by reason of their authorship or publication of this work. If medical or other expert assistance is required, the services of a competent professional person should be sought.

Acquisitions Editor: Tom Heine; **Developmental Editor:** Heather Healy; **Assistant Editor:** Claire Marty; **Copyeditor:** Annette Pierce; **Indexer:** Nan N. Badgett; **Permissions Manager:** Martha Gullo; **Graphic Designer:** Nancy Rasmus; **Graphic Artist:** Julie L. Denzer; **Cover Designer:** Keith Blomberg; **Photographer (cover):** Corey Rich/Aurora Photos/age fotostock; **Photographer (interior):** Neil Bernstein, © Human Kinetics, unless otherwise noted; **Photo Asset Manager:** Laura Fitch; **Visual Production Assistant:** Joyce Brumfield; **Photo Production Manager:** Jason Allen; **Art Manager:** Kelly Hendren; **Associate Art Manager:** Alan L. Wilborn; **Illustrations:** © Human Kinetics, unless otherwise noted; **Printer:** United Graphics

We thank The High School of St. Thomas More in Champaign, Illinois, for assistance in providing the location for the bleacher hop photo for this book.

Human Kinetics books are available at special discounts for bulk purchase. Special editions or book excerpts can also be created to specification. For details, contact the Special Sales Manager at Human Kinetics.

Printed in the United States of America   10 9 8 7 6 5 4 3 2 1

The paper in this book is certified under a sustainable forestry program.

Human Kinetics
Website: www.HumanKinetics.com

United States: Human Kinetics
P.O. Box 5076
Champaign, IL 61825-5076
800-747-4457
e-mail: humank@hkusa.com

Canada: Human Kinetics
475 Devonshire Road Unit 100
Windsor, ON N8Y 2L5
800-465-7301 (in Canada only)
e-mail: info@hkcanada.com

Europe: Human Kinetics
107 Bradford Road
Stanningley
Leeds LS28 6AT, United Kingdom
+44 (0) 113 255 5665
e-mail: hk@hkeurope.com

Australia: Human Kinetics
57A Price Avenue
Lower Mitcham, South Australia 5062
08 8372 0999
e-mail: info@hkaustralia.com

New Zealand: Human Kinetics
P.O. Box 80
Torrens Park, South Australia 5062
0800 222 062
e-mail: info@hknewzealand.com

E5327

For my father, Monroe, whose long walking strides caused me to run to keep up. And for my mother, Muriel, a great athlete herself. In her memory, I will personally donate 10 percent of my royalties on every book sold to Susan G. Komen for the Cure.

- Jason Karp

In memory of my grandmother, Gertrude Gallagher Smith, the remarkable matriarch of our family who was ahead of her time and a pillar of strength and inspiration to me and women everywhere. And to my first track and cross country coaches, Ben Newson and Dick Greene, who recognized and nurtured my talent and instilled a love for the sport, for which I am forever grateful.

- Carolyn Smith

Contents

Preface   vii
Acknowledgments   xi

Part I   **Physiology**

1	Performance Factors and Sex Differences	3
2	Menstrual Cycle, Hormones, and Performance	23
3	Pregnancy	35
4	Menopause	49
5	Older Runners	65

Part II   **Training**

6	Components of Training	79
7	Base Building	93
8	Acidosis (Lactate) Threshold Training	101
9	Aerobic Power Training for $\dot{V}O_2max$	107
10	Speed and Strength Training	113
11	Building Your Training Program	131

Part III   **Health and Wellness**

12   Female Athlete Triad   143

13   Injuries and Female Runners   157

14   Performance Nutrition
         and Female Runners   187

Appendix: Evolution of Women's Competitive Running   207
Index   211
About the Authors   217

Preface

As best-selling author John Gray so decisively pointed out, men and women seem to be from different planets. In addition to the many psychological and behavioral differences, it is evident from the time we are boys and girls that there are also many anatomical, physiological, hormonal, and metabolic differences between males and females. Many of these differences influence girls' and women's response to running, which raises the question: should women train differently than men?

The past few decades have seen a significant rise in the number of physically active women and the number of women competing in running races. Females now account for more than 5.4 million road race finishers nationwide and represent 53 percent of race fields compared to only 23 percent in 1989. Women now exceed the number of male participants in every race distance except the marathon. The half-marathon currently has the largest female percentage (57 percent) of any U.S. road distance, with the percent flipping to a female majority in 2005. By contrast, in 1985, less than 20 percent of half-marathon finishers were female. Of the nearly 468,000 runners who completed a marathon in the United States in 2009, 40.4 percent of them were female.

As a result of the "women's running boom," women's running performances have improved at a much faster rate than those of men, who have been running competitively for a long time. Over the first 40 years of women's official competition in the marathon (1971-2011), the world record improved by 46 minutes and 17 seconds (25.5 percent). In comparison, over the first 40 years of men's official competition in the marathon (1908-1948), the world record improved by 29 minutes and 39 seconds (16.9 percent). At the other end of the distance-running spectrum, women have decreased their time in the mile (1,600 meters) from 6:13 in 1921 to the current world record of 4:12.56, an improvement of 32.3 percent, while men have decreased their time in the mile from 4:28 in 1852 to the current world record of 3:43.13, an improvement of 16.7 percent. Interestingly, women are slightly closer to their male counterparts in the marathon (9.5 percent) than in the mile (13.2 percent), differences that have remained pretty stable since the 1980s.

In response to the popularity of running among women, a great deal of scientific research has been undertaken to understand what characteristics influence the difference in running performance between the sexes, a difference that averages 10.7 percent in favor of men across all running distances, from the 100 meters to the marathon. The research starts with the heart. During puberty, men's hearts grow larger than those of women, creating a larger, more powerful pump. Men also have more oxygen-carrying hemoglobin in their blood, owing to their greater blood volume. Together, the larger heart and greater blood volume create a cardiovascular system that supplies a greater amount of oxygen to the working muscles, giving men a higher aerobic ceiling (expressed physiologically as the maximum volume of oxygen consumed per minute, or $\dot{V}O_2max$). As a result, men are able to sustain a faster running pace. This cardiovascular advantage for men explains why the best female runners don't run as fast as the best male runners in distance races up to the marathon.

In ultramarathons, however, during which the race is run at a slower pace, a narrowing of race performances between the sexes occurs. Cardiovascular differences become less important, and other characteristics, such as fuel use by the muscles and the ability to dissipate heat, become more important. Ultramarathons may represent a unique opportunity for women to excel; scientific research has revealed that women have a greater capacity than men to metabolize fat and conserve their limited store of carbohydrate (glycogen), which may give them an advantage for very long endurance activities. Although men run significantly faster than women at race distances from the 5K to the marathon, they do not run significantly faster in races longer than a marathon and sometimes don't run faster at all. For example, while the women's 5K and marathon world records are 12.4 and 9.5 percent slower than the men's 5K and marathon world records, the women's 100K world record is only 5.3 percent slower than the men's world record. It seems possible that elite women could beat elite men in ultramarathons. Research is revealing that women ultramarathon runners seem to have a greater resistance to fatigue than do equally trained men whose performances are superior up to the marathon distance.

And then, of course, there's estrogen. Whether you are a miler or an ultramarathoner, estrogen is the single biggest factor that differentiates you from the guy running next to you in a race. It is a powerful hormone, influencing many aspects of your physiology, including metabolism, glycogen storage, lung function, and bone health. The more we learn about estrogen, the more runner friendly it seems. Indeed, estrogen is so important to bone health that its deficiency, which is often caused by irregular or absent menstruation caused by a high level of training, is the most significant risk factor for osteoporosis in active women.

Given the widespread effects of estrogen and the cyclic changing of a woman's hormonal environment, it is evident that women should train differently than men or at least alter their training to account for the hormonal changes. So women should no longer simply follow what men are doing. How the changes in estrogen and its sister hormone progesterone across the menstrual cycle affect endurance performance and what implications they have for training is a big part of what this book is about and distinguishes this book from all others on the subject. We wrote *Running for Women* with you, the female runner, in mind. It is the only book that takes an in-depth approach to training female runners and is the resource that all female runners and coaches need. The purpose of this book is to explain what makes female runners unique and examine how these differences affect training, performance, health, and wellness.

The book is divided into three parts. Part I sets the conceptual framework by addressing the physiology of women, beginning with women's differentiating cardiorespiratory, hormonal, metabolic, muscular, and anatomical characteristics. It then discusses how female physiology—menstrual cycle, pregnancy, menopause, and aging—changes the body and affects training and performance. Part II focuses on the principles and components of training and the types of workouts that target women's different training needs and goals. It discusses the best times of the menstrual cycle to do various types of workouts and proposes guidelines for how women can manipulate their training programs around their cycles to maximize results. It also shows how women can use sex differences to their advantage in training and competition. Finally, part III examines the health and wellness of female runners. It discusses the consequences of disordered eating, osteoporosis, and menstrual irregularities (collectively known as the female athlete triad) and includes chapters on common running injuries and nutrition. It also recommends preventive measures to minimize the risk of injury and disease.

In this book, you'll get the perspective of two highly respected doctors and practitioners. As an exercise physiologist, nationally recognized running coach and award-winning personal trainer, speaker, and writer, Dr. Jason has seen firsthand the success that female runners can have when manipulating their training in response to their unique physiology. As a university sports medicine physician, successful ultramarathoner, and U.S. Olympic Marathon Trials qualifier, Dr. Carolyn works with female athletes every day and can appreciate everything that female runners experience. Together, the authors bring a unique combination of research- and medical-based expertise, coaching experience and, at least for one of them, success as a female runner.

This book gives you the information you need to become a faster, better, and healthier runner. More than simply a book on training, what follows is an exploration of the question, "How does an understanding of female physiology influence your training and racing?" In other words, "What's the deal with estrogen?"

Acknowledgments

I'd like to thank the editorial staff at Human Kinetics, including Tom Heine, Heather Healy, and Laurel Plotzke Garcia; my wonderful agent, Grace Freedson; my twin brother, Jack, for inspiring me to be as good of a writer as he is and for not making nearly as many jokes as he could have about a man writing a book about women; the many women who shared their stories and provided insight to this male writer; and my mother, Muriel, for always telling me how proud she was of me.

- Jason Karp

I am grateful to the editorial staff at Human Kinetics for their patience, suggestions, and critical appraisal; to my parents and sister, all better writers than I will ever be, for supporting me when writing became challenging; to my husband for always keeping me grounded; to my 100K teammates who inspire me to keep going; and to all the female athletes I have had the privilege to work with and learn from.

- Carolyn Smith

Part I
Physiology

Performance Factors and Sex Differences

Although running may seem like a simple activity, improving your running performance is highly scientific. To be able to run longer than a couple of minutes depends on your ability to supply the working muscles with oxygen and the ability of the muscles to use the available oxygen to convert fuel into usable energy. Whether you run a mile or an ultramarathon, it's almost all about oxygen. Distance-running performance, in particular, involves the integration of cardiorespiratory, muscular, metabolic, and neurological factors that function cooperatively to efficiently transfer the production of energy into running speed.

This chapter first examines the basic physiology of distance running. Understanding how energy is produced for running is the basis for understanding how to train most effectively. After all, if you want to get faster or run without injury, every workout you do should have a specific, physiological purpose. The chapter then examines what makes female runners unique and shows you how to capitalize on that uniqueness. When training to run, it's important to consider sex because men and women have different physiological, hormonal, metabolic, and anatomical characteristics.

Energy Production

As you may have learned in a high school biology class, the energy to move your body comes from the chemical breakdown of a high-energy metabolic compound found in your muscles called adenosine triphosphate, or ATP. ATP is broken down into its two constituents: adenosine diphosphate (ADP) and inorganic phosphate (P_i). Because your muscles store only a small, emergency amount of ATP, you must constantly resynthesize it before you can break it down. The formation and resynthesis of ATP is thus a circular process: ATP is broken down into ADP and P_i, and then ADP and P_i combine to resynthesize ATP (figure 1.1). Simplistically speaking, running faster comes down to increasing the rate at which ATP is resynthesized so it can be broken down to liberate energy for muscle contraction.

Like many other animals, humans produce ATP through three metabolic pathways that consist of many enzyme-catalyzed chemical reactions. Two of these pathways, the phosphagen system and anaerobic glycolysis, do not use oxygen to create ATP and are therefore referred to as anaerobic. The third pathway uses oxygen to create ATP and is therefore referred to as aerobic.

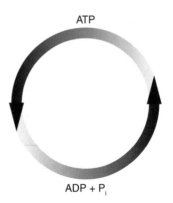

Figure 1.1 ATP breaks down into ADP and P_i, which recombine to create ATP again.

Phosphagen System

During short-term, intense activities, your muscles need to produce a large amount of power, creating a high demand for ATP. The phosphagen system, also called the ATP-CP system, is the quickest way to resynthesize ATP. Creatine phosphate (CP), which is stored in the skeletal muscles, donates a phosphate to ADP to produce ATP:

$$ADP + CP \rightarrow ATP + C$$

This process does not use carbohydrate or fat; the regeneration of ATP comes solely from stored CP. Because this process does not need oxygen to resynthesize ATP, it is anaerobic, or oxygen independent. As the fastest way to resynthesize ATP, the phosphagen system is the predominant energy system used for all-out sprinting that lasts 10 to 15 seconds. For all-out running that lasts between 15 and 30 seconds, both the phosphagen system and anaerobic glycolysis provide energy. However, because a limited amount of CP and ATP is stored in your muscles, fatigue occurs rapidly.

Anaerobic Glycolysis

Anaerobic glycolysis is the predominant energy system used for all-out running that lasts from 30 seconds to about two minutes (about 200 to 800 meters) and is the second-fastest way to resynthesize ATP. During anaerobic glycolysis, carbohydrate, either in the form of glucose (sugar) in your blood or its stored form of glycogen in your muscles and liver, is broken down through a series of chemical reactions. Every molecule of glucose broken down through glycolysis produces two molecules of usable ATP. Thus, this pathway produces very little energy, but the trade-off is that you get the energy quickly, so you can run fast.

You rely on anaerobic glycolysis when oxygen is not supplied fast enough to meet your muscles' needs for ATP. When this happens, your muscles lose their

Myths of Lactic Acid

As a runner, you have probably heard a lot about lactic acid, especially concerning its relationship to fatigue. Lactic acid gets a bad rap. Lactic acid is the final chemical product of glycolysis and is produced when oxygen is not supplied fast enough to meet your muscles' needs for energy. From the time Nobel Prize winners A.V. Hill and Otto Meyerhof discovered in the 1920s that lactic acid is produced during fatiguing muscle contractions in the absence of oxygen, lactic acid has been the scapegoat for fatigue. Before debunking the myth, let's deal with the semantics. Lactic acid does not exist or function as such inside your body. When lactic acid is produced in your muscles, it immediately converts to lactate, which is a different chemical compound.

No experimental evidence exists proving a cause-and-effect relationship between lactate and fatigue. Fatigue is caused by several things, depending on the intensity of the activity, none of which have to do with lactate. While lactate increases dramatically when you run fast, so do other metabolites, including potassium and the two constituents of ATP: ADP and P_i. Scientists have found that these other metabolites cause fatigue by affecting different aspects of muscle contraction. Part of the confusion likely results from the fact that scientists use blood lactate as an indirect measure of acidosis because measuring the lactate concentration in your blood is easy.

While lactate rises in your muscles when they rely heavily on anaerobic glycolysis for energy, which occurs during races from 400 meters to 10K, we often hear runners, coaches, and television commentators also talk about lactic acid in races like the marathon, especially when it comes to recovery strategies afterward to *flush out the lactic acid*. However, in half-marathons, marathons, and ultramarathons, lactate does not accumulate because you run those races at a speed below your acidosis threshold, the fastest sustainable aerobic speed above which acidosis occurs; see the section on metabolic factors (page 12) later in this chapter. At these distances, your muscles become depleted of glycogen. If no carbohydrate is left in your muscles, there is no glycolysis, and lactate cannot be produced. At the finish line of a marathon, your blood lactate level is no different than it was at the start line.

In races in which lactate does accumulate (400 meters to 10K), microscopic proteins transport the lactate to other places, such as the heart and liver, where it is used for fuel. Your heart uses lactate as a fuel and your liver, when it senses that your glycogen stores and blood glucose are running low, converts lactate into glucose so you can continue relying on glycolysis and maintain a fast running pace. Your liver is very smart.

Lactate has also been wrongly pegged as causing a sensation of burning in the muscles during intense exercise and muscle soreness in the days after a hard workout. Lactate does not cause muscle acidosis and so does not cause burning. As for the soreness, muscle and blood lactate return to their preexercise, resting levels in 30 to 60 minutes after your workout, so any lactate that accumulated during the workout is long gone by the time you feel sore. Muscle soreness is the result of training-induced microscopic tears in the muscle fibers, followed by inflammation. This is a normal part of training. The soreness typically worsens during the first 24 hours after exercise, peaks from 24 to 72 hours, then subsides in five to seven days as the muscles heal.

ability to contract effectively because of an increase in hydrogen ions, which causes the muscle pH to decrease, a condition called acidosis. The concentration of other metabolites, including potassium ions and the two constituents of ATP (ADP and P_i) also increases. Acidosis and the accumulation of these other metabolites cause several problems inside muscles. These include inhibition of specific enzymes involved in metabolism and muscle contraction; inhibition of the release of calcium, which is the trigger for muscle contraction, from its storage site in muscles; and interference with muscles' electrical charges, ultimately leading to a decrease in muscle force production and your running speed.

Aerobic System

Because humans evolved for aerobic activities, it's not surprising that the aerobic system, which is dependent on oxygen, is the most complex of the three energy systems. The metabolic reactions that take place in the presence of oxygen are responsible for most of the energy your cells produce. Races longer than two minutes (800 meters to ultramarathons) rely most heavily on the aerobic system. However, aerobic metabolism is the slowest way to resynthesize ATP. The aerobic system uses blood glucose, muscle and liver glycogen, and fat as fuels to resynthesize ATP. The aerobic use of carbohydrate produces 38 molecules of ATP for every molecule of glucose broken down. Thus, the aerobic system produces 19 times more ATP than does glycolysis from each glucose molecule. If that sounds like a lot, using fat gives you much more ATP—a whopping 130 molecules of ATP, give or take, depending on the specific fatty acid being used.

As a distance runner, your running performance, whether recreational or elite, depends mostly on the aerobic system. The more developed your aerobic system, the faster you'll be able to run before you begin to rely on the anaerobic energy pathways and experience the consequent fatigue. The next section takes a look at the factors involved in synthesizing ATP aerobically because these are the factors you'll want to improve with training.

Which pathway you use for the primary production of ATP depends on how quickly you need it and how much of it you need. Sprinting, for instance, requires energy much more quickly than jogging, necessitating the reliance on the phosphagen system and anaerobic glycolysis. Conversely, running a 10K or marathon relies more heavily on the aerobic system. Regardless of how quickly or slowly you run or the type of workout you're running, you never produce ATP through only one energy system, but rather by the coordinated response of all three energy systems contributing to different degrees.

Think of three dials that are always being adjusted to optimize the production of energy. When you race 100 meters, the phosphagen dial is turned up very high, while the other two dials are turned down low. When you run a marathon, the aerobic-system dial is turned up very high, while the other two dials are turned down low. When you race a 5K, the aerobic-system dial is turned up high, the anaerobic-glycolysis dial is turned to medium, and the phosphagen system dial is turned down low.

Cardiovascular Factors

Cardiovascular factors influencing running include those that affect the volume of blood your heart pumps and the transportation of oxygen to your muscles. When you run, your heart sends blood to places that demand it, such as your skeletal muscles. The amount of blood your heart pumps with each beat is called the stroke volume and is dependent on several factors: the heart's ability to contract quickly and forcefully so it can squeeze blood out of its left ventricle, the quick return of deoxygenated blood from the muscles back to the heart through the venous circulation so that oxygenated blood can be pumped out again from the heart, the amount of pressure in the left ventricle and in the aorta, and the size of the left ventricle.

Having a lot of pressure in the left ventricle as it is filling with blood is beneficial because it creates a stretch on the walls of the left ventricle, which will then contract more forcefully and push out a lot of blood. On the other hand, excessive pressure in the aorta creates a large pressure head that the heart must work against as it pumps blood. The larger the left ventricle, the more blood it can hold; the more blood it can hold, the more it can pump. One of the most elegant adaptations to distance-running training is an increase in the size of the left ventricle of the heart so it can generate a larger stroke volume. Since it was first documented in seven-time Boston Marathon winner Clarence DeMar, scientists and physicians have recognized that an enlarged heart as a result of endurance training, known as *athlete's heart*, is a positive physiological adaptation.

If you multiply your stroke volume by your heart rate (the number of times your heart beats per minute), you get cardiac output, the volume of blood your heart pumps per minute. How high your cardiac output is when you are running at your heart's maximum capability to pump blood (1.5- to 2-mile race pace [2,400-3,200 meters]) is extremely important for your success as a distance runner and is one of the key factors you want to improve.

Once the blood leaves the heart, its flow to the muscles depends on a number of factors. These include the redistribution of blood away from other, less important, tissues to the active muscles, and the resistance of blood flow through the blood vessels. It also depends on the adequate dilation of blood vessels, which depends on the interplay between two branches of your nervous system and their associated hormones: the sympathetic (excitatory, causing vasoconstriction) and parasympathetic (calming, causing vasodilation) nervous systems. Flow to the muscles also depends on the oxygen-transport capacity of the blood, which is determined by red blood cell volume and the amount of hemoglobin, which transports oxygen in the red blood cells; the amount of myoglobin, which transports oxygen in the muscles; and the density and volume of capillaries within the muscle fibers. The greater the network of capillaries around your muscle fibers, the shorter the diffusion distance is for oxygen from the capillaries to the mitochondria, the important microscopic factories responsible for aerobic metabolism.

Muscular Factors

Muscles are wonderfully complex structures responsible for functions such as metabolism and movement. Getting blood from the heart to the muscles is only half the story. Once oxygen is delivered to the muscles, the muscles have to use the oxygen to regenerate energy for muscle contraction.

Oxygen Use

The amount of oxygen muscles extract and use depends primarily on how many mitochondria the muscles have. The number of mitochondrial enzymes is also an important determinant of running performance because enzymes, through their catalyzing effect on chemical reactions, control the rate at which aerobic metabolism functions.

Together, the cardiac output and the amount of oxygen extracted and used by the muscles determine the volume of oxygen that muscles consume ($\dot{V}O_2$). As you increase your running pace from an easy jog to a hard run to running as fast as you can, $\dot{V}O_2$ increases, first very quickly and then more slowly, to keep up with the demand of the run until you reach the maximum volume of oxygen you can consume per minute ($\dot{V}O_2max$). Once you reach the maximum rate at which your muscles can consume oxygen, some of the energy needed to continue running at that pace is supplied to your muscles through anaerobic glycolysis. Because fatigue occurs much more rapidly when you start to rely on anaerobic metabolism, the higher your aerobic ceiling ($\dot{V}O_2max$), the better distance runner you'll be because you'll delay your reliance on oxygen-independent metabolism.

$\dot{V}O_2max$ is the single best indicator of a person's aerobic fitness. Since it was first measured in humans in the 1920s, it has become one of the most often measured physiological characteristics in the field of exercise physiology. Although having a high $\dot{V}O_2max$ alone is not enough to enable you to run a fast 5K, it gives you access into the club. You simply cannot run fast without a high $\dot{V}O_2max$. It is especially important for the middle-distance races, 800 meters to 5K, which are run at or close to 100 percent $\dot{V}O_2max$.

One of the biggest questions, even arguments, in the field of exercise physiology is whether $\dot{V}O_2max$ is limited more by cardiac factors or by muscular factors. While unfit people are equally limited by cardiac and muscular factors because they lack both a high blood flow to the muscles and abundant metabolic machinery, highly trained distance runners seem to be limited more by cardiac factors. After all, there is a structural limit to how big the left ventricle of the heart—and thus stroke volume and cardiac output—can become with training. Training appears to shift the limiting factors away from a metabolic restriction on $\dot{V}O_2max$ and toward a limit on oxygen supply. In part II, we'll discuss how you can decrease these limitations with training.

Having a high $\dot{V}O_2$max alone is not enough to improve your running. Runners with the same $\dot{V}O_2$max do not often cross the finish line together in races. In 1930, David Dill and his colleagues at Harvard University were among the first physiologists to show that marked differences exist in the amount of oxygen runners use when running at the same speeds and that these differences in *economy* of oxygen use could be a major factor explaining differences in running performance. Running economy is the volume of oxygen ($\dot{V}O_2$) you use when running at submaximum speeds. For example, when you run at a 10:00-, 9:00-, or 8:00-mile pace, you consume a specific amount of oxygen every minute to maintain each of those paces. And the amount increases the faster the pace.

Running economy is an important indicator of running performance and is influenced by several factors, including running mechanics, the proportion of slow-twitch fibers in the muscles, the density of mitochondria in the muscles, and body weight. If two runners have the same $\dot{V}O_2$max, but runner A uses 70 percent and runner B uses 80 percent of that $\dot{V}O_2$max while running at 8:00-mile pace, that pace feels easier for runner A because runner A is more economical. Therefore, runner A can run at a faster pace before feeling the same amount of fatigue as runner B. With the same $\dot{V}O_2$max and superior running economy, runner A would almost surely beat runner B in a race.

Muscle Contraction

Running performance is influenced not only by factors related to oxygen consumption, but also by factors related to muscle fiber recruitment and contraction, muscle force production, and resistance to fatigue. Muscle contraction begins with the nerves. The central nervous system sends a signal to a motor neuron, which integrates with muscle fibers. Under the action of a specific neurotransmitter, the signal propagates deep inside the muscle fibers, causing the release of calcium from its storage site and triggering muscle contraction by the complex interaction of specific microscopic proteins.

In 1957, Nobel Prize winner Andrew Huxley discovered how those microscopic proteins—actin and myosin (see figure 1.2, page 10)—interact. Myosin, which looks like a rowboat with oars at an angle, attaches to actin, which looks like two strings of pearls twisted together. The paddle portion of myosin, which contains ATP, binds to actin and, when ATP is broken down, pulls it so that actin slides past myosin. The mechanism is much like the movement of the oars of a rowboat, except that the water (actin) moves past the stationary boat (myosin). This movement happens among millions of actin and myosin proteins within each muscle fiber, with all of the actin proteins from opposing sides moving closer together, causing the entire muscle to shorten. The more actin and myosin proteins in your muscles, the more force they can produce. A boat with eight oars stroking the water is stronger and more powerful than a boat with two.

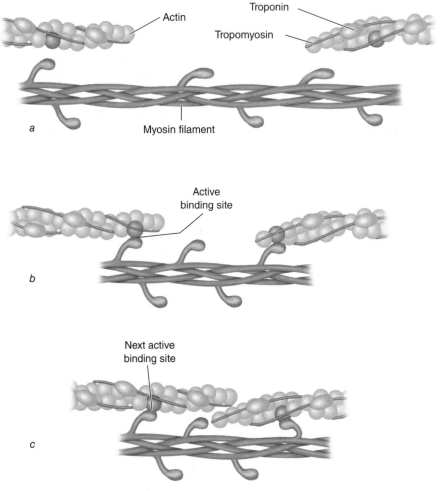

Figure 1.2 Myosin and actin use a ratchetlike action to shorten a muscle fiber from (a) a relaxed position, to (b) a contracting position, and to (c) a fully contracted position.

Types of Muscle Fiber

The specific types of fibers that make up individual muscles greatly influence your running performance over different distances and the way you adapt to training. Humans have three types of muscle fibers as well as gradations between them. The proportions among them are genetically determined. Slow-twitch (type I) fibers are recruited for aerobic activities because they have many characteristics needed for endurance, for example, a large network of capillaries to supply oxygen, lots of myoglobin to transport oxygen, and lots of mitochondria—the aerobic factories that contain enzymes responsible for aerobic metabolism. True to their name, slow-twitch fibers contract slowly, relatively speaking, and are resistant to fatigue. People can run for hours at a time because they rely on slow-twitch muscle fibers.

Fast-twitch (type II) fibers are recruited for anaerobic activities because they have many characteristics needed for strength, speed, and power, such as large stores of creatine phosphate and glycogen and an abundance of the enzymes involved in the anaerobic metabolic pathway of glycolysis. They contract quickly and fatigue easily. Fast-twitch fibers come in two forms: fast-twitch A (type IIa) and fast-twitch B (type IIb). Fast-twitch-B fibers are recruited for short, intense activities, such as sprinting, jumping, and lifting very heavy weights. They are also recruited during aerobic activities once the slow-twitch fibers and fast-twitch-A fibers have fatigued. Fast-twitch-A fibers possess both endurance and power characteristics and represent a transition between slow-twitch fibers and fast-twitch-B fibers. Fast-twitch-A fibers are recruited for prolonged anaerobic activities that require relatively high forces, such as running a long sprint and carrying heavy objects, and are also recruited during aerobic activities to help support the workload of the slow-twitch fibers. They are more resistant to fatigue than the fast-twitch-B fibers. In addition to the three major divisions of muscle fibers, hybrid forms of these fiber types also exist.

You can see the difference between the fiber types in the meat of turkey or chicken. The dark meat, so colored because of its myoglobin content, is composed of slow-twitch fibers, and the white meat is composed of fast-twitch fibers. But if you want to run a great marathon, don't reach for the dark meat too quickly. Unfortunately, the type of meat you eat has no impact on your endurance or sprinting ability. Muscle fiber composition is largely genetic. You are born with specific proportions of slow-twitch, fast-twitch-A, and fast-twitch-B fibers.

Distance runners have a greater proportion of slow-twitch fibers in the muscles used to run than sprinters do. However, the percentage of slow-twitch fibers varies a great deal among runners. There is some evidence, not completely validated, that women have more slow-twitch muscle fibers than men, which, if true, may contribute to greater long-endurance performance, while subtracting from their sprint performance. Although the proportions of slow-twitch and fast-twitch muscle fibers vary from person to person, both the structure and metabolic capacity of individual muscle fibers may be amenable to change with specific, extreme training.

For example, aerobic training increases the enzyme activity of the Krebs cycle in slow-twitch fibers, while sprint training increases the glycolytic enzyme activity of fast-twitch fibers. Although it does not seem possible to convert a slow-twitch fiber into a fast-twitch fiber or vice versa—making it impossible for an elite marathon runner to become an elite sprinter and vice versa—there does seem to be some plasticity between the fast-twitch fiber subtypes. For example, maximal or near maximal strength training has been shown to convert fast-twitch-B fibers to fast-twitch-A fibers, suggesting that training can cause a genetic transformation among the fast-twitch fiber subtypes.

Instead of recruiting individual muscle fibers to run, you recruit motor units—groups of muscle fibers innervated by a single motor neuron. All muscle fibers of a motor unit are of the same type: slow twitch, fast twitch A, or fast twitch B.

All of the muscle fibers of a motor unit either contract or they don't. There is no such thing as a partial contraction in which only some of the fibers contract. Like a light, fibers are either on or off. You vary the amount of muscle force by varying the number of motor units you contract and the frequency that the central nervous system recruits those motor units, not by varying their degree of contraction.

Motor units are recruited along a gradient dictated by the size of the motor unit, specifically, the size of the motor axon of the neuron supplying the motor unit. This condition is known as the size principle. Motor units with a small motor axon diameter, which contain slow-twitch muscle fibers, have the lowest firing threshold and are recruited first. Demands for larger forces or faster speeds are met by the recruitment of increasingly larger motor units. Motor units with the largest axon diameter, which contain fast-twitch-B fibers, have the highest firing threshold and are recruited last. Thus, regardless of your running pace, slow-twitch motor units are always recruited first. When you're jogging, slow-twitch motor units may be the only ones recruited. When you're running fast, such as during an interval workout or sprinting, slow-twitch motor units are recruited first, followed by fast twitch A and, if needed, fast twitch B.

Fast-twitch motor units are also recruited to pick up the slack of fatiguing slow-twitch motor units, even when the speed is slow. For example, when running long distances or even when holding a one-pound dumbbell in your hand, slow-twitch motor units are initially the only motor units recruited. But continue your run or hold that one-pound dumbbell long enough and the slow-twitch motor units will eventually fatigue, forcing recruitment of fast-twitch motor units to continue the task. Thus, the size principle gives us insight into how to recruit, and thus train, fast-twitch motor units: go intense, go fast, or go long. Recruiting fast-twitch motor units by running long enough to fatigue the slow-twitch motor units means that you won't experience the negative consequence of acidosis that usually accompanies the recruitment of fast-twitch motor units because the run is aerobic. We'll discuss more about different methods of training your slow-twitch and fast-twitch motor units in part II.

Metabolic Factors

At slow running speeds, oxygen is adequate to meet the demand of the muscle cells. At faster speeds, reliance on anaerobic metabolism for the production of energy is greater, and aerobic metabolism can't keep up. When this happens, hydrogen ions accumulate in the muscles and blood, decreasing the pH and causing metabolic acidosis and fatigue. The acidosis threshold signifies the transition between running that is almost purely aerobic and running that includes significant anaerobic metabolism. The acidosis threshold is often called the lactate threshold because, as noted earlier, lactate accumulates at the same time as acidosis develops and is easy to measure.

All running speeds have an anaerobic contribution, although when running slower than acidosis threshold pace the contribution is negligible. Thus, the acidosis threshold is an important determinant of distance-running performance because it represents the fastest speed you can sustain aerobically without a significant anaerobic contribution and the subsequent development of metabolic acidosis. The longer the race, the more important your acidosis threshold is because the more important it becomes to hold a solid pace for a long time.

The ability to metabolize fat also influences running performance because the muscles' preferred fuel—carbohydrate—is limiting, providing enough energy for only about 100 minutes of running. By contrast, humans' store of fat is virtually unlimited, with enough to fuel about five days of running or about 1,000 miles (1,610K) of walking for a 145-pound (66 kg) person with 18 percent body fat. At slow running speeds, some of carbohydrate's metabolic responsibility for regenerating energy is relieved by fat in the form of free fatty acids in the blood and triglyceride molecules inside the muscles. Even with the contribution of fat helping to delay the depletion of carbohydrate, running at a moderate pace, 70 to 75 percent $\dot{V}O_2max$, can only be sustained for two to three hours.

Physiological Sex Differences and Implications for Training and Performance

Sex is determined by sex chromosomes. Your cells have 46 chromosomes, distributed in 23 pairs. Despite what men and women think about each other, you and your male counterpart are more alike than you are different because 22 of the chromosomal pairs are the same in both sexes. However, it's that final pair—the sex chromosomes—that makes all the difference. Women have two X chromosomes and men have one X chromosome and one Y chromosome. The sex chromosomes are responsible for all of the sexual characteristics, including reproductive anatomy and the differences in muscle mass, heart size, and body fat between men and women. Table 1.1 (page 14) provides a summary of these differences for runners aged 20 to 30 years.

Hormonal Differences

Hormones are messengers that make cells act a certain way. The two major hormones that differentiate men and women are testosterone and estrogen. Indeed, testosterone is the single biggest factor that makes a man a man, and estrogen is the single biggest factor that makes a woman a woman. Estrogen, which was discovered in the 1920s, actually refers to a group of steroid hormones that include estrone, estradiol, and estriol. For most of your adult life, from menarche to menopause, the predominant estrogen is estradiol. Estriol is the primary estrogen during pregnancy, and estrone is produced during menopause.

Before puberty, the level of testosterone in the blood is similar between the sexes, which is why young girls can often run just as fast as boys. During puberty, however, things change. Testosterone creates taller, more muscular males, while estrogen increases fat deposition in the hips of females and the development of

Table 1.1 Physiological Sex Differences Between Women and Men (Aged 20-30 Years)

Physiological characteristic	Women	Men
Sex-specific hormones*	Estrogen: 30-200 pg/ml Progesterone: 0.5-15 ng/ml Testosterone: <500 pg/ml	Estrogen: <5 pg/ml Progesterone: <0.5 ng/ml Testosterone: 500-10,000 pg/ml
Anatomy	Wider hips Larger Q-angle	Wider shoulders
Average body fat	27%	15%
Essential fat	12%	3%
Maximum cardiac output	20 L/min	30 L/min
Hemoglobin*	13.7 g/dl (normal range is 12-16 g/dl)	15.8 g/dl (normal range is 14-18 g/dl)
Blood volume	4.5-5 L	5-6 L
Maximum oxygen consumption ($\dot{V}O_2$max)	34-41 ml/kg/min	40-48 ml/kg/min
Metabolism	Greater reliance on fat	Greater reliance on glycogen and protein during prolonged exercise

*pg/ml=picograms per milliliter, ng/ml=nanograms per milliliter, g/dl=grams per deciliter.

Adapted from R.A. Robergs and S.O. Roberts, 1997, *Exercise physiology: Exercise, performance, and clinical applications* (St. Louis: Mosby), 566.

breasts. While testosterone and other male-specific hormones, called androgens, occur in adult females, they do so to a much smaller degree than in males. After puberty, men have about 10 times the level of testosterone as women. Androgens are important hormones for protein synthesis, which explains why men grow larger muscles than women in response to strength training. These hormonal changes during puberty cause in part the differences in physical performance between boys and girls during adolescence that were minimized or even absent before puberty.

In addition to the development of secondary sexual characteristics, estrogen plays a variety of roles, including endometrial and uterine growth and vaginal wall thickening for the preparation of pregnancy, bone protection, blood coagulation, menstrual cycle functioning, cholesterol production, and salt and water retention, just to name a few. Even the pathology of certain diseases, such as breast cancer, are influenced by the actions of estrogen. Many of these estrogen-influencing roles have huge ramifications for female runners. For example, the most important determinant of bone mineral density in women is the circulating concentration of estrogen. Any condition that reduces estrogen concentration, e.g., amenorrhea, which is often a negative consequence of a large training volume, negatively affects bone remodeling, which explains why your risk for osteoporosis and fractures increases dramatically with amenorrhea and after menopause, when there is a lack of estrogen. Indeed, estrogen deficiency caused by amenorrhea is the most significant risk factor for osteoporosis in active women.

Studies have also shown that estrogen influences pulmonary function, body temperature, and the plasma volume of the blood, the latter affecting fluid retention and hydration status. The effects of estrogen on fluid distribution and control of body temperature may make running in the heat more challenging for women than for men. For example, when estrogen levels are high, baseline body temperature is reset to a higher value to prepare for the possible fertilization of an egg. As a result, you begin sweating at a higher body temperature. Your ability to dilate the small blood vessels under your skin also decreases, which compromises your ability to release heat.

Although estrogen is a woman's most significant hormone, other hormones also affect a woman's physiology. Progesterone, which is produced in the ovaries and in the placenta during pregnancy, supports many actions that prepare for the receipt of a fertilized egg and the development of the fetus. Its actions are often amplified in the presence of estrogen. Studies have shown that both estrogen and progesterone affect a woman's breathing during exercise. Progesterone in particular has been shown to stimulate breathing and increase the severity of asthma symptoms, which may increase the perception of effort during workouts.

Luteinizing hormone and follicle-stimulating hormone, which also exist in men to synthesize testosterone and maintain sperm production, function in women to stimulate ovulation, the production of progesterone, and the conversion of testosterone to estrogen. These hormones, along with the running-related influences of estrogen and progesterone throughout the menstrual cycle, will be discussed more in chapter 2.

Anatomical Differences

Your anatomy is largely influenced by your bones, which provide shape to your body. Like a fickle homeowner who can't decide whether the kitchen should be modeled in English country or art deco, bones constantly remodel themselves. Bone cells called osteoclasts remove small areas of old bone, a process called resorption, and other cells called osteoblasts synthesize new bone in its place, a process called formation. This cyclical process of bone resorption and formation occurs throughout your life. Formation exceeds resorption until age 25 to 30, when bone mineral density (BMD, the most-often measured indicator of bone strength) peaks for both sexes. However, the peak bone mineral density achieved by women is less than that achieved by men.

During your 30s, resorption begins to exceed formation, with BMD decreasing by about 1 percent per year. Nutrition, hormones, and physical activity also affect bone remodeling. Because bone strength is proportional to the square of its density, small reductions in BMD are associated with large reductions in bone strength. Therefore, you need to be more careful than male runners in how you progress with your training and increase running mileage, especially if you're experiencing irregularities in your menstrual cycle, which will reduce bone-protecting estrogen (see chapter 2).

Before puberty, body structure is similar between boys and girls. Until about 10 years of age, boys and girls are similar in body weight, height, leg length, and upper-arm circumference. During puberty, boys develop larger shoulders and girls develop larger, wider hips. Women's smaller shoulders make it more difficult to develop upper-body strength, giving women weaker upper bodies than men throughout adulthood. Because women have narrower shoulders and are typically shorter than men, they have a larger pelvic width-to-height ratio and shoulder-to-hip ratio then men.

Women's wider hips cause the femur (thighbone) to create a more pronounced angle between the pelvis and the knee than it does in a man. This angle is called the quadriceps angle, or Q-angle. A wide Q-angle pulls the patella (kneecap) off center from the tibia (shinbone). Tracking of the patella against the femur depends on the direction of the force produced by the quadriceps. A wide Q-angle causes more lateral movement of the patella as the quadriceps contract, which can potentially put female runners at a greater risk for knee injuries than male runners (see chapter 13).

A larger Q-angle also puts women at a mechanical disadvantage when running. After your leg lands on the ground, you must push off the ground to propel yourself forward. The application of muscular force has both a magnitude and direction. And the direction the force is applied has both a horizontal and vertical component. The more parallel your leg is to your body when it's on the ground, or the smaller the Q-angle, the greater the muscle force transmitted in the vertical direction to the tendons that move the bones.

Wide hips and a large Q-angle put the femur at an angle when the leg is on the ground. Thus, more force is dispersed in different directions, with some of the force of the muscles surrounding the femur (quadriceps in the front and hamstrings in the back) being lost in the horizontal direction rather than propelling you forward. If you ever watch elite female runners, you'll notice they have very narrow hips that more closely resemble those of male runners. Research has also shown that the hip width of very good female runners is similar to that of both athletic and even nonathletic males. Narrow hips allow runners to direct more of the muscular force into forward propulsion.

Women's anatomy also affects their stride mechanics. Research has shown that female runners take shorter strides than male runners when running at the same speed. Because running speed is equal to stride length multiplied by stride rate, female runners compensate for the shorter stride length by using a quicker stride rate than male runners. Although it's interesting that the combination of stride rate and stride length differs between female and male runners, it's not completely clear why women take shorter strides.

The obvious reason would seem to be that women are generally shorter than men and have shorter legs, so they take shorter strides. However, this is a misconception among runners—research has shown little correlation between both height and leg length and stride length. The fact is that taller runners don't take longer strides than shorter runners. Stride length is more a product of hip extension and how much force your muscles produce as you push off the ground. Therefore, something else must cause female runners to take shorter strides than male runners when running at the same speed.

Differences in Body Weight and Body Composition

How much you weigh is a balance between the amount of energy (calories) you consume (energy intake) and the amount of energy (calories) you expend (energy expenditure). To lose weight, energy expenditure must be greater than energy intake. To gain weight, energy intake must be greater than energy expenditure. If it seems as though it's harder for women to lose weight while men seem to drop weight easily, you're not dreaming. A clear difference exists in the ability of the sexes to balance energy. Women adjust their energy intake to match their energy expenditure and vice versa better than men, making weight loss, whether in response to a restricted energy intake (diet) or an increased energy expenditure (exercise) more difficult for women than men. Women may be more attuned to fluctuations in energy balance so that their bodies adjust their metabolism to maintain a certain weight or body composition. This balance of energy is probably a physiological or central nervous system process governed by a woman's need to hold on to a certain amount of fat to prepare for childbirth—evolution at work.

More of a woman's weight is composed of fat than a man's is. The total amount of fat available to the average female is much greater than that of the average male. Women need more fat than men—part of the trade-off for bringing new life into the world. Essential fat, which makes up approximately 3 percent of total body weight in males and 12 percent in females, is crucial for normal body functioning. It includes fat incorporated into nerves, brain, heart, lungs, liver, and mammary glands. Fat in these areas is essential for conduction of nerve impulses, metabolism, cell structure, and protection from trauma.

Nonessential fat, on the other hand, exists primarily within fat cells called adipose tissue, located just under your skin and around major organs. You also store fat within your skeletal muscles, called intramuscular triglyceride, which is the major source of fat used when you run because it is physically closer to the muscles' mitochondria than the adipose tissue fat, which makes it easier for the muscles to get energy quickly. Runners with a high percentage of body fat are at a disadvantage because fat is essentially dead weight, which increases the amount of energy required to run. Women must propel more body fat with less muscle mass than men. Small breasts are a characteristic of very good female runners because it minimizes the amount of dead weight. The greater percentage of body fat and less total muscle mass also contribute to the lower $\dot{V}O_2$max of women. Research has shown that percent body fat and skinfold thickness in specific areas of the body, e.g., below the scapula on the back, above the hip bone, and the abdomen, also influence training speed and race performance in female runners.

Greater body fat also slows the release of body heat while running because fat acts as an insulator. Although running is the best activity for decreasing body fat and a low percentage of body fat is necessary for improved running performance, women must balance the need for low body fat with good health. A body fat percentage that is too low can disrupt the menstrual cycle and increase the risk for bone injuries (see chapters 2 and 13). As with hip structure, the body composition of good female distance runners is more similar to that of average males and male distance runners than to that of average females.

Men's natural advantages in $\dot{V}O_2$max become less important over longer distances during which success depends on aerobic training and the ability to use stored fuel.

Cardiovascular Differences

Women have smaller hearts than men, even when comparing similarly trained runners. The larger heart gives men a greater stroke volume and cardiac output, contributing to a greater $\dot{V}O_2$max. Maximum cardiac output averages 20 liters per minute in trained women vs. 30 liters per minute in trained men. Men also have a larger blood volume and more hemoglobin in their blood to transport oxygen, 15.8 versus 13.7 grams per deciliter of blood. Together, the larger heart, greater blood volume, and greater blood hemoglobin concentration create a cardiovascular system that supplies more blood and oxygen to the running muscles, giving men greater cardiovascular endurance than women.

Although it may seem that a 2.1-gram difference in hemoglobin concentration is very small, it's actually a big difference. Each gram of hemoglobin can transport 1.34 milliliters of oxygen when hemoglobin is fully saturated with oxygen. On this trait, you're equal to your male counterpart—there is no evidence of a sex difference in the ability to saturate the blood with oxygen, which is dependent on the diffusion capacity of the lungs and the environmental altitude. The 2.1-gram difference between men and women means that men can carry 2.8 more milliliters of oxygen per deciliter of blood. Multiply this difference by the difference in maximum blood flow to the muscles between women and men who are running as hard as they can (i.e., a 10,000 milliliter difference in maximum cardiac output), and men send 280 more milliliters (a little more than one cup) of oxygen to the muscles every minute than women do.

While trained male runners have about a 15 percent higher $\dot{V}O_2$max than trained female runners, there is considerable overlap between the sexes: many trained female runners have a higher $\dot{V}O_2$max than untrained men. Furthermore, there is no difference between the sexes in the adaptations to training and the amount runners can improve their $\dot{V}O_2$max. Research has shown that $\dot{V}O_2$max can improve up to 20 percent with training in both men and women. While a trained woman will always have a lower $\dot{V}O_2$max than a similarly trained man, a trained woman may have a higher $\dot{V}O_2$max than a sedentary or recreationally active man. For races from 800 meters to the marathon, $\dot{V}O_2$max is extremely important. However, the longer the race, the less important it becomes, although it's still important, because race performance is less affected by the use of a large aerobic engine and more dependent on an efficient use of stored fuel.

Muscular Differences

When you were young, chances are some boy tried to show you his biceps. Although the biceps may be the poster boy for strong, attractive muscles, there are more than 600 muscles in your body, from the large vastus lateralis on the front of your thigh to the small orbicularis oculi that closes your eyelids and wrinkles the skin on your forehead. The most obvious sex difference when it comes to muscles is that women have a smaller muscle mass than men. Because muscular strength and power are proportional to the size of the muscle, women cannot produce as much muscular force or power as men. Therefore, men can sprint faster than women.

While the stores of ATP and creatine phosphate per pound of muscle and the ability to rapidly acquire ATP from the breakdown of creatine phosphate are the same between men and women, the total amount of stored ATP and creatine phosphate—and therefore the total energy available from these fuel sources—is greater in men because of their larger muscle mass. However, for a given unit of muscle mass, women produce the same amount of force as men because there is no sex difference in the amount of force that individual muscle fibers produce. The way that muscles contract in women is exactly the same as it is in men.

Metabolic Differences

Metabolism refers to all of the energy-requiring chemical reactions occurring inside your body. At any one time, trillions of reactions are going on inside of you, including the growth of new tissue, muscle contraction, and the breakdown of food for energy. The resting metabolic rate—the amount of energy needed during resting conditions—is lower in females because of their smaller body mass and muscle mass. When you run, your metabolic rate increases dramatically because of the increased demand for energy. The faster your metabolic pathways can use the available fuel to regenerate energy for muscle contraction, the faster you will be able to run any race.

While your nervous system controls your body's faster functions, like the initiation of reflexes and movement, hormones control the slower functions, like the regulation of growth and metabolism and the development of reproductive organs. Much of metabolism is under the direction of hormones, which act as conductors, initiating signals that lead to the transportation and use of fuel. And the two predominant fuels for running are carbohydrate and fat, which provide energy on a sliding scale. At slower speeds, your muscles rely more on fat and less on carbohydrate, and as you increase your running pace, the energy contribution from fat decreases while the energy contribution from carbohydrate increases.

Carbohydrate Metabolism

The hormone insulin is responsible for carbohydrate metabolism. Consuming carbohydrate elevates your blood glucose concentration and increases insulin concentration. The increase in circulating insulin, which is secreted from your pancreas, stimulates specific proteins to transport the glucose from your blood into your muscles, where it is either used for immediate energy by your cells or stored as muscle glycogen for later use. Males typically have more glycogen stored in their muscles. Longer races like the marathon are limited, in part, by the amount of stored glycogen. Therefore, the lower muscle glycogen in women's muscles can partly explain why they cannot run marathons as fast as men.

Research has shown that men also are more responsive to carbohydrate loading than women. In other words, women do not increase muscle glycogen as much as men in response to consuming more carbohydrate in their diets. However, some of this research is clouded by the fact that women consume fewer total calories than men, so the lack of glycogen storage may be due to a lower caloric or carbohydrate intake by women rather than an inherent sex difference in the ability to store glycogen. When women increase their total caloric intake as they also increase the amount of carbohydrate in their diets, they increase their muscle glycogen content by a similar amount as men. From a training perspective, while men simply need to increase the percentage of their calories coming from carbohydrate in order to *carbo load* and store more glycogen, women need to also increase the total number of calories in their diets to get the same effect.

Because carbohydrate is the predominant fuel source during running and the only fuel source at speeds faster than acidosis threshold, research has focused on how the hormonal differences between men and women affect insulin and alter carbohydrate metabolism. Most research has found that women use less carbohydrate than men when exercising at similar intensities.

When you finish a workout that severely lowers your muscle glycogen content, it's important to replenish the carbohydrates so you can resynthesize more glycogen to be prepared for your next run. In fact, refueling nutrient-depleted muscles is possibly the single most important aspect of optimal recovery from training and racing. Scientists first discovered in the late 1960s that endurance performance is influenced by the amount of stored glycogen in skeletal muscles, and that intense endurance exercise decreases muscle glycogen stores. The faster you can resynthesize muscle glycogen, the faster your recovery. Research has shown that the rate of glycogen synthesis in the first few hours following a workout (the time when you are best able to store glycogen because the cells are most sensitive to insulin) is similar between the sexes. This suggests that recovery rates between males and females are similar, at least the component of recovery affected by the resynthesis of fuel.

Fat Metabolism

As a consequence of not using as much carbohydrate during exercise, women rely more on fat than men. Indeed, it has been estimated that women use about 75 percent more fat than do men while running or cycling at 65 to 70 percent $\dot{V}O_2$max. Women get about 39 percent of their energy from fat during exercise at 65 percent $\dot{V}O_2$max, while men get about 22 percent of their energy from fat. However, the percentage of energy derived from fat varies significantly from person to person because factors such as training status, muscle fiber type, muscle glycogen content, and mitochondrial density all play a role.

While it is difficult to tease out the exact reasons for the difference between the sexes in the metabolism of carbohydrate and fat, it appears that estrogen is at least partly responsible. Research done on rats has shown that when male rats are given estrogen, they deplete less glycogen during exercise; the concentration of fatty acids in the blood increases, suggesting a greater availability of fat for energy; and they can exercise for longer periods before becoming exhausted. Increasing the amount of fatty acids circulating in the blood favors their use by muscle during exercise, resulting in a decreased reliance on muscle glycogen and blood glucose, thus delaying glycogen depletion and hypoglycemia, or low blood sugar, and postponing fatigue.

This switch in fuel use to a greater reliance on fat at the same running speed also occurs from endurance training. Training enhances fat use by increasing the mitochondria in your muscles, allowing for more aerobic metabolism and the sparing of muscle glycogen. This shift in the energy source for muscular activity is a major advantage in delaying the onset of fatigue in running events that are limited by the availability of muscle glycogen—marathons and ultramarathons. Because humans' carbohydrate stores are limited, the difference in metabolism between the sexes may give female runners an advantage for very long endurance activities, during which there is a greater need to conserve carbohydrate and a greater use of fat because of the slower pace. In 2002 and 2003, Pam Reed showed that science may be on to something, by winning the 135-mile (217K) Badwater Ultramarathon, beating all of the men. In shorter races, however, when there is a greater demand to generate energy quickly for muscle contraction, relying more on fat will slow the pace because energy is derived much more quickly from carbohydrate than from fat.

Protein Metabolism

The third macronutrient, protein, is often neglected in metabolism because it accounts for only 3 to 6 percent of the amount of energy expended while running. Rather, protein is used primarily for other things, such as building, maintaining, and repairing muscle, skin, and blood tissue, as well as aiding in the transportation of materials through the blood. Protein can be thought of as your body's scaffolding and cargo. However, it can be used for energy if inadequate amounts of fat and carbohydrate are available because the body's requirement for energy takes priority over tissue building. Although the amount of protein you use for energy may be small, even a small contribution to your daily run may be large if you run a lot and run often.

Exercise increases the use of amino acids from protein breakdown, and the amount of amino acids that your muscles use is inversely related to the amount of glycogen in the muscle. When glycogen is abundant, muscles rely on glycogen, but when glycogen is low, muscles begin to rely more on amino acids. Research has shown that females use less protein during exercise than do males. Because endurance-trained females use less muscle glycogen and rely more on fat than endurance-trained males, protein breakdown seems to be inhibited in females by virtue of the greater muscle glycogen.

Sex differences in distance running decrease as the level of performance increases. Although there may be huge differences between the average man and woman at your local 10K road race, at the elite level, there is only an 8 to 10 percent difference in running performance between men and women. For example, the average marathon times in the United States in 2009 were 4:24:17 for men and 4:52:31 for women; however, the world records are less than 12 minutes apart. (The record for men, set in 2011, is 2:03:38. The record for women, set in 2003, is 2:15:25.) The differences in body composition and the anatomical, cardiovascular, muscular, and metabolic characteristics between elite male and female runners are much smaller than the differences between runners in the general population.

The main reason you don't run a 10K as fast as the guy standing next to you on the starting line—even if your level of training is the same—is because of your smaller cardiovascular system and greater percentage of body fat. Fat percentage accounts for about 75 percent of the difference in running performance between the sexes, while $\dot{V}O_2$max accounts for about 20 percent. Given the many differences between male and female runners, women need to approach their training and racing differently than men to optimize their unique characteristics.

2

Menstrual Cycle, Hormones, and Performance

The menstrual cycle, which occurs monthly from menarche (age 11-14) until menopause (age 45-50), is the defining physiological characteristic of females. The levels of the four hormonal markers of the menstrual cycle—estrogen, progesterone, follicle-stimulating hormone, and luteinizing hormone—change continuously throughout the cycle as a complex interaction of positive and negative feedback mechanisms regulate the timing and amount of hormone secretion. With the large fluctuations in the concentrations of these hormones, the phase of the menstrual cycle significantly affects the female runner's hormonal environment and therefore her physiology. Indeed, research has shown that many aspects of physiology are affected by the phase of the menstrual cycle, including oxygen consumption, body temperature, hydration, and metabolism, as the sex hormones rise and fall. This suggests that the menstrual cycle affects how women respond and adapt to training.

Phases of the Menstrual Cycle

The menstrual cycle is usually 28 days and is divided in half by ovulation on day 14 as the ovum is released from the ovary. The first half of the cycle is the follicular phase, and the second half is the luteal phase (see figure 2.1, page 24). The exact length of the menstrual cycle can vary from woman to woman, cycle to cycle, and year to year. Changes in hormone levels can affect the length of the cycle. Teenagers and women in their 40s who are closing in on menopause tend to have low or changing progesterone levels, which can alter cycle length. Birth control pills, low body fat, weight loss, being overweight, stress, and intense exercise can also change the cycle length.

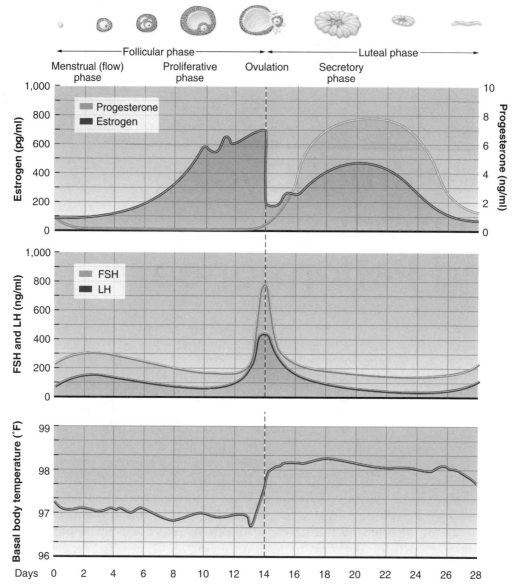

Figure 2.1 The fluctuation of estrogen, progesterone, follicle-stimulating hormone (FSH), luteinizing hormone (LH), and basal body temperature.

Adapted, by permission, from W.L. Kenney, J.H. Wilmore, and D.L. Costill, 2012, *Physiology of sport and exercise*, 5th ed. (Champaign, IL: Human Kinetics), 484.

Follicular Phase

The follicular phase of the menstrual cycle, which begins with the onset of menses (your period), typically lasts 14 days but can last 11 to 21 days. Following menses, which typically lasts 3 to 5 days, estrogen rises, peaking around day 14, right before ovulation. The burst of estrogen toward the end of the follicular phase causes a surge in luteinizing hormone around day 14 to initiate ovulation. During the follicular phase, the progesterone level remains low.

Luteal Phase

During the luteal phase of the menstrual cycle, which always lasts 14 days, progesterone rises. Estrogen drops after ovulation before rising again toward the middle of the phase. The increase in progesterone causes body temperature to increase to prepare for the fertilization of an egg. If fertilization does not occur, both estrogen and progesterone levels decrease abruptly. The luteal phase ends with the onset of menses, and the cycle starts all over again.

If you've ever felt bloated during your period, you can blame progesterone. The high concentration of progesterone during the luteal phase affects fluid balance, causing you to lose water and electrolytes. The rapid drop in progesterone as you shift from the luteal phase back to the follicular phase results in excess premenstrual water and electrolyte retention, causing you to feel bloated.

Premenstrual Syndrome

Premenstrual syndrome (PMS) comprises a variety of physical and psychological symptoms that occur toward the end of the luteal phase in the days leading up to menses. Many women of reproductive age experience PMS. Hormonally, PMS is characterized by a rapid drop in both estrogen and progesterone. The most common symptoms are headache, breast swelling and tenderness, bloating, fatigue, mood swings, and irritability. The specific cause of PMS is not known, although several theories exist, including progesterone deficiency, progesterone withdrawal, excessive amounts of estrogen, estrogen withdrawal, changes in the estrogen-to-progesterone ratio, changes in prolactin levels, a drop in the level of endorphins, and psychological issues.

Cramping, one of the more difficult menstrual issues for the female runner, is thought to be caused by an increase in prostaglandin, a hormone produced by the uterus that causes the uterus to contract. Birth control pills and over-the-counter anti-inflammatory drugs, such as ibuprofen or naproxen sodium, can reduce the severity of cramps by inhibiting the release of prostaglandin. Premenstrual irritability may be related to a high estrogen-to-progesterone ratio and premenstrual depression to a low ratio; however, research has been unable to document specific changes in the hormone levels in relation to the appearance of PMS symptoms. Breast tenderness may be due to an increase in prolactin, a hormone secreted by the pituitary glands. As you age, PMS symptoms may worsen as you approach menopause. The symptoms may also worsen when you experience major hormonal changes, such as those that occur immediately following childbirth or miscarriage or when taking oral contraceptives.

Although not a lot of research on the effects of exercise on PMS exists, the research that has been done has shown that exercise reduces its symptoms. Research examining the effects of exercise on mood has generally found that intense exercise performed regularly, especially running, is psychologically beneficial for women because it reduces tension and increases psychological well-being. However, there are women for whom exercise is ineffective at alleviating the effects of premenstrual mood swings.

Menstrual Irregularities

Many girls and women who train intensely and train a lot and have a low percentage of body fat experience irregular or even absent menstrual cycles, which
reduces estrogen levels. Research has shown that girls who start intense training before menarche delay their menstruation nearly a year later than girls who
already have menstrual periods when they start training. Once menstrual activity
commences, its continued occurrence is also sensitive to training. In response
to heavy training, the first change in menstrual cycle activity is a shortening of
the luteal phase, followed by cycles without ovulation and, finally, cessation of
menses, called amenorrhea. Amenorrhea, which is defined as having three or fewer
periods per year, results in constantly low levels of estrogen and progesterone. A
female runner with amenorrhea has about one-third the estrogen concentration
and about 10 to 20 percent the progesterone concentration of a normally menstruating woman. Thus, endocrinologically, an amenorrheic runner experiences
an estrogen-deficient state similar to that of a postmenopausal woman.

The incidence of menstrual irregularity or amenorrhea varies from woman to
woman. Some female runners can train at high volumes and never disrupt or lose
their menstrual cycle activity, while other women notice changes in cycle activity
with relatively little training. High training volumes, low body weight, and endurance sports such as distance running increase the incidence of menstrual irregularities. Long-distance runners in particular are at an increased risk for menstrual
irregularity or amenorrhea. Research has shown that consuming fewer calories
than you expend rather than the stress of exercise is responsible for the loss of
menstrual activity and that consuming enough calories to replace the calories
spent through exercise can prevent amenorrhea. Therefore, if you run a lot, you
need to increase the calories you consume throughout the day to keep up with
the large number of calories you expend by running.

One of the biggest ramifications of menstrual irregularity or amenorrhea is its
effect on your bones. Any disruption to the menstrual cycle can cause a decrease
in your bone mineral density, increasing the risk for osteoporosis and stress fractures. Estrogen is extremely important in facilitating the absorption of calcium
into your bones. Research has shown that female distance runners with irregular
or absent menstruation have significantly lower bone density than runners with
regular menstruation and even than nonathletes. Furthermore, several studies
have found a significant loss in bone density, particularly at the lumbar spine, in
amenorrheic athletes. A female runner with irregular menstrual cycles runs the
risk of decreasing bone mineral density to such an extent that stress fractures
occur with only minimal impact to the bones.

Menstrual irregularities greatly increase a female runner's risk for stress fractures. Therefore, if you have menstrual irregularities, you must take extra care in
planning your training program so you do not increase your running volume or
intensity too quickly, and you may need to increase your dietary intake of calcium
and vitamin D to protect your bones (see chapter 14).

Physiological Effects and Performance Implications of the Menstrual Cycle

While a man's hormonal environment is pretty stable, your hormonal environment is constantly changing. Physiological changes resulting from fluctuations in estrogen and progesterone caused by the menstrual cycle are exacerbated during exercise, especially if the exercise is intense. When you go for a hard run, the concentrations of estrogen and progesterone in your blood increase during both the follicular and luteal phases of the menstrual cycle. Low-intensity exercise, however, does not alter the concentrations of these hormones.

Body Temperature

The menstrual cycle exerts a large effect on body temperature. Humans have a unique ability to sweat, which maintains body temperature, allowing you to exercise in the heat. Other animals become incapacitated by high body temperatures if forced to run for too long in the heat. A positive adaptation to training is that your body's thermostat improves its ability to cool itself. When your body adapts, you sweat more when you run, and you begin sweating earlier in a run. Thus, any condition that decreases your ability to sweat will decrease your ability to dissipate heat while you run. The menstrual cycle is one such condition.

Body temperature changes rhythmically throughout the menstrual cycle, peaking during the luteal phase in response to the surge in progesterone. Indeed, many children are conceived under the direction of their mothers' body temperatures because a high body temperature signifies readiness for conception. Progesterone acts on your brain's hypothalamus, your temperature control center, which increases your temperature set point. A higher body temperature increases the threshold for dissipation of heat. In other words, your body must reach a higher temperature before your thermostat compensates and begins to cool itself. This is not a good thing when you are running on a hot and humid day and want to begin the cooling response as soon as you can. Research on rats has shown that estrogen has the opposite effect on the hypothalamus, decreasing body temperature, which explains why your body temperature is lower during the estrogen-dominant follicular phase.

Most studies have shown that the increased body temperature during the luteal phase remains elevated during exercise and when exercising in the heat. A higher body temperature during the luteal phase makes it more difficult to run in the heat during this phase because you don't begin sweating to dissipate heat until you have reached a higher body temperature. You are also less able to dilate the small blood vessels under your skin, which compromises your ability to release heat. Hyperthermia—an increased body temperature—is one of the factors that cause fatigue during prolonged exercise. Thus, long, intense workouts and races such as half-marathons and marathons in the heat, can be more difficult during the luteal phase of your cycle. The increased body temperature during the luteal phase can also increase your risk of developing heat illnesses such as heat exhaustion and heat stroke. Although, as previously noted, training improves your ability to regulate body temperature.

Cardiorespiratory Characteristics

When running in the heat, the increase in thermal strain is accompanied by a greater cardiorespiratory strain. Profuse sweating to increase evaporative cooling causes a loss of plasma volume from the blood, decreasing total blood volume. When blood volume decreases, stroke volume decreases. A decreased stroke volume compromises oxygen flow to your muscles, which decreases your running pace. To compensate for the decreased stroke volume, your heart must work harder to pump blood, and heart rate drifts upward in an attempt to maintain cardiac output and blood pressure. This rise in heart rate during prolonged running without an increase in pace is called *cardiac drift*. Heart rate rises three to five beats per minute for every 1 percent of body weight lost from dehydration.

The progesterone-induced increase in body temperature during the luteal phase can cause your heart rate to rise during your runs even if it's cool outside. Some studies have shown that women's heart rates are higher when exercising during the luteal phase, while other studies have shown that heart rate is not different between phases of the menstrual cycle. Regardless of whether your heart rate increases, your aerobic power ($\dot{V}O_2$max) does not change over the course of the menstrual cycle.

Both the thermal and cardiorespiratory strain of exercising in the heat, especially during the luteal phase of the menstrual cycle, means your ability to run for prolonged periods declines with an increase in environmental temperature. Therefore, it's better to run a long race like a half-marathon or marathon during the follicular phase of your menstrual cycle when your body temperature is lower, especially if the race is in a hot and humid environment.

If you bleed a lot during menstruation, it's possible that your blood's hemoglobin concentration may decrease, which can decrease your ability to transport oxygen in your blood. Because iron is an important component of hemoglobin, you may need to supplement your normal diet with iron. Many female runners exhibit athletic anemia, low blood iron levels caused by physical activity, especially if they lose a lot of blood during menstruation.

Metabolism and Muscle Glycogen

Variations in running performance caused by menstrual phase may largely be due to changes in exercise metabolism stimulated by fluctuations in the concentration of estrogen and progesterone. The magnitude of the increase in these hormones between menstrual phases and the ratio of estrogen to progesterone concentration appear to be important factors in determining an effect on metabolism. The research suggests that estrogen may improve endurance performance by altering carbohydrate, fat, and protein metabolism, with progesterone often acting antagonistically to estrogen. Estrogen promotes both the availability of glucose and uptake of glucose into slow-twitch muscle fibers, providing the fuel of choice during short bouts of exercise.

Your ability to run for a long time is greatly influenced by the amount of glycogen stored in your skeletal muscles, with fatigue coinciding with glycogen depletion. Research comparing the amount of muscle glycogen in women eating either a normal diet (2.4 grams of carbohydrate per pound of body weight per day) for three days or a high-carbohydrate diet (3.8 grams of carbohydrate per pound of body weight per day) for three days has shown that muscle glycogen content is greatest during the midluteal phase after both normal and high-carbohydrate diets. Muscle glycogen is lowest during the midfollicular phase. However, you can increase the amount of muscle glycogen in the follicular phase by eating a high-carbohydrate diet. During the luteal phase, your muscles rely more on fat than on glycogen for energy during submaximal exercise. Given both the greater muscle glycogen content and the glycogen-sparing effect of the midluteal phase, if you're planning to run a marathon or other long race, plan it to coincide with the luteal phase of your menstrual cycle.

Another ramification of the altered metabolism is the possible delay of

Certain times during the menstrual cycle provide greater muscle glycogen content and glycogen-sparing effects that enhance the ability to run long distances.

fatigue during submaximal exercise. Theoretically, with less reliance on carbohydrate for energy, less lactate, and therefore other metabolic byproducts, is produced. While some studies have documented that less lactate is produced during exercise in the midluteal phase, other studies have not. Interestingly, when men are given a synthetic version of progesterone, they produce less lactate during maximal exercise, suggesting that progesterone, which is elevated during the luteal phase, may lower lactate levels. Thus, while it has not been documented by research, it's possible that during the luteal phase it takes longer to fatigue during long runs or long races, which are performed below the acidosis threshold, because they rely less on carbohydrate and therefore produce less lactate and delay the associated increase in metabolites that cause fatigue.

Breathing

Because breathing is something we do without thinking about, we often take it for granted. However, controlling your breathing during exercise is a complicated matter. Ventilation, the movement of air into and out of the lungs, increases as a function of running speed. Run faster, ventilate more. Ventilation increases slowly when you run slowly and increases rapidly when you run fast because of the increased need to eliminate the metabolic production of carbon dioxide. This increase in ventilation is attributable to the initial increase in the amount of air per breath at slower speeds and an increase in breathing frequency at faster speeds.

Given the physiological demand for oxygen and the need to eliminate carbon dioxide at faster running speeds, humans have a large capacity to increase their breathing. At rest, you breathe about half a liter of air per breath and about 6 liters of air per minute, but when you're racing a 5K, you may breathe about 100 to 125 liters of air per minute. That's about 30 gallons of air entering the lungs each minute. Try filling a tub with 30 gallons of water in one minute. This should give you a lot more respect for the lungs.

Many runners get frustrated because they believe their lungs limit their ability to run. They claim they *can't breathe* while running and are forced to stop so they can *catch their breath*. Even trained runners sometimes feel this way. However, being unable to get more oxygen into your lungs doesn't limit your ability to run faster. Getting more oxygen to your muscles does.

During the luteal phase, progesterone concentration is at its highest. Because progesterone stimulates ventilation regardless of the intensity of your run and because runners typically base their perception of effort on how hard they're breathing, you may feel more winded during your luteal-phase workouts than during your follicular-phase workouts.

Besides making you feel like you're working harder when you run, increased breathing at rest has physiological consequences. Because you exhale carbon dioxide with each breath, increased ventilation decreases the partial pressure of carbon dioxide in your blood, altering your body's acid–base balance by elevating the pH. In response to this *respiratory alkalosis*, your kidneys compensate by excreting bicarbonate (your body's buffer to acidosis) in your urine to lower blood pH back to its normal physiological value and maintain acid–base balance. With a reduced buffering capacity of acidosis caused by having less bicarbonate, running performance in middle-distance races (800 meters to 5K), which include a significant anaerobic contribution resulting in acidosis, may be hampered during the luteal phase of the menstrual cycle.

The increased breathing during the luteal phase may also increase the oxygen demand of breathing itself because the muscles responsible for breathing need oxygen to work just like your leg muscles do. More oxygen being used by your breathing muscles means less oxygen available to your leg muscles to help you run. The increased breathing could hypothetically reduce running economy because you'll consume more oxygen to support the increased breathing rate. Most research, however, has not documented a change in running economy across the menstrual cycle.

Lung function after exercise is also affected by the phase of the menstrual cycle. Many women have more trouble breathing during the luteal phase when running. This has huge implications for runners with asthma, because exercise is a powerful trigger of asthma symptoms. Thus, the declining lung function in the luteal phase can negatively affect training and competition strategies in an asthmatic runner. Females with asthma experience a worsening of asthma symptoms and increased bronchodilator use during the midluteal phase. Interestingly, lung function and asthma symptoms seem to vary cyclically. Thirty-three to 52 percent of asthmatic women report a premenstrual worsening of asthma symptoms, and an additional 22 percent report that their asthma is worse during menses.

Muscle Contraction and Strength

Most research shows that muscle strength is not affected by the menstrual cycle. However, research shows that a woman's responsiveness to strength training is influenced by the menstrual cycle. For example, one study found that weight training (consisting of three sets of 12 repetitions) every second day during the follicular phase and once per week during the luteal phase of the menstrual cycle increased maximal quadriceps strength by 32.6 percent compared to just 13.1 percent by training once every third day over the whole menstrual cycle. The ratio of maximal strength to muscle cross-sectional area was also greater following the former training program (27.6 percent) than in the latter, more traditionally used program (10.5 percent).

Endurance Performance

The documented effects of the menstrual cycle on physiological characteristics is one thing; how they influence your running performance is quite another. As with most of the research on the menstrual cycle, the research on how it affects endurance performance is not totally clear. Survey-based research has shown that many female athletes do not report a noticeable decline in performance between phases of the menstrual cycle. However, many others report an improvement in performance during menstruation. The best performances have generally been reported to occur in the immediate postmenstrual days with the worst performances occurring during the premenstrual interval and the first few days of menstruation. However, this type of survey-based research should be interpreted with caution because many confounding variables surround the menstrual cycle, the perception of exercise effort, and women's inherent bias about the menstrual cycle, especially the premenstrual days.

Research that has actually measured performance in women is conflicting: Some studies show that the menstrual cycle influences performance, and other studies show that it does not. Endurance performance may be theoretically and often anecdotally better in the midluteal phase than in the early follicular phase; it may only be so when the ratio of estrogen to progesterone is high in the midluteal phase. Remember that both estrogen and progesterone are elevated in the midluteal phase. An improved performance also tends to occur in the late-follicular phase, which is characterized by the preovulatory surge in estrogen and suppressed progesterone. It seems that you can expect to perform better during times of the menstrual cycle when estrogen is the dominant hormone and perform the worst when progesterone is the dominant hormone.

Anecdotally, many of the female runners Dr. Jason has coached have experienced their worst training days in the few days leading up to and including menstruation. How your workouts and races are affected is highly individual. You may find harder workouts to be more challenging during your period, but easy running may actually improve your mood and alleviate physical symptoms associated with your period. Part II discusses how to manipulate your training and racing to accommodate the menstrual cycle.

Oral Contraceptives

Oral contraceptives, which supply a woman with synthetic sex hormones, are the most common form of birth control for women. Oral contraceptives mimic the normal menstrual cycle by increasing and then subsequently decreasing the concentrations of estrogen and progesterone on a set 28-day schedule leading up to menses. The three types of oral contraceptives are monophasic, biphasic, and triphasic. Monophasic pills, the most commonly used, provide fixed doses of estrogen and progesterone over 21 days, followed by seven days of placebo. These pills regulate the hormonal environment, decreasing hormonal fluctuations across the cycle, which can provide a controlled environment for the runner and minimize potential variations in physiological variables. Biphasic pills switch the dosage of the hormones once during the 21-day cycle. Triphasic pills supply three different doses of estrogen that are increased throughout the cycle. Oral contraceptives reduce the natural production of estrogen, progesterone, luteinizing hormone, and follicle-stimulating hormone, which inhibits ovulation and prevents pregnancy.

In addition to preventing pregnancy, oral contraceptives force a regular 28-day cycle, which makes it easier to plan your training and races. Some research has shown that runners consume less oxygen while running at submaximal speeds, i.e., their running economy is improved, when taking oral contraceptives. However, both the maximum ability to consume oxygen ($\dot{V}O_2max$) and running performance do not seem to be affected.

Because oral contraceptives supply estrogen, it's possible, at least theoretically, that they can reduce the risk for bone injuries associated with menstrual irregularities by increasing bone mineral density. However, research examining the effects of supplemental estrogen provided by birth control medication on bone mineral density has shown mixed results. Some studies have shown that it has no effect, some studies have shown an increased bone mineral density, and still other studies have shown a decreased bone mineral density, especially when contraceptives are taken during late adolescence or early adulthood.

In premenopausal women with normal menstrual cycle activity, oral contraceptive use does not seem to benefit bone health. In other words, if you have a normal menstrual cycle, your estrogen level is already adequate to protect your bones; supplying more estrogen from a pill is not going to make your bones stronger. Benefit to bones seems to be specific to active women with menstrual irregularities who have compromised skeletal health. Another benefit may come for women at the onset of menopause. Use of oral contraceptives at this time may increase bone mineral density.

One of the possible side effects of oral contraceptives that can affect your running is the potential to gain weight. Studies on physically active women have found that oral contraceptives, when taken either as a single, fixed dose of estrogen or as multiple doses over the menstrual cycle, increase body mass and percent body fat. But the weight gain doesn't seem to be permanent and can return to what it was when women stop taking the pill. One study found that women's body weight increased by nearly four and a half pounds (2 kg) after six months of oral contraceptive use, but returned to normal only one month after stopping.

Another side effect of oral contraceptives is a progesterone-mediated increase in body temperature, much like what occurs during the luteal phase of the menstrual cycle. Because temperature regulation is an important factor in long races, the increase in body temperature set point caused by oral contraceptives can affect your ability to run in the heat. While monophasic and biphasic oral contraceptives do not affect $\dot{V}O_2max$, triphasic contraceptives have been shown to decrease $\dot{V}O_2max$ during the time between what would be preovulation and postovulation (if the women were ovulating). This could potentially impair performance in the postovulatory period for someone taking the triphasic version of the pill.

3

Pregnancy

Pregnancy is a part of the life cycle for many women. Not long ago, doctors told women not to exercise for fear of harm to mother and baby. Thankfully for women runners, this advice is changing. Research indicates that more than 40 percent of pregnant women in the United States participate in some type of weight-bearing exercise (running, aerobics, stair climbing) during pregnancy and at least half of them continue beyond the sixth month of pregnancy. The decision to run during your pregnancy should be a personal one determined by your priorities, lifestyle, past experiences, and support system. Learn everything you can about running during pregnancy as you make your decision.

Pregnancy results in profound anatomical and physiological changes that provide nutritional support to the developing fetus and prepare a woman's body for delivery. Some of these changes can affect your ability to run. If you run while pregnant, the first difference you'll notice is the extra weight in the front of your body. This shifts your center of gravity, changing your running mechanics and making you more likely to lose your balance. The extra weight also increases the forces exerted on your hip and knee joints and contributes to back pain caused by the excess curvature (lumbar lordosis) that develops in the lower back. Your heart rate is higher than usual because the heart must work harder to send oxygen to the placenta.

While participation in running continues to increase and guidelines for pregnant runners become more relaxed, data on how much running is too much for a pregnant runner are still limited. Given that endurance exercise causes an increase in core temperature and a redistribution of blood flow of at least 50 percent from less important tissues to active muscles and it depletes muscle glycogen (energy) stores, the medical concern is that these changes associated with exercise could compromise the growth and development of the fetus. For example, when you're not pregnant, the redistribution of blood away from less active organs and to the active muscles to meet the increased demand for oxygen is not a problem. When you are pregnant, however, that redistribution of blood means blood is also directed away from the placenta. Because the developing fetus cannot breathe, it must get all of its oxygen from the placenta, so you don't want to divert blood away from the placenta. Studies are underway to find answers to the question of how much running is too much. In the interim, what is a pregnant runner to do?

History of Exercise Recommendations During Pregnancy

Recommendations for exercise during pregnancy have undergone significant modifications since 1985. Initial guidelines placed restrictions on exercise intensity and duration, limiting women to a heart rate of less than 140 beats per minute and restricting exercise to 15 minutes or less. Following publication of numerous studies that showed maternal benefits from regular exercise during pregnancy and safety to the health of the baby, guidelines were relaxed in 1984. Although restrictions on heart rate and exercise duration were removed, these guidelines offered only cautious approval to women wanting to engage in exercise while pregnant.

In 2002, the most progressive guidelines to date were released. These guidelines recommend that in the absence of either medical or obstetrical complications, pregnant women who exercised before they were pregnant should participate in 30 minutes or more of moderately intense exercise on most, if not all, days of the week. Running, along with cross-training, such as swimming, stationary cycling, and cross-country skiing are now recommended and acceptable forms of exercise. Although upper limits on physical activity and intensity do not yet exist, the guidelines do give consideration to competitive athletes and their more strenuous training schedules as long as they remain under close obstetric supervision.

As the guidelines have evolved, acceptance by the medical profession is growing. It's understandable, however, why the medical community has been slow to endorse exercise, and running in particular, during pregnancy. Research in this area is inherently difficult. There are ethical concerns about research involving pregnant women, and much of the data comes from research on animals. Human studies have been difficult to compare because of differences in study design; maternal fitness levels; varied exercise activities, intensities, and duration; and the time during the pregnancy the exercise is performed. Despite these difficulties, when everything is evaluated together, clear maternal benefits can be gained from running during your pregnancy.

Benefits of Exercise During Pregnancy

Frequent complaints of pregnancy, including nausea, heartburn, insomnia, varicose veins, and leg cramps are reduced in women who remain active during their pregnancy. Other common discomforts of pregnancy, including fatigue, back pain, swelling of the extremities, and shortness of breath are also lessened. Exercising while pregnant can greatly impact a woman's cardiorespiratory fitness. A study of women runners who continued to run during their pregnancy improved their maximal aerobic capacity 8 to 10 percent more than that of a group of nonpregnant runners followed over the same period.

Exercise during pregnancy has also been associated with a reduced risk of developing certain obstetrical complications, including preeclampsia, pregnancy-induced hypertension, and gestational diabetes. (See table 3.1, page 38, for more information on these conditions.) However, a study in Dutch women published in 2009 calls into question the possibility that the risk of preeclampsia may be decreased. Women engaging in more than four and a half hours per week of physical exercise in the first trimester showed a significantly greater increase in the risk of developing severe preeclampsia than women participating in less physical activity. This suggests that an upper limit for exercise may exist during the first trimester. Future studies are needed to clarify these findings. While a relationship between exercise and length of labor has not been demonstrated, exercise during pregnancy has been associated with better tolerance of labor and a lower risk of Cesarean-section childbirth.

Running can reduce some of the common complaints and discomforts of pregnancy.

Erik Isakson/Blend Images/age fotostock

Circumstances That Prevent Training and Racing

Despite the liberalization of these guidelines, legitimate medical conditions that already exist or develop during pregnancy could prohibit you from running and racing while pregnant. Significant heart and lung disease, persistent bleeding in the second and third trimesters, and ruptured membranes are just some of these conditions. Table 3.1 contains a complete list. Several other conditions require a careful evaluation of the risks and benefits before you continue your running program. The most common of these include severe anemia, being extremely underweight, poorly controlled thyroid disease, and inappropriate fetal size and

Table 3.1 Conditions That Prohibit Running During Pregnancy

Condition	Description
Significant heart disease	Conditions that interfere with the heart's ability to circulate blood through the cardiovascular system Examples include the following: • Congestive heart failure • Uncontrolled high blood pressure
Restrictive lung disease	A category of lung diseases in which it is difficult to fully expand the lungs, often resulting from conditions that make the lungs stiff or the respiratory muscles weak Examples include the following: • Pulmonary fibrosis (scarring of lungs) • Muscular dystrophy • Obesity
Incompetent cervix or cerclage	An incompetent cervix dilates prematurely. A cerclage is a procedure that involves stitching the cervix closed.
Risk for premature labor	Risk of delivering before 37 weeks of gestational age Possible risk factors include the following: • Previous history of premature labor or preterm birth • Carrying more than one fetus • Being underweight • Problems with the placenta
Persistent second- and third-trimester bleeding	Early persistent bleeding usually indicates a problem with the cervix or placenta and increases the chances of preterm labor.
Placenta previa after 26 weeks of gestation	A low-lying placenta that covers the cervix and partially or completely blocks the cervical opening
Ruptured membranes	The amniotic sac that surrounds the fetus in the uterus is leaking.
Preeclampsia	A condition that affects all organs of the body Symptoms include the following: • Elevated blood pressure • Elevated protein in the urine • Swelling of the hands and face
Pregnancy-induced high blood pressure	Elevated blood pressure that develops during the second half of pregnancy and may reduce blood flow to the placenta

development. Although these conditions will not necessarily prohibit you from running during your pregnancy, experiencing them will require close monitoring by your obstetric provider.

Circumstances can develop that mean you should stop exercising. You should be aware of how important it is to change your running regimen if changes in your pregnancy make this necessary, and you need to know the warning signals that require an evaluation by a physician. In pregnant women these warning signs include the following:

- Vaginal bleeding
- Breathlessness at rest or out of proportion to the effort
- Dizziness
- Headaches
- Chest pain
- Racing heart
- Muscle weakness
- Significant swelling in feet or legs
- Uterine contractions that occur more than 30 minutes after exercise
- Decreased fetal movement
- Pelvic, hip, or worsening back pain
- Chronic fatigue
- Leakage of fluids

Many women continue running during pregnancy until it becomes too uncomfortable to do so. When this occurs, consider switching to nonweight-bearing exercises, such as pool running or swimming.

Physiology of the Pregnant Runner

The physiological and anatomical changes a woman experiences during pregnancy include an expanding uterus and increases in estrogen, progesterone, and other hormones. Although several adaptations occur, those related to the musculo-skeletal, cardiorespiratory, and metabolic systems are worth mentioning. The most obvious change is weight gain. Weight gain coupled with weight-bearing exercise increases the forces exerted on the hip and knee joints. While there is no conclusive evidence that joint damage occurs as a result of these increased forces, consider changing the type of exercise if persistent joint pain develops.

Increased circulating hormones loosen the tendons and ligaments, increasing joint mobility. Although this helps prepare the body for delivery, theoretically it could increase the risk of muscle strains and joint sprains. While this has been demonstrated with certain joints in the hand and wrist, no data support this hypothesis for lower-extremity muscles and joints. Despite the lack of data, women should be aware of these possibilities as they continue to run during pregnancy and use caution or consider modifying running drills that are overly jerky or bouncy or are high impact.

Traditionally, heart rate has been used as the standard guide to measure exercise intensity. However, the cardiorespiratory changes caused by pregnancy suggest that

Monitoring Intensity

Because of the variability in maternal heart rate responses to exercise, target heart rates should not be used to monitor exercise intensity. Rather, a better measure of intensity is effort level using either the *talk test* or perceived effort, known as the Borg rating of perceived exertion (RPE). This is an effective approach because most pregnant women will voluntarily reduce their exercise intensity when exercise is self-paced.

Most runners are familiar with the talk test as a measure of intensity. The intensity level is appropriate if you are able to carry on a conversation while exercising. If talking is difficult, the intensity is too hard. The rating of perceived exertion, developed by Gunnar Borg, is a scale that ranges from 6, no exertion at all, to 20, maximal exertion. The RPE measures the intensity of physical activity by reporting how strenuous the activity feels. The greater the exertion feels, the greater the number you report. Exercising at 12 to 14, or somewhat hard, is a safe level of exertion for most pregnant women, although highly trained runners can exercise at levels in the range of 14 to 16, or hard. While most runners use objective measurements of intensity like pace and heart rate, it's even more important when pregnant to be in tune with your body and also use subjective measurements like RPE.

this may not be a reliable guide for pregnant women. During pregnancy, resting heart rate increases 10 to 15 beats per minute. And it has been shown that during maximal exertion, the heart rate doesn't increase to the same degree it would if the woman were not pregnant. During lower-intensity exercise, both the blunted and the normal heart rate response to exercise has been exhibited. These conflicting findings make the use of heart rate monitoring to guide exercise intensity difficult.

Metabolism increases to support the increased work of pregnancy, which results in increased energy needs of 300 calories or more per day. Regular exercise will further increase these daily requirements. While running during pregnancy will minimize excess weight gain, pregnancy is not a time to lose weight. It is important to gain the recommended amount of weight and evaluate nutritional needs for exercise to ensure you are getting adequate calories. A good rule of thumb is that for each mile (1.6K) run or each three miles (5K) cycled, you need an additional 100 calories during the first half of pregnancy and 150 calories during the second half of pregnancy.

It is important to consume adequate amounts of carbohydrate because glucose is the primary energy source controlling fetal growth. As a result of this fetal need, pregnant women use carbohydrate at a greater rate, both at rest and during exercise, than nonpregnant women. Indeed, pregnant women are predisposed to low blood glucose levels (hypoglycemia) during exercise lasting more than 45 minutes. For this reason, it is also important to incorporate sport drinks or fruit juices into your exercise and postexercise recovery.

During pregnancy, your body temperature increases because of increased metabolism. During exercise, further increases in body temperature occur in proportion to the intensity of the exercise. Although there has been concern that increased maternal temperature caused by exercise is associated with congenital defects, this has not been demonstrated in humans. Nevertheless, it is prudent to avoid becoming overheated and refrain from running in hot, humid conditions. Staying hydrated while running is critical to temperature regulation.

Running During Pregnancy

From conception until delivery, multiple physiological changes occur to accommodate fetal development. Some of the common changes of pregnancy include increases in blood volume, cardiac output, and heart rate and a decrease in the resistance of blood flow through the blood vessels. Despite the increases, by the time maternal blood reaches the capillaries of the placenta, its oxygen saturation (which is nearly 100 percent as blood leaves the mother's lungs) has decreased considerably. Fetal blood is less than half saturated with oxygen because the placenta takes a lot of the oxygen. To compensate for this, a fetus has a special type of hemoglobin that allows it to extract more oxygen from the mother's blood.

This section explores the physiological changes more specifically and their impact on your running performance as you progress through each trimester of pregnancy. The training recommendations are based on what science and medicine have learned thus far. Recognize that these are guidelines; some runners may tolerate more exercise, others less. Women should confer with their health care provider before adopting any of the recommendations.

First Trimester

Although you don't look pregnant during the first trimester, most women certainly feel pregnant. Shortly after conception, hormone levels change and your body and uterus begin adaptations that support the growth of the placenta and the developing fetus. These changes cause the symptoms that many women experience in the first trimester, including fatigue, morning sickness, and headaches.

Cardiovascular changes, including an increase in maternal blood volume and resting heart rate and stroke volume, occur early in the first trimester. This increase in maternal blood volume delivers more oxygen and nutrients to the fetus. As you learned in chapter 1, stroke volume is the amount of blood your heart pumps with each beat. Stroke volume begins to rise in the first six to eight weeks of your pregnancy and increases as much as 10 percent by the end of the first trimester. Resting heart rate also increases by 10 to 15 beats per minute. Because cardiac output (the amount of blood your heart pumps per minute) is directly affected by stroke volume and heart rate, cardiac output consequently increases early in pregnancy. This response is further enhanced as a result of the decreased resistance of blood flow through the blood vessels that occurs during pregnancy.

Because fetal size and therefore its oxygen and nutrient needs are small in the first trimester relative to the other trimesters, increases in cardiac output create a

Appropriate Expectations for Exercise

Whether you consider yourself a recreational or competitive runner, you generally come into pregnancy with a well-established fitness routine. You should take into consideration your current level of fitness and activities, environmental conditions, and gestational age when you plan your running program. Your goal should be to maintain a good fitness level throughout your pregnancy without trying to reach peak fitness.

Although no generally agreed-upon formula exists, most women who experience uncomplicated, healthy pregnancies can continue to run at prepregnancy running levels. Although women who have attained a high level of fitness before becoming pregnant can typically tolerate higher-intensity training, they should be careful about engaging in activities that are more intense than those achieved prepregnancy. An obstetric care provider should supervise high-intensity training and frequent doctor visits are often required. All women runners, whether recreational or competitive, should expect their overall exercise performance to decline somewhat as their pregnancy progresses.

circulatory reserve, which is why most women are able to run in the first trimester. In fact, some women report that running feels easier in the first trimester than it does before pregnancy. Although running may feel easier, you should listen to your body and not overdo it. Focus on a running intensity that is comfortable and doesn't cause you to become too short of breath during the exercise.

Your running goals in the first trimester should be to maintain fitness levels and prepregnancy activities. Recommendations that can support these goals include running three to five times per week for 30 to 60 minutes per session. Because research is lacking in this area, recommendations for intensity are difficult to make. Basing intensity on effort can balance safety concerns with fitness desires. Running at a moderately hard to hard intensity, or a 12 to 14 on the Borg RPE scale, can achieve this balance. The pregnancy-induced symptoms in the first trimester, including nausea, vomiting, and fatigue, may require that you adjust your training. Nausea and vomiting are often referred to as *morning sickness*, although these symptoms can occur at any time of the day. In most women, symptoms are mild and go away after the middle of pregnancy. Decreasing training by 5 to 10 percent often allows women to continue to run until symptoms subside. You can also adjust the time of day that you run.

If you are a competitive runner, you likely desire a more strenuous training schedule. Be aware that because of the changes that occur during pregnancy, you will have difficulty maintaining your prepregnancy level of performance and thus need to set reasonable and flexible goals. The more frequent, longer, and more intense workouts of a competitive runner put you at risk of overheating, heat illness, and dehydration. Dehydration can prompt uterine contractions. As a competitive runner, be aware of these risks and make adjustments to prevent them.

Although competition during pregnancy is not encouraged, numerous reports show women participating in marathons early in pregnancy and elite athletes tolerating high levels of endurance and interval training without compromising fetal growth or complicating the course of pregnancy. Based on these reports, training recommendations for competitive runners in the first trimester include four to six running sessions per week. Duration can increase to 90 minutes per session with intensity not to exceed a hard effort, or 14-16 on the Borg RPE.

Second Trimester

During the second trimester, the size of your uterus increases rapidly to accommodate the growing fetus. Accompanying this rapid growth, pregnancy can become more uncomfortable as the body makes room for the growing uterus and the muscles and supporting pelvic structures are stretched. By the end of this trimester, the fetus will be almost four times as big as it was at the end of the first trimester. Maternal and fetal oxygen and nutrient needs increase during this time of fetal, uterine, and placental growth.

Cardiac output continues to rise during the second trimester. By 20 to 24 weeks of pregnancy, cardiac output is 30 to 50 percent greater than before pregnancy. Further increases in heart rate and stroke volume account for this continued increase in cardiac output. By the middle of the second trimester, the increase in stroke volume will peak, increasing by as much as 30 percent over prepregnancy levels. Total blood volume continues to rise in a linear fashion. These two adaptations allow adequate supplies of nutrients and oxygen for the fetus both at rest and when running.

During pregnancy, blood flow is distributed preferentially to the uterus, kidneys, and skin and increases with gestational age. Running results in a redistribution of this blood flow away from the uterus to skin and exercising muscles and is directly proportional to the intensity of the running. These opposing effects could compromise blood flow to the fetus and affect fetal growth and development. However, thanks to the increases in cardiac output and blood volume and placental adaptations that result in greater extraction of oxygen and nutrients, these effects are minimized, particularly during running at moderate intensity. Indeed, studies have shown that placental adaptations are greater in women who maintain a regular exercise regimen through the second trimester of pregnancy. Whether these placental adaptations are effective with prolonged, high-intensity running remains unclear.

The increased metabolic demands of pregnancy result in increased resting oxygen requirements. The expanding uterus puts pressure on the diaphragm, increasing the work of breathing. These factors combined, result in decreased oxygen availability for aerobic exercise and a decline in maximal exercise performance. Most pregnant runners feel like running gets more difficult at the end of the second trimester, a feeling that persists until delivery.

Guidelines for Pregnant Runners

Running can be beneficial for both mother and baby, for both physical and emotional reasons. To minimize risk to the developing fetus and contribute to a safe and enjoyable running experience, pregnant runners should adhere to the following recommendations:

- Run with a partner. If you need to run alone, always tell someone when and where you are running and carry a cell phone, if possible.

- Wear proper clothing and shoes. Running clothes that are lightweight and breathable, a supportive running bra, and well-fitting, cushioned, supportive running shoes will minimize the discomforts of increased weight and enlarged breasts that occur with pregnancy.

- Running while pregnant causes a greater need for bathroom stops. Plan your running routes so you can stop when you need to.

- Include a warm-up and cool-down as part of your running routine. This will help you protect your muscles and joints from injury and allow your body's breathing and heart rate to adjust to the demands of exercise.

- Pay attention to hydration, nutrition, and feelings of heat stress during continuous running that exceeds 45 minutes. Consume sport drinks during these activities.

- Drink plenty of fluids before a run. Adequate hydration is important because dehydration increases your risk of premature contractions. Monitor hydration by weighing yourself before and after your workout. For every one pound (0.45 kg) lost, consume 16 ounces (0.5 L) of fluid. Make up fluid loss before the next workout. Another way to monitor hydration is urine color, which should be light yellow.

- Don't exercise in the fasting state. Your body needs fuel to support your pregnancy and your running. Too little fuel will result in hypoglycemia (low blood sugar) as you and your fetus compete for energy. Eating frequent small meals to help maintain adequate caloric intake is often more comfortable than eating three large meals and can reduce the nausea that often accompanies pregnancy.

- To avoid overheating, don't run in hot or humid conditions. In hot and humid weather, your body's cooling system is less efficient, which can result in both you and your fetus becoming overheated. Running indoors in the air-conditioning is a better alternative.

- Listen to your body and make training adjustments as necessary. Barring medical issues, you should be able to run consistently up through six months of pregnancy. Many women can run right up until delivery.

- Do not try to increase your mileage or speed during pregnancy. Rather, consider it a time for maintaining the status quo and enjoying the changes in your body.

- If you're tired, slow down. If you are still tired, stop. If you have weird pains, talk to your doctor if you are worried.

- Maintain the rate and amount of weight gain recommended by your physician. Running while pregnant can help keep your weight gain to a minimum.

- Running while pregnant may cause pain or soreness in your pelvic region. If the pain is severe, check with your doctor.

You can safely continue to run during the second trimester. It may even be possible to increase your training by 5 to 10 percent above what you were doing in the first trimester. However, as your uterus gets larger, your center of gravity shifts forward, making you more prone to losing your balance. To minimize the risk of falling, choose flat running routes and surfaces that have few obstacles. Recommendations for intensity and duration for both recreational and competitive runners in the second trimester are identical to those of the first trimester, with the exception of total weekly time spent running, which can be increased by 5 to 10 percent assuming you are tolerating the mileage without increased fatigue, shortness of breath, or back or joint pain. Some women runners experience preterm labor with strenuous training. Because of this, competitive athletes with a history of or a risk of preterm labor should proceed cautiously with strenuous activity in the second trimester.

Many women runners include weight lifting as part of their fitness routine. Studies suggest that it can be continued safely, and women are encouraged to continue these activities in the second trimester. If you choose to continue strength training, train all major muscle groups through low-resistance and high-repetition exercises using resistance bands, free weights, or machines. Emphasize continuous breathing throughout the exercise and avoid holding your breath while lifting. Perform exercises in a sitting position. Increased blood volume can cause pooling in the lower extremities during prolonged standing, which will cause you to become lightheaded.

As the uterus increases in size, the enlarged uterus obstructs the return of blood to the heart, which results in decreased cardiac output. This is particularly evident when lying on your back. For this reason, after the fourth month of pregnancy, avoid performing exercises while lying on your back. Lying on your side is acceptable.

Third Trimester

By the third trimester, most physiological adaptations have peaked. The decrease in these adaptations, your enlarging uterus, increasing weight, and the hormones that are preparing your body for delivery will affect your running. Although total blood volume continues to expand, by the third trimester the increase in resting heart rate has plateaued and resting stroke volume and cardiac output begin to decrease. The enlarging uterus continues to push on the diaphragm, causing a decrease in vertical chest height by as much as 1.5 inches (4 cm). As a result, the volume of air that remains in the lungs after each exhalation falls considerably in late pregnancy. This causes a decrease in oxygen reserve, making higher intensity and prolonged running more challenging.

While some women are able to run through the end of their pregnancy, others are not. Regardless, running in the third trimester should be moderate. It is important to keep yourself hydrated and cool. Although the fetus will be buoyed by the movement of the uterus and amniotic fluid during running, consider switching to a lower-impact activity if you experience low back, hip, or other joint pain.

Continuing some form of exercise throughout pregnancy is beneficial. The better shape you are in before delivery, the easier it will be to get back in running shape after the baby is born. Yet, the third trimester is often a time to alter your running program. Recognize that every runner is different and the alterations you make to your running will depend on how you feel. Many women runners decrease the frequency and duration of their workouts. Others substitute nonweight-bearing activities.

Your running goals, therefore, in the third trimester, should be to maintain your exercise level, giving consideration to reducing impact. The discomforts of pregnancy for some women are minimal, and they are able to continue to run during the third trimester. If you are one of those women and are able to continue to run, frequency, intensity, and time goals should not exceed three to six days per week, 30 to 60 minutes per session, and an intensity level of moderate to moderately hard, which corresponds to 11 to 13 on the Borg RPE scale.

Some women find running uncomfortable during their third trimester. If that's the case, substitute activities that are less traumatic to the joints and ligaments. Exercises such as stationary and recumbent cycling and swimming are alternatives you can substitute using the same frequency, intensity, and duration guidelines as you would with running during the third trimester. Swimming is a particularly good alternative to running because the buoyancy of the water decreases forces on joints, minimizes heat stress, and controls leg swelling. Ongoing research examines the effect of more-intense cycling activities typically seen in spinning classes on pregnancy during the third trimester.

Postpartum Exercise

Postpartum refers to the time after delivery of your baby, which is usually six weeks long. Unless you are breastfeeding, most of the changes of pregnancy have resolved and your body has returned to its prepregnancy state during this time. If you breastfeed, expect some of the changes of pregnancy to persist until you stop breastfeeding. Immediately following delivery, the resistance of blood flow through the blood vessels increases markedly. Resting cardiac output, stroke volume, and heart rate all begin to fall dramatically, and your blood volume decreases.

Within the first week, women lose a significant amount of weight because of the decrease in plasma volume (the fluid portion of the blood). By two weeks, most of the pregnancy-induced cardiovascular adaptations have returned to normal. Simultaneously, changes in the reproductive organs occur. By three weeks postpartum, the size of the uterus and other reproductive organs near the size they were before pregnancy; however, the uterus never completely returns to its prepregnancy size. Resuming exercise following delivery has maternal benefits, including improved cardiorespiratory fitness, facilitated weight loss, increased positive mood, reduced anxiety and depression, and increased energy. Because pregnancy and vaginal delivery are risk factors in the development of urinary

Postpartum Depression

Postpartum, or postnatal, depression occurs in about 13 percent of women following childbirth. It usually resolves itself spontaneously in three to six months, but about one in four affected mothers are still depressed one year after giving birth. Several therapies used to treat depression in general have been used to treat postpartum depression, including antidepressants, counseling, and exercise. Although running is good for you during pregnancy, no significant association seems to exist between postpartum depression and having been physically active before or during pregnancy or both. However, physical activity has been shown to alleviate symptoms of postpartum depression, as it does for depression in general, so even though you may not feel like running if you have postpartum depression, it will likely help alleviate your symptoms.

incontinence, pelvic floor exercises started immediately postpartum may also reduce the risk of future urinary incontinence.

How quickly women may return to exercise and running postpartum varies. The timing of return to running after delivery depends on the type of delivery, delivery complications, and how quickly a woman recovers from the fatigue and discomfort of her labor. Some women return to activities within days of delivery while others need more time. Avoid a quick return to running if you had a Cesarean section, a complicated vaginal delivery, or an extensive episiotomy. Waiting four to six weeks allows the surgical repair to heal, the pelvic floor muscles to strengthen, and the soreness at the episiotomy site to resolve. No studies demonstrate that rapid resumption of activities postpartum in women with uncomplicated pregnancies or deliveries causes adverse effects. Further, no conclusive data support that women must wait until the six-week postpartum visit to resume running. Additionally, breastfeeding mothers may safely return to running as soon as they feel up to it and as long as it does not impair their milk production.

Because most women who have been pregnant have lost conditioning, gradual resumption of exercise is advised for most. It is common for women to need to reduce intensity and the length of their running sessions, at least initially. The competitive athlete with an uncomplicated pregnancy may resume training soon after delivery without trouble. When resuming activity postpartum, women should listen to their bodies and confer with their health care providers.

Breastfeeding and Exercise

Resuming your running after having your baby is good for your health and mood and will not have a negative impact on your baby as long you follow a few simple guidelines when exercising in the postpartum period. To ensure adequate milk production, be sure to consume enough calories and do not drop weight too quickly. While you are nursing, a good rule of thumb is to take in 500 calories in excess of what you needed to maintain your weight before you were pregnant. You are consuming sufficient calories if your baby is gaining weight. You should also consume 1,000 milligrams of calcium per day. Your health care provider may suggest that you continue your prenatal vitamin. Stay hydrated before, during, and after activity. If your urine is pale and you are not constipated, your hydration is adequate.

You can also adjust your feeding schedule in response to your baby's receptivity to your milk. Lactic acid increases in the breast milk of women exercising at maximal intensity. (Mild to moderately intense exercise during the postpartum period will not cause an accumulation of lactic acid in breast milk.) Although there are no known risks or harmful effects to babies if they consume lactic acid, controversy exists about whether the short-term increase makes the breast milk less palatable to the nursing infant.

If your baby doesn't like your postexercise milk, nurse before running, postpone feeding until at least one hour after running, or use a breast pump to extract milk before your run to use afterward. Feeding your baby before you exercise minimizes any discomfort engorged breasts might cause during exercise. Lactic acid disappears from breast milk 60 to 90 minutes following exercise, so nursing at least 90 minutes after a run may make your milk more palatable. Additionally, some babies don't like the taste of sweat, so after exercise you may need to rinse your breasts or take a shower before nursing.

To ensure your own comfort while running, be sure to wear a supportive bra with cotton nipple pads that fits well but does not compress your breasts too much. A bra that is too tight can obstruct and plug your breast ducts and lead to mastitis, a painful infection in the breast.

Menopause

4

While menarche describes the onset of menstrual periods, menopause is the time when women have their last menstrual period. It occurs because women no longer produce adequate amounts of estrogen. Although this loss of circulating estrogen can result in physical and psychological changes and increase your risk of osteoporosis and heart disease, the onset of menopause does not need to be a time to slow down and does not mean you need to stop doing the activities you enjoy. Menopause is a unique experience for every woman. Some women may experience symptoms that can challenge their running activities, while other women will move through it with little difficulty. Menopause does not require you to abandon your running activities. In fact, menopause is an ideal time to become a runner. At a time that can be emotional for many women, running can provide an outlet for that emotion and can make you feel empowered and accomplished. In addition to the physical benefits of running, including the important benefit to your bones, running provides numerous psychological, emotional, cognitive, and spiritual benefits.

Unfortunately, little data exist to show definitively whether regular running affects menopausal symptoms, such as hot flashes. The available data suggest that regular aerobic exercise improves your mood and sleep, both of which can be beneficial during the menopausal transition. Whether menopause affects your running performance is also unclear. Many women complain that they are unable to maintain their same running pace once they reach menopause. However, it is more likely that this slowing of pace is due to the effects of aging rather than the effects of menopause.

Remember, menopause is a normal part of every woman's life. Understanding the physiology of menopause, the available treatment options, and the possible training adaptations will allow you to run well into your postmenopausal years.

Defining Menopause

Menopause is the time in a woman's life when the ovaries stop producing eggs and her menstrual periods end. As the ovaries stop working, the level of estrogen falls. Menopause usually occurs between ages 45 and 55, with the average age being 51 years. Several terms describe the stages before and after your menstrual periods end.

Perimenopause refers to the time before menopause when your menstrual periods first begin to change and hot flashes develop. In the early phase of this transition, irregular cycles develop, characterized by a cycle length of more than seven days different from your normal cycle length. For example, cycles may occur every three weeks or every five to six weeks instead of every four. Hot flashes, described as a sudden sensation of heat in the upper chest and face that spreads throughout the body, occur during this transition. During the latter stages of this transition phase, cycle length increases. Commonly, intervals of amenorrhea of more than 60 days will occur. Perimenopause generally starts 5 to 10 years before menopause and ends 1 year after your final menstrual period. As your hormone levels fluctuate during this stage, there may be times when your daily run does not go as well. You may feel more fatigued or have difficulty running in warmer temperatures because of hot flashes. If this occurs, you may need to adjust your daily or weekly training routine by going out for shorter runs, running during cooler times of the day, or running on a treadmill in an air-conditioned environment.

Menopause is a natural biological process and is the permanent end of menstruation and fertility. By definition you have gone through menopause when you have had no menstrual period for 12 consecutive months. In the months to years preceding menopause, characteristic symptoms occur, including hot flashes, night sweats, sleep problems, and vaginal dryness. If you are 45 years or older and you are not having regular menstrual periods, it is likely you are menopausal, especially if you are having menopausal symptoms such as hot flashes or night sweats. Conversely, if you are 40 years old and you stop having your menstrual period, you should speak with your health care provider. While it is possible to become menopausal at 40 years or younger (a condition known as premature menopause), it is important to determine whether the loss of menstrual cycles is due to menopause or something else. Premature menopause results in more years without the benefits of estrogen and places you at greater risk for health problems later in life, such as osteoporosis and heart disease. The symptoms of menopause are well documented. Less well understood is how these symptoms affect your running performance. During this phase, some women experience a slower pace, increased aches, prolonged recovery, and declining energy. And although this can be discouraging, the best strategy is to keep running, making necessary adjustments along the way. The good news is that many runners report that performance effects during the menopause transition often resolve when menopause is complete.

Postmenopause is the time after menopause. During these years, the physical effects of aging become more apparent (addressed in chapter 5) and symptoms associated with diminished levels of estrogen, such as vaginal dryness, will persist. You will also be vulnerable to diseases associated with decreased estrogen levels, most notably, osteoporosis. With life expectancy close to 80 years for women, you can expect to be postmenopausal for approximately one-third of your life. Our overall health is tied to both our physical and emotional health. Running allows you to work on both. Accept and be comfortable with your changed body. Running when you are postmenopausal will improve your mental well-being and enhance your physical health by strengthening and toning your muscles, assisting with weight management, reducing your risk of heart disease, and helping you prevent osteoporosis.

Physiology of Menopause

Women are born with a finite number of eggs (oocytes) that are contained within the ovaries. From the time of birth until menopause, these oocytes are lost at a steady rate. Of the approximately 2 million oocytes in your ovaries at birth, only 400 reach ovulation during your reproductive years. The other 99 percent undergo degeneration and are unresponsive to your hormones. This degeneration is the result of the biological phenomenon of programmed cell death. That is, in the early embryological stages, the body produces more oocytes than will ultimately be needed later in life.

As you learned in chapter 2, during a normal menstrual cycle, the ovary, through a complex process, produces estrogen and progesterone in response to the pituitary hormones follicle-stimulating hormone (FSH) and luteinizing hormone (LH). This production of estrogen and progesterone depends on the presence of responsive, or viable, oocytes within the ovary. Between menarche and menopause, the level of responsive oocytes declines. By the onset of menopause, there are no further responsive oocytes in the ovaries. It is this inevitable depletion in responsive oocytes and resultant resistance to pituitary hormone levels that contribute to menopause and its resulting symptoms. The most significant result is the dramatic decrease in circulating estrogen levels.

Although estrogen is a hormone produced in the ovaries, its role in your physiology is rather extensive. Receptors for estrogen are found in your vagina, uterus, ovary, bladder, skin, bone, heart, blood vessels, and breasts. When estrogen levels are low or absent, cells within these tissues become inactive. Symptoms develop because organ systems are unable to respond due to the decreased levels of circulating estrogen. The range and severity of symptoms that women experience during perimenopause and menopause vary from woman to woman. Although you may not experience all or any of the symptoms that can occur, becoming familiar with the changes will give you a better understanding of what may occur. The most common symptoms of menopause include the following.

- **Hot flashes.** Hot flashes are the most common menopause-related symptom and usually begin in the perimenopausal transition period. You will experience a sudden sensation of heat in the upper chest and face that spreads throughout the body. Hot flashes last for several minutes, are often associated with sweating, and can occur several times per day. Although their cause is not fully understood, it is believed that hot flashes occur because of changes in the hypothalamus, the part of the brain that regulates the body's temperature. Estrogen plays a role in regulating brain chemicals that control body temperature. As estrogen levels diminish, the hypothalamus mistakenly senses that you are too warm. As a result, a chain of events is triggered to cool you down. In an attempt to dissipate body heat, blood flow to your skin surface increases. This produces the sensation of heat that you experience and can cause you to perspire.

  Too little data exist to show definitively whether regular running affects hot flashes. Anecdotally, women runners report that hot flashes tend to be less severe and tend to occur during times of stress rather than while running and when they are relatively relaxed. You can minimize the discomforts of hot flashes by wearing lightweight clothing or dressing in layers so you can peel some off, running during cooler times of the day, and drinking iced fluids. Because hot flashes cause you to perspire, it is important that you stay hydrated, drinking more fluids on days when hot flashes are more frequent.

- **Night sweats.** Hot flashes that occur during sleep are called night sweats and can cause you to perspire heavily and wake you because you are hot or cold. Frequent awakenings result in disrupted sleep, which can lead to fatigue and irritability.

- **Sleep disturbances.** Some women experience sleep disturbances around menopause. Sleep problems include trouble falling or staying asleep even if night sweats are not a problem. Sleep disturbances are likely related to fluctuating levels of circulating estrogen. Research suggests that estrogen replacement can improve sleep during menopause in some women. Poor sleep patterns can result in a lack of energy and cause you to become discouraged about your running. It is important to be flexible in your training and make adjustments when energy levels are low.

- **Vaginal dryness.** The lining of the vagina is sensitive to estrogen levels. Consequently, decreases in estrogen levels before and during menopause can cause the tissues of the vagina to become thin and dry, causing symptoms of vaginal irritation, dryness, itchiness, and pain.

- **Urinary incontinence.** Involuntary leaking of urine (incontinence) becomes more common as you age. While weakening of the pelvic muscles, nerves, and ligaments that are a part of the aging process can contribute to the problem, low estrogen production associated with menopause increases the risk for urinary incontinence. Without estrogen, the tissues that line the urethra (a short, muscular tube that carries urine from the bladder to the surface of the body) become thin and irritated. The thin and irritated tissues become weak and are not strong enough to hold back urine. Postmenopausal women frequently experience incontinence during running. To help control your symptoms, urinate immediately before your run, plan bathroom stops along your running routes, and use pads or protective garments while running. Your health care provider can also teach you about Kegel exercises, which help strengthen the pelvic muscles that control the flow of urine.

- **Mood swings.** Some women experience symptoms of mood swings, tearfulness, and feeling blue or discouraged during the menopause transition. These symptoms may be related to fluctuating hormonal levels, sleep disturbances, or a combination of these factors. Little evidence supports that menopause contributes to true clinical depression. However, if you have had clinical depression in the past, you may be vulnerable to recurrent depression during the menopause transition. Talk to your health care provider if you have symptoms of depression that will not go away. Indeed, running can improve your emotional health. Studies have demonstrated less psychological distress, improved well-being, improved energy, and less fatigue in postmenopausal women who run.

Heart Disease and Menopause

Before menopause, your risk of heart disease is less than that of your male counterparts. After menopause, however, your risk of heart disease increases dramatically. In fact, heart disease rates are two to three times greater for postmenopausal women than they are for premenopausal women. This dramatic increase in heart disease rates after menopause suggests that estrogen provides some cardioprotective benefits. Indeed, the benefit of estrogen on heart health is due to many factors.

One factor appears to be caused by estrogen's effects on cholesterol. Cholesterol is carried to and from the liver by molecules called lipoproteins, including low-density lipoproteins, or LDL, and high-density lipoproteins, or HDL. LDL transports cholesterol from your liver to the organs that require it, depositing the excess cholesterol in the blood vessels where it can block arteries. When cholesterol sticks to the walls of the arteries, there is less room for blood to flow through, which increases blood pressure and can slow or block blood flow to the heart. HDL, on the other hand, is like a garbage collector—it removes unused cholesterol from the blood vessels, bringing it back to the liver to be recycled. Having a high ratio of LDL to HDL and a high level of total cholesterol are associated with a high risk for heart disease. Estrogen protects your heart by lowering LDL levels and increasing HDL levels. The loss of estrogen in menopause changes this ratio of LDL to HDL, increasing your risk of heart disease.

Osteoporosis and Menopause

Osteoporosis is a serious health issue affecting postmenopausal women and is a major health problem in the United States. Characterized by low bone mass and compromised bone strength, osteoporosis predisposes you to an increased risk of fracture. (See chapters 12 and 13 for information about stress fractures.) The World Health Organization (WHO) has established diagnostic criteria for osteoporosis based on bone mineral density (BMD) measurements from dual-energy X-ray absorptiometry (DXA), the gold standard test for measuring bone mineral density. BMD is reported as the number of standard deviations from the average for normal young adults of the same sex. This information is known as a T-score.

According to the WHO, the definition of osteoporosis in a postmenopausal woman over the age of 50 is a BMD T-score that is equal to or lower than 2.5 standard deviations below the average peak bone mass of a normal, 30-year-old female. Low bone mass, or osteopenia, is a T-score between 1.0 and 2.49 standard deviations below the average peak bone mass of a normal, 30-year-old female. Stated another way, BMD at any given age is a function of both peak bone mass reached by the age of 30 and how much bone is subsequently lost.

For example, if a woman's T-score for her hip is more than one standard deviation below the average peak bone mass for the hip in a healthy, young adult female, she has lost bone mass and is at a higher risk of fracture to this site than is a woman whose T-score is better. However, women do not have to have T-scores that meet the definition of osteoporosis to be at risk for osteoporotic-type fractures. Even a loss of one standard deviation of bone mass can significantly increase your risk of a spine fracture or hip fracture.

The majority of peak bone mass is achieved during childhood and adolescence and plateaus by age 30. From then on, bone loss occurs gradually for the remainder of your life but accelerates at menopause. Beginning two to three years before menopause and continuing for up to five years afterward, bone loss occurs at a rate of 2 percent per year. The greatest bone mineral lost in postmenopausal women occurs during the first five years after menopause. After five years, bone loss slows to 1 to 1.5 percent per year. By age 80, you will have lost up to 30 percent of your peak bone mass. To reduce your risk of osteoporosis, you need to acquire as much bone mass as possible before menopause and minimize bone loss after menopause.

Although age-related bone loss depends on multiple factors, including family history, diet, and exercise, it is the low estrogen levels associated with menopause that make women so susceptible. Bone remodeling is an active, lifelong process in which old bone is removed from the skeleton (a process known as bone resorption) and new bone is added (known as bone formation). Estrogen, calcium, and exercise play important roles in the remodeling process, which is normally in balance. Weight-bearing exercise, such as running, along with adequate calcium intake help to build bone mass, and estrogen slows the process of bone breakdown.

With menopause, the lower levels of circulating estrogen result in a loss of inhibition of bone resorption. Thus, bone breakdown is accelerated without a compensatory increase in bone formation. The result is a decrease in bone mass, which reduces bone strength and increases the risk of fracture. While BMD is an important determinant of fracture risk, additional factors increase your risk for osteoporotic fractures. Having multiple risk factors from the following list in addition to decreased BMD puts you at greater risk for fracture:

- Age of 50 to 90 years old
- Another fracture after age 40
- History of hip fracture in parent
- Current cigarette smoking
- Alcohol intake of more than two drinks per day (Excessive alcohol interferes with bone remodeling by inhibiting the normal formation of new bone. This leads to bone loss, higher risk of fractures, and slower healing of bone breaks.)
- Inadequate calcium and vitamin D
- Body mass index of less than 21 (Body mass index is based on your height and weight as shown in the following equation.)

$$\text{BMI} = \text{body weight in pounds} \times 703 \div (\text{height in inches})^2$$

To prevent osteoporosis, you need to slow or stop loss of bone mass and increase bone mineral density and bone strength. Strategies include regular weight-bearing exercise, adequate intake of calcium and vitamin D, and bone strengthening drugs.

Do Men Need Estrogen?

The fact that women need estrogen for strong bones and men seemingly do not can seem confusing. Part of the explanation is that men have bigger and longer bones and that they have testosterone, the male sex hormone needed for developing peak bone mass and maintaining bone mass. Men, like women, accumulate the majority of their bone mass in adolescence and early adulthood. Because men typically have larger skeletons, they accumulate more bone mass than women by the time their bone mass peaks.

Yet, estrogen also regulates bone metabolism in men. Most estrogen in men is converted from testosterone. However, unlike amenorrheic or postmenopausal women who experience a sharp decline in estrogen and resultant bone loss, a comparable drop in men's testosterone levels does not occur. Rather, men's testosterone levels decline slowly and usually only in response to advancing age. Thus, without dramatic hormonal changes, bone loss doesn't occur and bone strength can be maintained. So, yes, men need estrogen too.

Menopause and Running

To reduce your risk of osteoporosis, you need to acquire as much bone mass as possible before menopause and reduce the rate at which bone is lost after menopause. Although genetic factors are important to peak bone mass, you can take several steps to maximize bone mass. Bone responds best to activities that generate high rates of stress on the bone.

Because bone is lost rapidly in the years surrounding menopause, it is important to take measures to reduce this loss. Regular running reduces the rate of bone loss in postmenopausal women. A long-term study in women masters runners (those over age 40) demonstrated that levels of bone mineral density can be maintained through consistent running.

Running can maintain women's bone density during and after menopause.

Hormone Replacement Therapy

Hormone replacement therapy refers to treatment with prescription hormonal medications, namely, estrogen or estrogen in combination with progesterone, to restore your decreasing hormone levels. Estrogen use to treat symptoms of menopause dates back to the 1950s. Twenty years later, researchers recognized that postmenopausal women on estrogen therapy were at an increased risk of developing uterine cancer. Since then, progesterone has been combined with estrogen. Progesterone prevents the uterine lining (endometrium) from thickening and reduces the risk of uterine cancer to the same level as that of someone not using hormones. Today, estrogen supplementation alone is reserved for women who have undergone a hysterectomy, and estrogen plus progesterone therapy is used in women with an intact uterus. Hormone therapy, or HT, encompasses both estrogen therapy and estrogen plus progesterone therapy.

Although HT has been prescribed for many years as a treatment for menopausal symptoms and to treat or reduce the risk of certain diseases, its use has not come without considerable controversy surrounding the risks and benefits. One of the largest and most well-known studies bringing attention to HT use was the Women's Health Initiative, conducted by the National Institutes of Health. The primary goal of the study was to determine whether HT would reduce the risk of cardiovascular events, such as heart attacks and strokes. Although the study demonstrated significant benefits of HT use, significant risks were also demonstrated, prompting the researchers to discontinue the study three years early. Since then, follow-up analyses and further studies have attempted to better clarify the risks and benefits of HT use. Although consensus has been reached regarding the use of HT to relieve menopausal symptoms, the use of HT to prevent complications of menopause such as osteoporosis and heart disease remain controversial.

HT and Menopausal Symptoms

Considerable evidence demonstrates HT to be the most effective treatment for the menopause-related symptoms of hot flashes and night sweats and the disrupted sleep that accompanies these symptoms. In fact, if you are healthy and postmenopausal, HT is recommended as a treatment option for your symptoms. However, based on current evidence, HT should be used for the shortest amount of time possible to relieve symptoms. Generally, this is considered to be two to three years and not more than five years.

HT and Heart Disease

Previously, it was believed that HT lowered the risk of heart disease, primarily because of its positive effects on cholesterol. However, numerous studies have failed to unequivocally demonstrate this finding. Several studies have shown that HT may increase the risk of heart disease, stroke, and blood clots, while others suggest that the impact of HT on heart health may be affected by how old you are when you start HT. Recent studies suggest that if you start HT closer to the onset of menopause, your risk for developing heart disease might be reduced; whereas, if you initiate HT more than 10 years beyond menopause, your risk for heart disease is increased. Current recommendations are cautious and indicate that HT should not be used to prevent heart disease.

HT and Osteoporosis

The benefits of HT on bone mineral density are well established. Numerous studies evaluating the effects of HT in postmenopausal women have consistently demonstrated increases in bone mineral density. Increases in lumbar spine BMD have ranged from 3.5 percent to 6.8 percent, while increases in hip BMD have ranged from 1.7 percent to 3.7 percent. When HT is combined with either strength training or aerobic exercise, further increases in bone mass have been demonstrated. Numerous studies have also indicated that HT reduces fracture risk in postmenopausal women by as much as 27 percent. This risk reduction has been proven regardless of type or dose of HT or whether HT is given as a tablet or in the form of a patch. Although fractures caused by osteoporosis typically occur later in the postmenopausal years, it's important to address bone health as early as possible. The benefits of HT are particularly effective when started during the first five years after the onset of menopause.

Several alternative therapies have been developed to prevent osteoporosis. However, because of the proven bone-protective benefits, HT is approved for the prevention of postmenopausal osteoporosis. Although it is recommended that HT be used for the shortest amount of time possible when used to control menopausal symptoms, the bone-protective benefits depend on long-term use. Indeed, a 3 to 6 percent loss in bone mineral can occur during the first year after stopping HT. Continued long-term use of HT should still be considered for bone effects, as long as you weigh the benefits and risks against those of alternative therapies. It's important to speak with your health care provider about the best option for you.

Nutrition and Bone Health

While adequate consumption of calcium and vitamin D are important to female runners regardless of age, an adequate intake of calcium along with vitamin D is essential for bone health at menopause and beyond. (See chapter 14 for more information on calcium and vitamin D.) The important role that calcium and vitamin D play in preventing bone loss and reducing fracture risk in postmenopausal women is well established. Calcium also enhances the effects of exercise on bone mineral density. Postmenopausal women who exercise and take calcium experience less bone loss than women who take calcium supplements alone.

Calcium availability depends on the amount of calcium you ingest. Although the recommended daily intake of calcium when you are menopausal is at least 1,200 milligrams per day, most menopausal women consume about half that amount. In fact, female endurance runners are among the athletes most prone to inadequate calcium intake. Additionally, your ability to absorb calcium in your gut declines in your menopausal years. Finally, the decreased estrogen levels as a result of menopause also increase the amount of calcium you excrete in your urine. This combination of circumstances makes it imperative that you increase your daily calcium intake in the years leading up to and following menopause.

No amount of calcium benefits bone health, however, without vitamin D. In fact, vitamin D is essential for calcium absorption in the gut. Unfortunately, several studies have noted vitamin D deficiency in postmenopausal women. Vitamin D can be produced in the body through the interaction of sunlight with your skin. However, age, where you live, and time of year all affect the skin production of vitamin D. Older women who live in northern latitudes produce less vitamin D than younger women living in the south. Additionally, sunscreen blocks this chemical reaction, contributing to a deficiency of vitamin D.

Dietary sources of vitamin D are limited to fortified foods and fatty fish. (See chapter 14 for more on nutrition and vitamin D.) Therefore, using a supplement containing vitamin D is the best way to ensure adequate vitamin D stores. Several studies in postmenopausal women have found that vitamin D doses of 600 to 800 International Units per day along with a calcium supplement reduced the rate of bone loss and the risk of hip fractures. It is recommended that vitamin D supplementation should include at least 800 to 1,000 International Units per day.

Training Considerations

As you've learned, menopause induces a loss of bone mineral density, but by adjusting your training, you can slow this inevitable consequence. Combining running with strength training can enhance your bone health. Training recommendations for female runners before and after menopause to maximize bone health include the following activities:

- Strength-training exercises that focus on the large muscles of the back, hip, thigh, upper arm, and forearm
- Weight-bearing activities, such as continuous running or running with intermittent walking

If you have suffered bone loss, strengthening the muscles surrounding the bone can reduce your risk of falling. In fact, weight-bearing exercise along with strength training is the best strategy to reduce the risk of falling and subsequent fractures because of the simultaneous ability to increase bone mass, increase muscle strength, and improve balance. The following general training recommendations can help keep your training on track during the menopausal transition:

- **Be flexible in your training routine.** There may be days you don't feel well. Take a day off or substitute with yoga or another gentle activity. Enhance your motivation by running with a partner or listening to music.
- **Substitute nonweight-bearing exercises.** As you get older, your risk of injury increases because of age-related changes in your muscles and joints. Periodically substituting nonweight-bearing exercises, such as swimming or cycling, will give your body a rest. Although not effective at improving or maintaining bone density, it will benefit your cardiorespiratory fitness.
- **Minimize your risk of falling.** Osteoporotic fractures commonly occur in the shoulder and wrist because of falls, so be sure to run in well-lit areas and on even surfaces. Running on a track is a nice option. If you choose to run on trails, avoid routes with lots of roots and rocks.
- **Keep a log of your activity and diet.** Metabolism slows as you get older. If you are struggling with weight gain, this will allow you to better gauge your caloric intake and daily expenditures and make necessary modifications.
- **Manage the stress in your life.** Plan to run fewer races or race shorter distances such as a 10K instead of a half-marathon. Treat yourself to a massage. Eat a balanced, nutrient-rich diet.
- **Incorporate jumping activities into your routine.** Exercises such as box jumps (see chapter 10) or skipping enhance your bone mass. Use box heights less than one foot high (30 cm) to minimize your risk of injury.
- **Remain committed to your running and strength-training program.** The bone benefits from exercise may not persist if you discontinue your exercise.

Strength Training

To maximize your bone health, incorporate strength training into your training routine. Although it is debatable whether running can increase bone mineral density in postmenopausal women, strength training can maintain and increase bone mineral density.

To achieve benefits to bone health, exercises must target the large muscle groups of the back, hip, and thigh, as well as the shoulder and arm. Training sessions must be high intensity and include an adequate number of repetitions (8 to 12) and sessions (2 to 3) per week. Strength training can be done with machines, free weights, and resistance bands. An easy and safe way to train is to use weight-lifting machines and exercises such as leg press, leg extensions, hamstring curls, squats, and back extensions. Intensity is often expressed as a percentage of the maximum amount of weight you can lift just once for a given exercise. This is known as your 1-repetition maximum (1RM). Positive effects on bone have been shown at intensities of 70 to 90 percent 1RM. For example, if the maximum amount of weight you can lift in a leg press is 100 pounds (45 kg), 70 percent 1RM equals 70 pounds (32 kg). (See chapter 10 for specific strength-training exercises.) Postmenopausal women should avoid strength-training exercises that require bending forward from the waist or too much twisting of the spine. In addition to exercises using machines, squats, hamstring curls, and calf raises as described in chapter 10 are good strength-training exercises for postmenopausal women.

Running: Your Weight-Bearing Activity

Just as it does in the premenopausal state, a running program during menopause must include the principles of frequency, intensity, and time. To improve bone mass and to lessen the effects of aging, you should include exercise bouts that incorporate higher intensities than those used when you were younger. Figure 4.1 provides a training plan for menopausal and postmenopausal recreational runners, and figure 4.2 (page 62) provides a training plan for menopausal and postmenopausal competitive runners. These training plans focus on specific considerations, including strength training, that will help you maintain or enhance your running performance in your menopausal and postmenopausal years. (See chapter 5 for more about the importance of strength training for older women.)

Figure 4.1   Training Plan for Menopausal and Postmenopausal Recreational Runners

Frequency

Running or running with intermittent walking should be performed three to five days per week. Running can continue daily depending on your training and experience. Higher intensity exercise such as strides (short, fast runs 50 to 100 meters in length), jumping drills such as single-leg hops (see chapter 10), or skipping should be performed one to two times per week. Regular skipping or power skipping can be used. Power skipping is performed like regular skipping but it uses a more forceful drive up of the leading knee.

Intensity

Intensity should be at 60 to 85 percent of maximum heart rate or at a moderately hard to hard effort.

Time

Minimum session length should be 30 to 60 minutes per day. Longer session lengths will be required if you intend to participate in half-marathons or marathons.

Strength Training

Perform strength-training exercises two or three times per week. Include 8 to 10 exercises that focus on the large muscles of the back, hip, thigh, upper arm, and forearm at each session. An easy and safe way to train these muscles is to use weight-lifting machines and exercises like leg press, leg extension, leg curl, squats, back extensions, biceps curl, and seated chest press (see chapter 10). For each exercise, perform 8 to 12 repetitions at 70 to 90 percent 1RM. Complete two or three sets per session with one to three minutes of rest between each set.

Cross-Training

As you age, the ability of your musculoskeletal system to adapt to the stresses of running is less efficient and requires more rest. Cross-training activities such as cycling, swimming, pool running, and using an elliptical machine allow you to reap the cardiorespiratory and psychological benefits of exercise while at the same time giving your body a break from running.

Sample Training Week

Monday	Tuesday	Wednesday	Thursday	Friday	Saturday	Sunday
30-45-min run with strides	Strength training	45-60-min run or run with intermittent walking	Off or cross-training	30-45-min run and strength training	45-60-min run and jumping drills	30-min run or cross-training or off

Figure 4.2   Training Plan for Menopausal and
Postmenopausal Competitive Runners

Frequency

Run five to seven days per week. Although there are no published guidelines for upper limits to weekly mileage for menopausal women, older postmenopausal women will probably find that they cannot tolerate the high-mileage weeks (more than 40 miles [64K] per week) of their younger years. However, if you were running 30 to 40 miles (48-64K) while you were premenopausal, there is no reason you should not be able to continue running this volume as long as you adequately recover and stay injury free.

Intensity

Intensity should be 70 to 85 percent of maximum heart rate or at a moderately hard to hard effort. Incorporate no more than two interval workouts per week. (See chapter 6 for a description of interval workouts.) These could include shorter intervals up to three minutes or longer intervals such as mile repeats depending on your fitness and competitive goals. Base your interval pace on your current race times, not those you obtained when you were younger.

Time

Weekly mileage goals will determine session length. At a minimum, each session should be 30 minutes per day. Sessions of up to several hours are acceptable if your goal is to run long-distance races such as a marathon.

Strength Training

Perform strength-training exercises two or three times per week. Choose 8 to 10 exercises that focus on the large muscles of the back, hip, thigh, upper arm, and forearm at each session. Also perform exercises such as the hamstring curl, squat (see chapter 10), lunge, leg press, leg extension, single-leg extension, back extension, biceps curl, triceps extension, chest press, overhead press, and seated row. *Running Anatomy* by Joseph Puleo and Patrick Milroy (2010, Champaign, IL: Human Kinetics) is a good resource to learn more about strength training for running. For each exercise, perform 8 to 12 repetitions at 70 to 90 percent 1RM. You should complete two or three sets per session with one to three minutes of rest between each set.

Cross-Training

As you age, your bones and muscles require more rest to adapt to the stresses of running. Cross-training allows you to reap the cardiorespiratory and psychological benefits of exercise while also giving your body a break from running. Consider activities such as cycling, swimming, pool running, and using an elliptical machine.

Racing

Racing is a great alternative to an interval workout and allows you to share your passion with other women. Remember that other women in your age-group are experiencing similar physiological changes, so your competitors are likely experiencing the same effects on their performance. As you age, your ability to recover between training and racing sessions takes longer. Be sure to schedule adequate recovery time between races. Some postmenopausal women find that running shorter races such as 5Ks or 10Ks brings the same amount of pleasure as longer races without the added training stresses or time commitments.

Sample Training Week

Monday	Tuesday	Wednesday	Thursday	Friday	Saturday	Sunday
Off	Interval workout (50 min total running time)	60-75-min run	45-60-min run and strength training	Off or cross-training	5K race	45-60-min run and strength training

5

Older Runners

Running can be a lifelong sport. And although it is unlikely that you will run as fast as you did when you were in your 20s, you can still run and even remain competitive as you age. Older women comprise a significant number of participants in road races, and women runners in their 50s, 60s, 70s, and beyond have demonstrated impressive athletic performances. Women 45 years old and older comprise 22 percent of half-marathon and marathon participants and 21 percent of all road race finishers. This increased participation and resultant success of older female runners has led to a better understanding of the training response as you age and of effective training strategies.

Physiology of Aging

Considerable research on aging and physical activity has been conducted in recent years. In addition to the biological effects of aging, lifestyle factors, such as diet and exercise, can affect the aging process. Poor lifestyle choices like smoking, lack of exercise, and an unhealthy diet exacerbate the effects of aging, while being physically active delays the effects of aging. Running when you are older positively influences physiological functions and improves your health and quality of life.

As you age, certain physiological changes occur that decrease your ability to respond to stresses the same way you did when you were younger. Exercise capacity is diminished, recovery from effort is prolonged, and body structures are less capable and resilient, putting you more at risk for injury. After age 30, most physiological functions decline at a rate of approximately 0.75 to 1 percent per year. This decline in physical capacity is characterized by decreases in $\dot{V}O_2max$, maximal cardiac output, muscle strength and power, and flexibility and an increase in body fat.

While there is no doubt that you will slow down as you age, how much of that slowdown can you attribute to the aging process and how much can you attribute to how you train as you get older? Considerable evidence shows that up to 50 percent of this decline is not caused by aging, but rather to deconditioning. With proper training, you can lessen the physiological effects of aging and remain competitive for a very long time.

Older people readily adapt and respond to endurance and strength training. Endurance training improves cardiorespiratory function and enhances exercise capacity. Strength training helps prevent the loss of muscle mass and strength normally associated with aging, and, along with weight-bearing exercise, prevents bone loss and improves balance, thereby reducing the risk of fractures and falling. Stretching improves flexibility and joint health. As noted in chapter 4, running can improve your mood and enhance your well-being. Although you will not run as well or as fast as you did when you were younger, running when you are older will allow you to perform at a higher level than your sedentary counterparts.

Cardiorespiratory Fitness

As you learned in chapter 1, maximal oxygen uptake, or $\dot{V}O_2$max, is a measure of the maximum volume of oxygen you can consume per minute and is an indicator of your aerobic fitness. As you age, your aerobic fitness begins to decline. It is estimated that $\dot{V}O_2$max decreases by 8 to 10 percent every 10 years after the age of 30 in healthy, sedentary adult women. However, deceases in $\dot{V}O_2$max associated with aging can vary, particularly if you remain active. In a study of 70-year-old women runners, $\dot{V}O_2$max levels were equivalent to those of sedentary 20-year-olds. Regular physical activity, not sex or age, therefore, is the primary determinant of cardiorespiratory fitness. The more physically fit you remain, the slower your rate of decline.

Decreased $\dot{V}O_2$max occurs because of decreases in maximal heart rate with age, although resting heart rate remains unchanged. Aging makes the heart muscle stiffer, which impairs the heart's capacity to pump blood. Because of the lower maximum heart rate and impaired contractility of the heart, cardiac output and stroke volume are lower in older adults than in younger people. Additionally, the ability of your muscles to extract and use oxygen is reduced with advancing age. Decreased muscle mass also contributes to the fall of $\dot{V}O_2$max with age.

Return of heart rate to baseline after activity takes longer in an older runner than it does in a younger runner. This slower return of heart rate to the resting level requires longer recovery periods during interval training and a longer cool-down after sustained running.

Muscle Mass and Strength

Men and women generally attain their highest strength levels between the ages of 20 and 40, after which the strength of most muscle groups declines, slowly at first and then more rapidly after age 50. Muscle strength decreases approximately 8 percent per decade after age 45, with greater strength losses occurring in women

Regular aerobic and strength training can significantly reduce the fitness declines that come with aging.

than in men. In both men and women, lower-extremity strength declines more rapidly than upper-extremity strength. The loss in muscle strength is particularly important for older women. One study demonstrated that 40 percent of inactive women between 55 and 64 years old were unable to lift 10 pounds. The loss of muscle strength associated with age is the result of significant reductions in muscle mass.

Sarcopenia is the decline in skeletal muscle mass due to aging. This age-associated loss in muscle mass is due to a decrease in size and loss of muscle fibers and a loss of motor units. When muscle mass is lost, it is replaced by connective tissue and fat. A loss in functioning motor units as you age contributes to the loss in muscle fibers. A motor unit includes the motor nerve and all the muscle fibers it connects to. Motor nerves die as you age. When they die, all the fibers within the motor unit lose their connection. This is known as denervation. This denervation causes the muscle fibers to deteriorate, resulting in a decrease in muscle mass. When a motor nerve dies, an adjacent motor nerve that continues to survive, usually a type I motor nerve, may connect to these deteriorating fibers. This process is called motor unit remodeling. Motor unit remodeling leads to less efficient motor units. Loss of motor neurons is directly related to a loss in strength and muscular power.

Loss of muscle fiber results in a loss of both type I (slow twitch) and type II (fast twitch) muscle fibers with a larger reduction in type II fibers. Because of declining fitness levels and a lack of intense physical training in older people, the reduction of type II fibers is greater because they aren't recruited. Because type II fibers contribute to strength and speed, muscle strength declines. In other words, use it or lose it.

Sarcopenia and strength loss, therefore, reflect the combined effects of motor unit deterioration and persistent decreases in regular muscle loading and activity. However, you can offset these effects with strength training. Muscle responds to vigorous strength training and can achieve marked and rapid improvement even in the ninth decade of life. Studies have demonstrated strength improvements in older women ranging from 2 percent to 72 percent. As with younger women, the frequency, intensity, and duration of strength training determines the magnitude of strength adaptations in older women.

Flexibility

Flexibility describes the ability of a joint to move through its full range of motion and depends on bony structures, muscle, and connective tissue. Collagen and elastin are components of connective tissue that form ligaments and tendons. The amount of collagen in ligaments and tendons decreases as you age. This results in stiffness, a loss of flexibility, and a decreased ability of these structures to withstand stress. As a result, older runners are more susceptible to strains, sprains, and tendon ruptures in the case of an inappropriate training program or a failure to include adequate amounts of rest between training sessions. An extended warmup, proper flexibility exercises, and a gradually progressive exercise program can alleviate these risks.

Regardless of age, flexibility is highly adaptable and can improve. Range-of-motion exercises significantly increase flexibility in older women. After only three to four weeks of regular stretching two or three times per week, improvement in range of motion is seen.

Body Composition

Changes in body composition occur as you age, including increases in the amount of body fat and decreases in the amount of lean body mass. These changes are the result of a slower metabolic rate. Metabolic rate decreases by about 10 percent from age 20 to 65, and another 10 percent during the later years of life. Decreased metabolic rate is mainly caused by decreases in lean body mass, which is more common in women than men.

Although increased body fat and decreased lean mass occurs as people age, increases in lean body mass can occur in older adults. In an analysis of more than

1,300 adults over the age of 50, 20 weeks of strength-training exercise resulted in a 2.2-pound (1 kg) increase in lean body mass. Although this increase may appear minimal, it is significant when you consider the nearly half-pound (0.23 kg) annual decline in lean body mass that occurs in older, nonactive adults. Exercise, particularly strength training, can help maintain body composition in older female runners, who can have 10 percent to 15 percent less body fat than sedentary women of the same age.

Bone Loss

As discussed in chapter 4, bone loss is a serious problem in older women. In post-menopausal women, the rate of bone resorption exceeds the rate of bone forma-tion, resulting in loss of bone mass. In women, bone mass decreases 20 percent by age 65 and 30 percent by age 80. Exercise is important in the prevention and treatment of osteoporosis. Bones adapt to stresses placed on them. Endurance and strength-training exercise can offset bone loss in older women.

Thermoregulation

As you age, your ability to dissipate heat (because of reduced and delayed sweat responses) decreases, resulting in decreased heat tolerance. A reduced thirst sen-sation is also associated with aging, which can cause you to become dehydrated. Dehydration coupled with reduced or delayed sweating will make you more sus-ceptible to heat illness. To minimize your risk of dehydration, it is important to drink fluids before, during, and after your run. As an older runner, training during the coolest part of the day, drinking an adequate amount of fluid in hot weather, wearing light-colored clothing, monitoring urine for evidence of dehydration, and recognizing the signs and symptoms of heat stress are important. Urine should be pale in color and not dark yellow. Worrisome symptoms of heat illness include headache, nausea, dizziness, weakness, rapid breathing out of proportion to the effort, and rapid heart rate.

Postural Stability

Postural stability involves a complex interaction between your sensory, motor, and higher brain functions. As you age, there is an impairment of the feedback control mechanisms that maintain balance, which can increase the risk of falls. Running, strength training, and flexibility exercises positively affect the feedback control mechanisms as you age, improving reaction times, balance, and agility.

Older Runners and Training Effects

Exercise improves physiological responses at any age. Several factors affect your physiological response, including your fitness level, genetics, and the specific type of training. Although it was previously believed that aging hindered the ability to improve muscular strength and aerobic capacity, research over the past 30 years has changed our understanding. Training can improve cardiorespiratory and muscular function in older men and women.

Several long-term studies have evaluated changes in $\dot{V}O_2$max in older runners. While $\dot{V}O_2$max decreases with age, the rate of decline is affected by the intensity and consistency of training. After adjusting for age, $\dot{V}O_2$max is greater among people who train regularly than among people who remain sedentary. Runners who continue to train at a high intensity experience smaller losses in $\dot{V}O_2$max than do runners who decrease their training. Training intensities of 60 percent to 80 percent of maximum heart rate minimize losses in $\dot{V}O_2$max, and greater intensities demonstrate a decreased rate of decline. Maintaining exercise intensity, therefore, rather than a higher volume of training, is the key to minimizing the loss of aerobic fitness as you age. In older women, high-intensity training recruits type II muscle fibers, which increase muscle mass, and enhances the muscles' ability to extract and use oxygen. These adaptations contribute to enhanced aerobic capacity.

You can realize the cardiorespiratory benefits of running even if you start training later in life. Endurance training can increase aerobic capacity in older women similar to that in younger women. You can expect years of improvement,

Even for those who start training later in life, running can provide many health benefits.

particularly if you maintain your training over time and adjust your exercise intensity as your conditioning improves.

Logically, you cannot maintain the same level of training when you reach 60 or 70 that you were capable of when you were 20. Yet, the success of older runners suggests that incorporating what you have learned as you have aged as a runner can keep you running at a high level for a long time. Listening to your body, not running through pain, incorporating higher-intensity with lower-volume training, and ensuring adequate and ample recovery periods will extend your years of peak performance. In other words, training smarter, not longer, will allow you to set new age-group personal records and achieve new goals. You can still reap the benefits of smarter training even if your goals don't include age-group records. Following a smarter training program will maintain your cardiorespiratory fitness and enhance your overall health.

While maintaining exercise intensity is the key to decreasing the effects of aging on your aerobic fitness, strength training can help offset the loss of muscle and strength associated with normal aging. Several studies have demonstrated that strength training in older women is effective for increasing muscle mass, including growth of type II fibers, which are most at risk of being lost or detrained during aging. Strength-trained older athletes maintain a fiber-type pattern similar to that of younger athletes, whereas older endurance athletes who are not strength trained appear to lose type II fibers.

Training intensity, expressed as a percentage of 1-repetition maximum (1RM), the maximum amount of weight you can lift only once for a given exercise, is a significant predictor of strength gains, and greater intensity leads to greater gains. Although women will gain strength at intensities of 60 percent 1RM, greater strength will be gained at intensities of 80 percent to 90 percent 1RM. To increase lean body mass, increase training volume. More sets of resistance exercises result in greater increases in lean body mass. The number of sets and repetitions as well as the intensity, duration, and frequency of strength training will determine the gains in strength and lean body mass in older female runners.

Training Recommendations

Whether you are a recreational or competitive runner, you must carefully consider the design of your training program as you age. The training principles for older runners are similar to those for younger runners. If you are a 40-minute 10K runner, it makes little difference whether you are 25 or 55; you still train like a 40-minute 10K runner. The biggest training differences are in the amount of recovery between workouts, the change from high-volume training to lower-volume and more high-intensity training, and the inclusion of strength training to target your fast-twitch muscle fibers. To achieve cardiorespiratory benefits and increase muscle strength, lean body mass, and bone mineralization, it is essential that your running program incorporate activities that improve aerobic capacity, strength, range of motion, and flexibility. Table 5.1 (page 72) provides a sample training program appropriate for older runners.

Table 5.1 Sample Training Plan for Older Runners

Week	Monday	Tuesday	Wednesday
1	Off	• 15-20-min warm-up • 4 × 400 m at mile pace (or 90-95% of maximum heart rate) w/ 2:1 rest:work interval • 10-min cool-down • Strength training	60 min cross-training
2	Off	• 15-20-min warm-up • 5 × 400 m at mile pace w/ 2:1 rest:work interval • 10-min cool-down • Strength training	50-min run
3	Off	• 40-min run • Strength training	45-min run plus strides
4	Off	• 15-20-min warm-up • 6 × 400 m at mile pace w/ 2:1 rest:work interval • 10-min cool-down • Strength training	50-min run
5	Off	• 15-20-min warm-up • 6 × 400 m at mile pace w/ 2:1 rest:work interval • 10-min cool-down • Strength training	50-min run
6	Off	• 45-min run • Strength training	40-min run plus strides
7	Off	• 15-20-min warm-up • 7 × 400 m at mile pace w/ 2:1 rest:work interval • 10-min cool-down • Strength training	50-min run
8	Off	• 15-20-min warm-up • 7 × 400 m at mile pace w/ 2:1 rest:work interval • 10-min cool-down • Strength training	40-min run

Thursday	Friday	Saturday	Sunday
Cross-training or off	• 20-min warm-up • 4 × 800 m hill at 5K pace effort • 10-min cool-down	• 30-min cross-training • Strength training	60-min run
Off	• 50-min fartlek	• 30-min cross-training • Strength training	60-min run
Off	• 30-min run or cross-training • Strength training	• 40-min cross-training	50-min run
Off	• 60-min fartlek	• 30-min cross-training • Strength training	60-min run
Off	• 20-min warm-up • 5 × 800 m hill at 5K effort • 10-min cool-down	• 30-min cross-training • Strength training	65-min run
Off	• 35-min run or cross-training • Strength training	• 40-min cross-training	55-min run
Off	• 20-min warm-up • 5 × 800 m hill at 5K effort • 10-min cool-down	• 30-min cross-training • Strength training	65-min run
Off	• 60-min fartlek	• 30-min cross-training • Strength training	70-min run

Although you might have been able to get away with an inadequate warm-up or two hard running days in a row when you were younger, training rules that apply to all runners are particularly important to older female runners. Adopting the following recommendations will ensure a safe and positive running experience.

- **Warm up.** Always include a warm-up of 10 to 15 minutes of easy running.
- **Cool down.** Be sure to cool down after exercise until your heart rate is less than 100 beats per minute.
- **Emphasize recovery.** This includes longer rests between intervals and more easy days between high-intensity training. Consider fewer actual running days per week. The most important training strategy is one that focuses on more recovery between hard training sessions and hard training weeks.
- **Be flexible.** Older runners are at an increased risk for injury. Listen to your body and be flexible with your training schedule.
- **Keep things in perspective.** Challenge yourself with realistic age-based and time-based goals.
- **Mix it up.** Incorporate nonweight-bearing forms of cross-training, such as water running, cycling, and swimming, to reduce wear and tear and maintain cardiorespiratory fitness.

Intensity

Older runners need to follow a careful progression in intensity and duration. Focus more on high-intensity training and less on training volume. Perform a combination of moderate and more intense running at least three days per week. Sessions should last 30 to 60 minutes or longer, depending on your training and racing goals. Intensity should feel somewhat hard to very hard, which corresponds to 60 percent to 90 percent of your maximum heart rate.

Older runners should also limit hard training sessions to two sessions per week. Hard training sessions should incorporate a range of speeds, depending on your running goals. Examples of hard training sessions for the recreational runner include five to seven strides incorporated into a run or a fartlek (speed play) workout or running hard up a hill several times. For a competitive runner, long or short intervals, acidosis threshold pace, fartlek, or hill repeats are all effective high-intensity workouts. Always tie the intensity of your speed work to current performances and never do more than two progressively hard weeks in a row. In other words, your build-up is slow: two consecutive and progressively harder weeks consisting of a total of four interval or high-intensity workouts, followed by a recovery week of easier running.

Strength Training

Older runners should commit to strength training. Because of the inevitable loss of muscle mass, you must focus on strength training to delay or reverse this decline.

Improvements in muscle strength gained through strength training reverse quickly, so this component of your training should be a priority. Squats, hamstring curls, and calf raises as described in chapter 10 are a good place to start. The exercises described in chapter 12 are also beneficial.

You can perform strength training with free weights, body weight, machines, and resistance bands. Exercises must target the major muscle groups of the chest, shoulders, back, hips, legs, trunk, and arms. A safe and effective training load for older female runners is 75 percent 1RM. Perform 8 to 12 repetitions of each exercise. Two to four sets are recommended, although a single set of each resistance exercise can be effective in older women who are new to strength training. Incorporate rest intervals of two to three minutes between each set of repetitions. Rest at least 48 hours between sessions for any single muscle group.

Train each major muscle group two or three days per week, and perform each exercise through a full, pain-free range of motion. Optimal strength development occurs when the muscle is worked from a fully stretched to a fully contracted position. Gradually increase resistance and frequency as you gain experience and strength. If you are new to strength training, start with fewer repetitions and lower intensity one or two times per week until comfortable, then gradually increase training volume and intensity.

Stretching

Joint flexibility decreases as you age. Although some disagreement exists surrounding the benefits of stretching on joint range of motion, particularly in joints that are stiff or less mobile, in older runners stretching is essential. Several types of flexibility exercises can improve range of motion. However, in older athletes, static stretching, which involves slowly stretching a muscle to the point of tightness and holding the position for a certain amount of time, elicits greater gains in range of motion than other types of stretching. Although holding a stretch for 10 to 30 seconds enhances range of motion in most people, older runners may see greater improvements by holding the stretches for 30 to 60 seconds. Stretch every muscle group, including the shoulder, chest, neck, trunk, low back, hips, front and back of the legs, and ankles. See chapter 13 for detailed descriptions of various stretches.

Always stretch after aerobic or strength training or as a stand-alone program. (See chapter 13 for suggestions about dynamic stretches that are appropriate to perform prior to a workout.) The goal is to attain 60 seconds of total stretching time per flexibility exercise by adjusting duration and repetitions according to your needs. For example, 60 seconds of stretching time can be met by one 60-second stretch, two 30-second stretches, or four 15-second stretches. You should stretch at least two or three times per week; greater gains in range of motion occur with daily stretching. Flexibility exercises are most effective when the muscle is warmed through light activity or through external methods such as moist heat packs or hot baths.

Nutrition and Hydration

Little research exists on the energy needs of older women who exercise. In general, runners over 50 should follow the dietary reference intake (DRI) regarding carbohydrate, protein, and fat, adjusting for energy expenditure (see chapter 14). The DRI suggests dietary carbohydrate should be in the range of 45 percent to 65 percent of total calories, fat in the range of 20 percent to 35 percent of total calories, and protein making up the rest of the calories. A falling metabolic rate may require fewer calories to minimize fat gain, although the age-related decline in resting metabolic rate can be reduced in older women who remain physically active.

A lower caloric intake must not occur, however, at the expense of important vitamins and nutrients, particularly calcium, vitamin D, and B vitamins. As explained previously, calcium and vitamin D are essential to maintaining bone health as you age and your daily needs increase. Vitamin B_6 performs a variety of functions in your body, such as metabolizing protein and amino acid, and is essential for good health. Requirements for this vitamin are greater in older women. Your ability to absorb foods containing vitamin B_{12} becomes less efficient as you age, resulting in decreased circulating levels of vitamin B_{12} in the body when you are older. Other B vitamin needs may increase in older women, especially women who exercise regularly. A well-balanced, varied diet that takes into account your energy needs will satisfy your nutritional requirements. Given the uncertainties surrounding vitamin and mineral needs in older female runners, you should consider a daily vitamin supplement. Speak with your health care provider to determine what may be best for you.

In addition to nutrition, you should pay special attention to fluid intake. Aging brings physiological changes to your thirst sensation, your sweating rate, and how your kidneys respond to fluids and electrolytes. Although there are no published recommendations for fluid intake for older female runners, follow hydration guidelines for younger runners.

Part II
Training

Components of Training

Despite the simplicity of putting one foot in front of the other, running is extremely complex. When done correctly, it is a scientific endeavor to maximize your endurance and speed. Whether you want to run around the block or qualify for the Boston Marathon, how you train can dramatically affect your performance. Running should be planned and systematic; nothing is done for the sheer sake of variety. While running just to run will certainly make you fitter, understanding all of the training components and putting them together in a systematic training plan will give you the blueprint for competitive success. It's the difference between building a house by placing bricks here and there and having a blueprint laid out beforehand. As New York Yankees catcher Yogi Berra once said, "If you don't know where you're going, you might not get there."

Functional changes take place only in the organs, cells, and intracellular structures that are stressed during physical activity. If you want bigger biceps, doing squats won't help. Muscles adapt to the specific demands placed on them. But running is not just about muscles. It's also about movement. In addition to the cardiorespiratory, metabolic, and muscular changes that take place from running, there is also a neuromuscular aspect to it, with your central nervous system being the primary player. Your brain needs to learn to communicate with your muscles to perform the specific task of running, and your muscles need to learn to produce force at specific joint angles, which influence the amount of force muscles can produce. This process is referred to as motor learning, or neuromuscular memory. Therefore, you need to train the entire movement pattern, rather than the strength or endurance of individual muscles or single joint movements.

For this reason, you need to run to be a good runner, and you need to ride a bike to be a good cyclist. Running won't help you become a better cyclist any more than riding a bike will help you become a better runner. The movement patterns of the two sports are completely different and therefore differ in their motor unit (muscle fiber) recruitment patterns and the muscles' ability to produce force. For example, cyclists, because of their pronounced flexed posture at the hip joint, move their hip flexors and quadriceps muscles at short lengths, while runners, because of their upright posture, move their hip flexors and quadriceps muscles at long lengths. The chronic use of these muscles at different lengths during these different activities results in different relationships between muscle length and the forces they can produce at those lengths.

The same concept holds true for cross country and trail running and to track and road running. If you're training for cross country or trail races, you should run as much as you can on cross country courses that include grass and dirt. You need to accustom your muscles and tendons to the terrain on which you plan to race. Good runners will run well regardless of the terrain, but doing all of your running on trails to prepare for a marathon on the road is like a tennis player practicing on a hard court to prepare for a tournament on a clay or grass court. The way a tennis player's feet move and the way the ball bounces on a clay or grass court are different from how they react on a hard court, just like running on trails is different from running on the road. You need to train on the surface you plan to race on.

Although training movement certainly needs to be specific to your racing environment, this specificity-of-training principle does not always hold true in an endurance sport like distance running when it comes to the speed at which you train. That's because endurance sports are volume based, so they require a large volume of work performed slower than race pace. To handle a lot of volume, you have to run slower than race pace most of the time. Although it may seem logical to run at 10K race pace as often as possible to get faster for a 10K, it's not the best way to improve your 10K time. You don't do workouts to practice running faster. You do workouts to improve the physiological characteristics that will allow you to run faster in the future. Now let's take a look at the different types of running workouts.

Aerobic Capacity Training

For distance runners, the aerobic system is the predominant energy system used to resynthesize ATP for muscle contraction. The rate at which you resynthesize ATP is limited by your aerobic capacity. Therefore, your development as a distance runner begins with aerobic training, which comprises the majority of your training. Not only does the majority of your improvement come from increasing your aerobic fitness, a high aerobic capacity is beneficial to doing anaerobic work. A runner with a well-trained aerobic system will recover faster from the anaerobic training than one who lacks a high level of aerobic fitness. Every month and every year of training should build on what came before it, with each year creating a larger aerobic base to lift your level of performance to a higher peak.

Mileage

To become a better distance runner, the number of miles you run each week is the most important component of your aerobic training. Running lots of miles stimulates many physiological, biochemical, and molecular adaptations. Think of these adaptations as your body's attempt to cope with the demand of running often. If you run every day, or at least regularly, your body must develop mechanisms to meet the demand you've created. Running lots of miles does many things to increase your aerobic capabilities, which will improve your performance from 800 meters to the ultramarathon.

Physiological Adaptations

One of the initial adaptations of increasing your mileage is an increase in your blood volume. With a greater amount of blood circulating through your body comes a greater number of red blood cells, which transport oxygen. Inside a red blood cell is a protein called hemoglobin, which carries oxygen to your working muscles. These changes to your blood improve your blood vessels' ability to transport oxygen. Endurance training also stimulates the storage of more fuel (glycogen) in your muscles, increases the use of intramuscular fat to spare glycogen, and creates a greater capillary network for a more rapid diffusion of oxygen into your muscles.

Additionally, through the complex activation of gene expression, endurance training increases your muscles' mitochondrial density and the number of aerobic enzymes contained within them. These changes increase your aerobic metabolic capacity. Mitochondria are important because that is where aerobic metabolism takes place. They are like aerobic factories. The discovery of the link between an increase in the enzyme activity of the mitochondria and an increase in mitochondria's capacity to consume oxygen, first made in 1967 in the muscles of rats, has provided much insight into the ability of skeletal muscles to adapt.

Limitations of Adaptation

Generally, the greater the demand, the greater the adaptations. In other words, the more you run, the more adaptations you'll make. But only up to a point. Unfortunately, your ability to adapt to a training stimulus doesn't occur indefinitely. There will come a point, which is specific to each runner, when more training does not lead to more adaptations and faster race times. For example, research has shown that although mitochondrial density is highly modifiable, a threshold exists above which further increases in training volume do not result in further increases in mitochondrial density. The main difference between Olympic athletes and the rest of us is that Olympic athletes continue to make physiological adaptations because of their genetic ability to adapt with more and more training, even when running more than 100 miles (161K) per week. Most of us will stop adapting far short of 100 miles per week.

Although many scientists have acknowledged there is an upper limit to the volume of training that causes further adaptations, research has not documented at what point these adaptations stop occurring in response to the demand. In other words, how much mileage do you need to run? The answer depends on several factors, primary among them being your genetically determined propensity to continually adapt to greater amounts of running and the amount of running that you can physically and psychologically handle.

There is also a load of training, again specific to each runner, that leads to injury. The human body is great at adapting to stress as long as that stress is applied in small doses. When the stress is too severe, or not enough recovery has preceded the new stress, injury can result. Another unique characteristic of Olympic runners is that they can tolerate very high training loads without getting injured. Most runners would likely get injured if they attempted to run 100 miles (161K) per week.

Research has shown that runners who run a lot tend to be more economical, which has led to the suggestion among scientists that running high mileage, more than 70 miles (113K) per week, improves running economy, which is the amount of oxygen needed to run at a given speed. Because it's difficult to prove cause and effect, it is not entirely clear whether high-mileage runners become more economical by running more miles or are innately more economical and can therefore handle higher mileage without getting injured. Another possibility is that high mileage improves economy through more repetition of the running movements, which optimizes biomechanics and muscle fiber recruitment patterns. Additionally, as many runners will tell you, a great side effect of running is weight loss because running burns more calories than just about everything else. Weighing less decreases the amount of oxygen needed to run at a given pace (i.e., it improves your economy). This is one of the main reasons that the best runners are thin: less weight provides an economical advantage.

Much of the research on the biochemical adaptations to endurance training has been done on animals. For example, the mitochondrial enzyme content of rats has been shown to reach its maximum adaptation at running 60 minutes per day five days per week. A study published in *European Journal of Physiology* in 1998 on horses training for 34 weeks found that increases in muscle fiber area and the number of capillaries per fiber plateaued after 16 weeks of training. After the first 16 weeks, the horses were divided into two groups: a control group and an overload training group, which trained with higher mileage. Both groups increased mitochondrial volume and $\dot{V}O_2$max with the increased mileage over the next 18 weeks, but there was no difference in those variables or in muscle fiber area and capillarization after 34 weeks despite the twofold difference in training volume between groups over the final 18 weeks. Clearly, there is a limit to muscles' adaptive response to training.

Obviously, the less trained you are, the more you can expect to improve by increasing your mileage. Research has shown that weekly mileage ranging from 5 to 75 miles per week can explain 86.5 percent of the difference in $\dot{V}O_2$max between runners and that runners training more than 60 miles (97K) per week run significantly faster in races from 10K to 90K than runners who run less than 60 miles per week. Although it is likely, and even probable, that running more mileage leads to a higher $\dot{V}O_2$max and faster race times because of all of the previously described adaptations, we cannot conclude cause and effect from cross-sectional studies comparing separate groups of runners. It's likely that genetically gifted runners who have a high $\dot{V}O_2$max are capable of running more miles and run faster races. Having said that, however, it is likely that if you are running less than 30 miles (48K) per week, both your $\dot{V}O_2$max and your race times will improve with more mileage.

Body Composition

Running more is not better only for your running performance. If you're a runner who wants to lose weight in addition to getting faster, your weekly mileage will also influence your body shape. Data from the National Runners' and Walkers' Health Studies, the largest series of research studies on the relationship between running and health, found that women who averaged more than 40 miles (64K) of running per week had a 10 percent lower body mass index (an indicator of body weight for height and the most popular measurement to determine obesity) than those who ran fewer than 10 miles (16K) per week. They also had 8 percent lower waist circumferences, 7 percent lower hip circumferences, 4 percent lower chest circumferences and 18 percent smaller bra cup measurements (which, as previously discussed, is an advantage for female distance runners because it reduces the amount of fat they have to carry). In every age group studied, from 18 to 24 years to over 50 years, the more miles the women ran, the lower their body mass index and chest, waist, and hip circumferences.

Many other studies have also shown that how much you weigh is directly linked to the amount of exercise you do. When it comes to distance running, there is a lot of truth to the motto, "the more the better." However, unlike men, who can run to their heart's content, female-specific factors such as amenorrhea, the female athlete triad (osteoporosis, disordered eating, menstrual irregularities; see chapter 12), pregnancy, and menopause all contribute to how much mileage you can handle without getting injured. For example, amenorrhea and menopause are both characterized by a lack of estrogen, which has a protective effect on bones. Trying to increase your running mileage during these conditions can put you at an increased risk of stress fractures, so you need to be careful about how or even whether you increase the volume of your training.

Despite all of the benefits obtained from your weekly mileage, if you want to be a successful runner, the consistency of your weekly mileage is just as important as the mileage itself. Whether you are running for fitness and weight loss or training for the Olympics, weekly mileage loses its value if there are constant interruptions to training. If you've ever been injured and forced to take time off from running, you know how quickly fitness is lost. With consistent training, you introduce a constant need for adaptation. If you remove the training stimulus, not only are there no further adaptations, there also is no longer a reason to keep the adaptations that have occurred. So your body gets rid of them. It will take you much longer to see results if you run two days this week, four days next week, three days the week after, six days the week after that, two days the following week, and so on. If you want to see results, you must consistently apply the training stress—week after week, month after month, year after year.

Long Runs

Long runs are significantly longer than any of your other runs and should typically be about one-third of your weekly mileage. In simple terms, long runs improve your endurance by running longer than you are used to. From a physiological perspective, long runs cause a sustained push of oxygen into the muscles, stimulating muscle capillarization—an expansion of your existing capillary beds and the creation of new capillary beds. Long runs also severely lower muscle glycogen and stimulate a greater reliance on fat. In the case of marathon training, long runs prepare muscles and connective tissue to handle the stress of pounding the pavement for 26 miles (42K) and callous you psychologically for running for a long time.

Lowering your muscles' store of carbohydrate (glycogen) presents a threat to the muscles' survival because carbohydrate is your muscles' preferred source of fuel. The human body responds rather elegantly to situations that threaten or deplete its supply of fuel, synthesizing and storing more than what was previously present, thus increasing endurance for future efforts. It's like emptying a full glass and getting a refilled larger glass in its place. (Much like some cocktail parties.) The more glycogen you have packed into your muscles, the greater your endurance and the more capable you will be at maintaining your marathon pace to the finish line.

Long runs can also train fast-twitch muscle fibers. Traditionally thought of as the muscle fibers for sprinting, fast-twitch fibers are also recruited when the slow-twitch fibers fatigue. If you run long enough, your slow-twitch fibers will fatigue, causing some fast-twitch fibers to be recruited to pick up the slack so you can maintain the pace.

Acidosis (Lactate) Threshold Training

Training your acidosis (lactate) threshold, or AT, increases the running speed at which acidosis occurs, enabling you to run at a higher percentage of your $\dot{V}O_2$max for a longer time. Increasing your AT pace allows you to run faster before you fatigue because it allows you to run faster before oxygen-independent metabolism begins to play a significant role. With training, what was once an anaerobic pace becomes high aerobic.

Imagine two runners who have similar $\dot{V}O_2$max values but different AT paces. If runner A and runner B both have a $\dot{V}O_2$max of 60 milliliters of oxygen per kilogram per minute (ml/kg/min), but runner A's AT is 70 percent of $\dot{V}O_2$max and runner B's AT is 80 percent of $\dot{V}O_2$max, runner B can sustain a faster pace and will beat

Balancing Motherhood and Training

When you don't have children, you can run whenever you want or whenever your job allows. Having children, of course, makes training a different matter. Regardless of how old they are, sometimes it's just impossible to squeeze in a run. Kids get sick, there's always another load of laundry to do, and let's not forget chauffeur duties to everything from Little League practice to ballet. Once in a while, it's okay to miss a run because you have family obligations. The important thing is to remain flexible and levelheaded through it all. Like many runners, you may become irritable when you don't run. But don't let a missed run get you down or ruin your week. And don't feel guilty about taking the time to run. Running makes you a better mom. Every mother needs an outlet and time to recharge so she can come back and be a nurturer and caregiver. Balancing motherhood and running comes down to prioritizing and planning. Here are strategies to try:

- **Plan.** Coordinate with your spouse or someone else to watch the kids while you go for a run.
- **Buy a jogging stroller.** When your kids are young, they can often accompany you on a run.
- **Become a (very) early-morning person.** Some of your best running can be done in the morning, before anyone in the house is awake. Early-morning runs are a great way to start your day.
- **Run at night.** If you can't run first thing in the morning, try running after your kids have gone to bed.
- **Buy a treadmill.** Although not as enjoyable as running outside, running on a treadmill gives you the benefit of never having to leave your house. Your kids can be in view for your entire workout.
- **Create a network.** Establish a system of people who can watch your kids: grandparents, other parents, gym kids clubs, babysitter, husband (or ex-husband), or other moms who run.
- **Take your kids to the track.** They can run around and you can see them during your workout.

runner A. Also, a runner with a lower $\dot{V}O_2max$ can run the same speed or faster than a runner with a higher $\dot{V}O_2max$ if she has a higher AT.

Although $\dot{V}O_2max$ has received most of the attention among runners and coaches, the acidosis threshold is actually more important because it exerts a greater influence on performance and is more responsive to training than is $\dot{V}O_2max$. Although a high $\dot{V}O_2max$ is your VIP card, having that VIP card is not enough. To be a good distance runner, you need to have other tools in your physiological arsenal to succeed among the other VIP members. We have tested many athletes in the laboratory who have an elite-level $\dot{V}O_2max$, but few of them were capable of running at the elite or even sub-elite level because they did not have a high AT. Indeed, research has shown that AT is the best physiological predictor of distance running performance.

The longer the race for which you're training, the more important it is to train your acidosis threshold. Because the mile is much faster than your AT pace, improving your AT doesn't play as large a role in improving your mile time. However, a well-run half-marathon and marathon are only a bit slower than AT pace, so it becomes more important to increase the pace you can maintain for an extended time. If you're training for the half-marathon and marathon, your AT should be the focus of your training. The keys to success for the longer distance races are (1) getting your AT pace as fast as you can and (2) being able to run as close to your AT pace as possible for as long as possible. Training the AT shifts it to a faster speed, enabling you to run faster before oxygen-independent metabolism (and fatigue) begin to play a significant role. See chapter 8 for more information on measuring your AT and workouts to develop it.

Interval Training

Interval training has been shown to induce some of the same peripheral muscular adaptations as continuous aerobic training, such as an increased number of mitochondria and enzymes. Possibly the greatest use of interval training, however, lies in its ability to target individual energy systems and physiological variables, improving specific aspects of your fitness level. Interval workouts alternate high-intensity work periods with low-intensity recovery periods. Four variables can be manipulated within an interval workout:

- Time (or distance) of each work period
- Intensity of each work period
- Time of each recovery period
- Number of repetitions

Although many athletes used interval training in the first half of the 20th century, it was distance runner Emil Zàtopek of Czechoslovakia, winner of the 10,000 meters at the 1948 Olympics and the 5,000 meters, 10,000 meters, and marathon at the 1952 Olympics, who popularized this method of training. However, it wasn't until the 1960s that famous Swedish physiologist Per-Olof Åstrand discovered, using a stationary bicycle in a laboratory, what many coaches and runners already knew—that by breaking up a set amount of work into smaller segments, they could perform a greater volume of work at a higher intensity. Sounds obvious, but Åstrand's simple observation is the basis for interval training.

Preceding Åstrand's work by 30 years was the attention given to interval training by German coach Waldemar Gerschler and physiologist Hans Reindell of Germany's Freiburg University. When they studied interval training in the 1930s, they focused on its cardiorespiratory aspects and believed that the stimulus for cardiorespiratory improvement occurs during the recovery intervals between work periods rather than during the periods of activity, as the heart rate decreases from an elevated value. Thus, the emphasis of the workout was placed on the recovery interval, prompting Gerschler and Reindell to call it an *interval workout* or *interval training*. Gerschler and Reindell's original interval training method consisted of running periods ranging from 30 to 70 seconds at an intensity that elevated the heart rate to 170 to 180 beats per minute, followed by sufficient recovery to allow the heart rate to decrease to 120 beats per minute, signifying the readiness to perform the next work period.

During the recovery interval, your heart rate declines quickly because you've stopped running fast, but you have a lot of blood returning back to the heart. Because the heart rate declines rapidly, there's a greater filling time in the left ventricle to accommodate the return of the large volume of blood to the heart, resulting in a brief increase in stroke volume (the amount of blood the heart pumps with each beat). The increase in stroke volume places an overload on the heart, which makes the heart stronger, and enables the skeletal muscles to be cleared of waste products quickly because of the elevated rate of blood flow when there is little demand for activity from the tissues. Because stroke volume peaks during the recovery interval, and because there are many recovery intervals during an interval workout, stroke volume peaks many times, providing a stimulus for improving maximum stroke volume and thus the capacity of the oxygen transport system.

Interval training can also improve your ability to regenerate ATP via anaerobic metabolic pathways, increasing your anaerobic fitness and speed. In addition to the large aerobic contribution to distance-running races, there is a significant involvement of anaerobic metabolism because most races are run at speeds faster than the acidosis threshold for most runners (with the notable exceptions being the half-marathon, marathon, and ultramarathon). When your pace exceeds the rate at which the heart and blood flow can provide oxygen to the muscles, some of the energy for muscle contraction is regenerated through anaerobic means.

When this happens, several problems begin to arise inside your muscles. Primary among them is that the muscles lose their ability to contract effectively because of an increase in hydrogen ions, causing acidosis. As you learned in chapter 1, acidosis has several side effects: It inhibits the enzyme that breaks down the energy molecule (ATP) inside muscles, which decreases muscle contractile force; it inhibits the release of calcium (the trigger for muscle contraction) from its storage site in muscles; and it inhibits the production of ATP from the metabolic pathway glycolysis by inhibiting the most important enzyme in glycolysis. Other metabolites, including inorganic phosphate (P_i), ADP, and potassium, also accumulate when you are running fast. Each of these cause specific problems inside muscles, from inhibition of specific enzymes involved in muscle contraction to interference with muscles' electrical charges, ultimately leading to a decrease in muscle force production and your running speed.

Given the many fatigue-inducing factors associated with oxygen-independent metabolism, it's important to develop your anaerobic capacity once you have

Running With a Group

Much has been written about the loneliness of the long-distance runner. During your training miles alone on roads and trails, you can learn how to become your own psychologist, how to *work in* rather than *work out*. Although running by yourself has its perks and gives you a chance—maybe the only one you have all day—to be alone, sometimes it helps to train with a group. Group training offers camaraderie and accountability, resources and a network for running-related information, and encouragement and motivation. Running with a group can also help you become faster because it's easier to push yourself with other runners around you. You'll also feel a sense of belonging to a team if you decide to join a formal group that trains together and competes together in races. Some groups even offer formal coaching.

If you decide to join a group, many options exist, from small, informal groups that include runners of all levels to large, competitive, fee-based clubs that meet at a track for coach-led formal workouts. Owing to the popularity of the marathon, training groups specifically geared toward training for a marathon are among the fastest-growing types of running groups. If you're interested in running a marathon, national organizations like Team in Training (www.teamintraining.org), which is charity based, and USA Fit (www.usafit.com), which is fee based, have local chapters in nearly every major U.S. city. Both offer weekly group long runs and a written training schedule for their members.

If you're interested in something more informal, hundreds of local groups meet around the country, and most of them meet regularly for runs of various distances based on runners' abilities. Perhaps the easiest way to find a group to run with is by doing an Internet search. Use search terms such as *running clubs* and your city and state. For a more specific search, add terms like *recreational, coach, fee, competitive,* or *trail*. Also check out Road Runners Club of America (www.rrca.org), which lists running clubs throughout the United States. Many running shoe stores lead informal groups that meet in front of their stores for weekly runs. The store's staff may also know of other clubs or coaches in the area.

developed yourself as aerobically as possible. Anaerobic-capacity training causes a high degree of muscle acidosis so that you enhance your buffering capacity, it increases the number of enzymes that catalyze the chemical reactions in anaerobic glycolysis so that glycolysis can regenerate ATP more quickly for muscle contraction, and it increases running speed by recruiting fast-twitch muscle fibers. We'll discuss specific interval workouts to target improvements in the acidosis threshold, $\dot{V}O_2max$, and anaerobic capacity and power in chapters 8 through 10.

Interval training reaps many health-related benefits, including improvement in vascular health and reduction in cardiovascular disease risk factors. Because it has a huge effect on metabolism and calorie burning, it also has a huge potential to help you lose fat. Its intense nature disrupts your body's homeostasis, making interval training more effective than continuous running for increasing metabolic rate following a workout as homeostasis is reestablished. The more intense the workout, the greater and longer the postworkout elevation in metabolism because recovery is an aerobic process. Interval training increases the number of proteins that transport fatty acids across the mitochondrial membrane. It also increases enzyme activity in skeletal muscle and the muscle oxidative capacity of carbohydrate and fat to the same extent as or more than traditional continuous aerobic training. Finally, it turns on the signaling cascade that leads to the synthesis of fat-burning mitochondria, which has been traditionally thought to occur only in response to aerobic endurance training. Decreasing your body fat will improve your running performance.

Other Types of Training

Other types of training, such as hills and fartleks, are great additions to your training program. You can use hill training to prepare for races with hills and to improve muscle strength and power. You can use fartleks to learn different paces, work on race tactics, practice responding to other runners' surges (if done in a group), add variety and fun to your training, and to shift into more formal speed work.

Hills

The feel of your heart pounding in your chest and your shortness of breath at the top of a hill attest to what hills provide for your cardiorespiratory system. But they also provide a great workout for your skeletal muscles. Hill training increases leg muscle power, can be used as a transition into more formal speed work, improves the performance of the heart because heart rate can easily climb to its maximum when running up a hill, and uses the muscles of the legs, arms, and trunk in ways that are different from running over flat terrain. Because hill running uncouples the effort from the speed (i.e., you're running relatively slow even though you're working hard), the exact pace is not as important as the effort. When you run hills, aim for a specific effort rather than a specific speed.

Hill training, which uses eccentric muscle contractions on the downhills, helps build strength and power.

Even though running uphill seems harder because your heart must do more work to send blood and oxygen to the muscle mass that is working against gravity, downhill running actually causes the biggest problems. If you've ever run a race with long or steep downhills, you know what running downhill can do to your legs. The reason downhills are so tough is because of the gravity-induced eccentric muscle contractions, during which your muscle fibers are forced to lengthen, causing them to tear. Eccentric contractions are also unique in that fewer muscle fibers are active than in other types of muscle contractions, causing the force generated to be distributed over a smaller area of muscle. A greater force over a smaller area equals greater tension, which causes even more damage.

The forces of impact and braking are also greater during downhill running than during uphill and flat running. Therefore, running downhill carries a greater risk of overuse injury than uphill or flat running. The muscle damage decreases your muscles' ability to produce force, which slows your pace on the flat and uphill portions of the race and leads to delayed-onset muscle soreness, which includes an inflammatory response and lasts for a few days following the race as your muscle fibers heal. The good news is that damaging muscle fibers with eccentric contractions makes them heal stronger, protecting them from future damage. Although you can expect your muscles to be sore after the first time running downhill, subsequent downhill workouts will cause less soreness. Proper technique when running downhill can alleviate some of the impact. Although it's tempting to lean back with your feet landing far out in front of your body, it's actually better to lean forward, allowing gravity to pull you. Your feet should land as close to directly underneath your hips as possible to minimize braking.

Hill workouts come in many forms, including the following:

- **Hill run.** This workout is a steady run that includes hills of various lengths and grades.
- **Long hill intervals.** These are repeats of a half-mile to 1-mile (800-1,600 m) gradual uphills.
- **Short hill intervals.** These are repeat sprints up a short, steep hill.
- **Uphill and downhill intervals.** This workout includes repeats of a combination of uphills and downhills.
- **Short downhill intervals.** These are repeat sprints down a short, gradual slope.
- **Hill accelerators.** This workout repeats runs up a short hill, accelerating the last 50 meters of the hill and the next 100 meters after reaching the top of the hill.
- **Hill bounding.** This is repeated bounding uphill.

Fartleks

Fartlek, from the Swedish words *fart*, meaning speed, and *lek*, meaning play, dates back to 1937 when it was developed by Swedish coach Gösta Holmér, who used it as part of Sweden's military training. Fartleks are continuous runs during which you pick up the pace at different times, when you reach specific landmarks, or just based on how you feel. Distances, speeds, and recovery periods may vary within the same workout. Fartleks can be as structured or as unstructured as you like.

Tapering Before Competition and Increases in Training Load

The most effective adaptations occur when you are recovered from previous training and best prepared to tolerate a subsequent overload. You can't train hard all the time. While you improve your fitness during periods of hard training, you also increase your fatigue. Periodic decreases in training load, called tapers, give your body time to adapt to the training stress and allow accumulated fatigue to diminish, making you ready for a higher load of training. How much or how long you need to taper depends on the severity of the training load that precedes the taper, your level of fatigue, and the distance of your upcoming race. Usually a week is sufficient, with a longer taper for longer races.

7

Base Building

A base is something on top of which a structure is built. If the base is weak, the structure falls apart. If the base is strong, the structure will have greater stability and will be able to be built taller without risk of toppling over. As a runner, your base is your aerobic fitness. The better your base of aerobic fitness, the more solid a runner you will be, whether you are recreational, elite, or somewhere in between.

Volume

To run fast or to improve your endurance, you first must spend a lot of time running slowly. This may seem counterintuitive, but it's the volume of training that ultimately dictates your performance capacity. And to accomplish a large training volume, you must perform most of your running at a relatively slow pace. Lots of easy, aerobic running forms the basis of any distance runner's training program. Indeed, the number of miles (or the amount of time) you run each week is the most important part of your training. While increasing your weekly running volume has the obvious benefit of improving your endurance so you can run longer faster, it also improves running economy (the amount of oxygen you use to run at a given pace), which is an often under-recognized parameter influencing running performance. When you run a lot, you increase your muscles' metabolic machinery needed to use oxygen. The constant repetition of the running movements also has an important neural effect, making you a smoother runner. Running more also burns more calories, which will help you to lose weight. Because the more you weigh, the more oxygen it costs to transport that weight over a given distance, the weight loss further reduces the amount of oxygen you need to run at a given pace.

Initially running slowly is a difficult concept for many runners to understand. Although speed work gives runners more bang for their buck and improves performance faster than simply running lots of miles, short-term success may likely occur to the detriment of your long-term development and consistency of performances. The more you attend to the qualities of aerobic metabolism, the more you will ultimately get from your subsequent speed work and the better your performance will be.

Think of your training as a pyramid, with the base of that pyramid being your aerobic-fitness level. The bigger the aerobic base is, the higher the peak of the pyramid is as the base pushes the peak up (see figure 7.1). To improve your running, the biggest difference in your training from year to year must be the size of your base. Focusing on the peak of the pyramid by adding more speed work or by trying to run your workouts faster will never make you as good a runner as if you first focus on the base. As a woman, you may even be able to get more from your base because women readily adapt to endurance training. Your aerobic fitness also affects your recovery. Because recovery from faster running is an aerobic process, being more aerobically fit allows you to recover faster both during the rest periods of your interval workouts and following each workout.

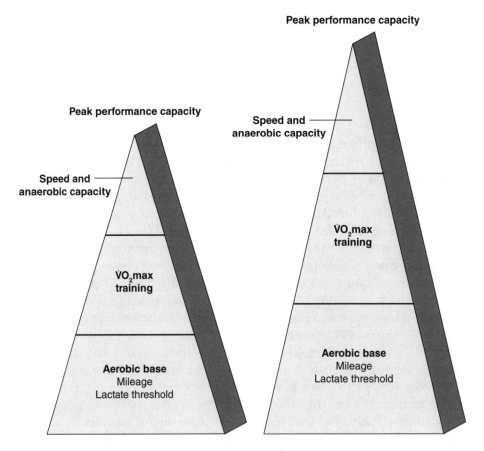

Figure 7.1   A larger aerobic base results in higher performance capacity.

Determining Pace and Intensity

Because the duration of effort is one of the key factors that arouse the biological signal to elicit adaptations that ultimately lead to improvements in your running performance, the amount of time (or number of miles) spent running is more important than the pace at which you run. Therefore, your runs should be easy enough to allow you to increase your weekly mileage over time. The single biggest mistake competitive runners make is running too fast on their easy days. By doing so, you add unnecessary stress to your legs without extra benefit and you won't be able to run with as much quality on your harder days. Speed-type runners (runners who fare better at shorter races) experience a greater difference between their race pace and easy running pace than endurance-type runners (runners who fare better at longer races).

Because many of the cellular adaptations associated with aerobic training are volume dependent, not intensity dependent, the speed of easy runs is not as important as their duration. Slowing your easy runs has at least three benefits: (1) it decreases your chance of injury, (2) it allows you to get more out of your harder days because there is less residual fatigue, and (3) it allows you to increase your overall weekly mileage. Remember that it is the volume of aerobic running, not the speed, that represents the major stimulus for adaptation. If you have a heart rate monitor, aerobic runs should be 70 to 75 percent of your maximum heart rate. Instead of running the same amount every day, make some days longer than others. For example, if you run 30 miles (48K) per week, it's better to alternate longer runs with shorter runs rather than run 5 miles (8K) per day six days per week. Some days give yourself a little more stress, some days a little less.

Deciding How Much to Run

So, how much mileage do you need to run to acquire an adequate aerobic base? That's a great question. Dr. Jason gets asked that question many times, and the answer depends on several factors, including your genetically determined propensity to continually adapt to aerobic training, the amount of time you have to run, the specific racing distance for which you are training, and your running goals (i.e., how good of a runner do you want to be?). Obviously, the longer the race for which you're training, the more mileage you need to run.

Interestingly, however, no proportional relationship exists between weekly mileage and racing distance. In other words, if you're training for a half-marathon, don't expect to run half as much as you would if you're training for a marathon. Even though the marathon is twice as long as a half-marathon and more than four times as long as a 10K, marathon runners don't run double the weekly mileage that half-marathoners run and don't run four times as much as 10K runners. Even for shorter races, you need to run a lot. The best 5K runners in the world run almost as much as the best marathon runners. The reason for this is that any race that takes longer than three minutes to run is primarily influenced by the aerobic

Buying Running Bras

Female runners come in all sizes from slender to full figured, from small bosomed to those more amply endowed. Along with a good pair of running shoes, a quality sports bra is essential to running in comfort, especially when you're logging a lot of miles. Current improvements in fabric and structure make it possible to find a sports bra to fit every body type.

Because running is a dynamic and high-impact sport, a female runner needs a bra that provides support, stability, and comfort. Fabrics such as spandex, which provide stretch where needed, and breathable materials such as Coolmax and Supplex that wick moisture and keep a runner dry, add to the comfort factor.

Females with small to medium-sized breasts fare best with a compression sports bra, which holds the breasts close to the chest wall, restricting their movement during running. Larger-breasted females should select an encapsulation sports bra. These bras limit the motion of the breasts by closely surrounding and separating each breast.

It is best to shop at an athletic or running specialty store for the best selection and to select a bra designed for runners. Try on several sizes to find the one most suited to your body. A bra with wide straps and a wide bottom band provides the best support and minimizes bounce as you run. It also will not dig into your skin as you exercise. A racerback- or T-back-style bra provides maximum freedom of movement. Avoid bras with inside seams that can chafe when you run. A good sports bra enhances your running experience from base building to race day.

system. The shorter the race, the more critical anaerobic training becomes, but for all distance races, aerobic metabolism is king.

The best way to determine how much aerobic training you need is to slowly and systematically increase your mileage from month to month and year to year, taking care to note how you respond to the training stimulus. If you're already running a lot (more than 40 miles [64K] per week), don't increase your mileage unless your prior training and racing experience gives you reason to believe that you will continue to improve with more mileage. If you haven't reached a plateau in your performance at 40 miles (64K) per week, there's no reason yet to increase your mileage to 50 miles (80K).

Despite what many runners believe, more is not always better; more is only better if you continue to adapt to more. In general, female runners do adapt to more; however, increasing your running mileage should still be done systematically and with reason behind it. While some female runners thrive off more speed work and are better at short-distance races than long-distance races, female runners, in general, tend to adapt to and fare better with more aerobic training. That is as long as they take precautions to avoid injury, such as consume adequate iron, pay attention to menstrual irregularities, and take in adequate calories. Of all the women Dr. Jason has coached, nearly all of them have been the endurance type, with endurance rather than speed as their strength, which makes them better suited for a longer aerobic base-building period and longer races.

Even at the elite level, while there are certainly women who excel at the middle distances (800 meters, 1,500 meters, mile), the best female distance runners tend to be of the long-distance variety (5K to marathon). This characteristic of good endurance among female runners is likely a metabolic issue and caused by women's estrogen-enhancing use of fat during exercise. Therefore, although it is often tempting to do speed work in an attempt to get faster, your initial focus should be on more aerobic training because that will likely give you a greater return on your investment. If you haven't been running for very long, aerobic base building may be the only type of training you do for a while.

Increasing Weekly Mileage

As you work on building your aerobic base, be careful when you increase your mileage because many female runners get injured when increasing their weekly mileage, more so than when increasing their intensity. Increase your mileage by no more than 1 mile (1.6K) per day per week. For example, if you currently run 20 miles (32K) in four days per week, run no more than 24 miles (39K) the next week by adding 1 mile (1.6K) to each of the four days. Do not run 24 miles (39K) the next week by adding all 4 miles (6.4K) to only one day of running. If you're a highly trained runner, you may be able to get away with adding more miles more quickly, especially if you have experience running more miles. If you're a new runner or an older runner or are prone to injury, run the same mileage for three to four weeks before increasing it. Give your legs a chance to adapt and habituate to each level of running before increasing the level.

Whether you run the same mileage for a few weeks or increase the mileage slightly for a few weeks, back off the volume by about a third for one recovery week before increasing the training load. For example, if you have been running 30 miles (48K) per week for three weeks, back off to 20 miles (32K) for one week before increasing to more than 30 miles (48K) the next week. Think of this strategy as taking one step back at the end of each training cycle so you can take two steps forward during the next one. Over time, your weekly mileage progression will look like this:

> Weeks 1 through 4: 30-30-30-20 miles (48-48-48-32K)

> Weeks 5 through 8: 35-35-35-23 miles (56-56-56-37K)

> Weeks 9 through 12: 40-40-40-26 miles (64-64-64-42K)

As you can see, the weekly mileage increases over time, but it does so systematically, which is the key for adaptation and preventing injuries.

Given the importance of aerobic development to running success, the base-building phase should be the longest phase of your training program. It takes

For any race lasting longer than three minutes, runners need to train by running a lot to create a solid base of aerobic fitness.

longer to develop endurance than to develop speed. Depending on your starting point and your running goals, you may want to devote 8 weeks (experienced) to 16 weeks (beginner) to base building. If you're training for a marathon and you've never run before, you may want to spend an entire year on base building.

Long Runs

As discussed in chapter 6, long runs stimulate the synthesis and storage of more glycogen in your muscles to improve your endurance. The base-building phase of your training is the primary phase during which you should focus on long runs. During each week of base building, make one run significantly longer than any of your other runs, especially when training for longer races. If you're a masters runner (over age 40), you may need more than one week between long runs because you may need more time to recover. While you should try not to let your long run comprise more than about 30 percent of your weekly mileage, this rule can be broken in the name of necessity if you plan to run only a few times per week. But you need to be careful because the main reason runners get injured is because they are not systematic in how they apply the training stress. Never make your long run three to four times the length of any other run during the week. You must have enough mileage during the week to support the long run on the weekend. Marathon training groups around the United States commonly increase the length of the long run without proportionally increasing the weekly mileage, and that's one major reason so many of the runners who belong to those groups get injured.

For your long runs, run at a comfortable, conversational pace (about two minutes per mile slower than 5K race pace, or about 70 to 75 percent of your maximum heart rate). Lengthen your long run by 1 mile (1.6K) each week for three or four weeks before backing off for a recovery week. If you're a new runner, you may need to run the same distance at least two or three times before increasing the distance. If you run more than about 40 miles (64K) per week, or if you run faster than about 8:00-mile pace, you can add 2 miles (3.2K) at a time to your long run. Because your legs have no concept of distance, only of intensity and duration, the amount of time you spend on your feet is more important than the number of miles you cover. Because women rely less on glycogen and more on fat during submaximal exercise, you may need to run longer than your male counterpart to severely lower muscle glycogen to stimulate its greater synthesis and storage.

Running a lot can make you fatigued. When increasing mileage, make sure you get adequate recovery. Interestingly, all adaptations from training occur during the recovery from your training, not during the training itself. The older you are, the more time you need to recover from training, so the longer you need before increasing the volume. While young runners can get away with training mistakes because they recover quickly from high training loads, older runners must be more careful with how and when they increase their training loads.

Hills and Fartleks

While you're building your mileage, you can integrate hills and fartleks into your base building. Use these types of runs toward the end of your base building, once you have reached your goal mileage. For example, during the second half of your base building, do at least one run per week on a hilly course or do a long hill interval workout (see chapter 6). You can also replace one of your easy running days with a fartlek, during which you play with different speeds for varying amounts of time. If we add to the training outline above, your base-building phase can look like this:

> Weeks 1 through 4: 30-30-30-20 miles (48-48-48-32K)
> Weeks 5 through 8: 35-35-35-23 miles (56-56-56-37K)
> Weeks 9 through 12: 40-40-40-26 miles (64-64-64-42K)
> Weeks 13 through 16: 40-40-40-26 miles (64-64-64-42K), with alternating weeks of hills and fartleks

Special Considerations

As a woman, there are specific things you need to consider when creating your base. Because estrogen has such a big effect on bone health, one thing to consider during your base building is the time of the month that you increase your mileage. Try not to increase your weekly mileage during menses (the early part of the follicular phase; days 1 to 5) and the latter part of the luteal phase (week 4) because those are times of the month when your estrogen concentration is low. Conversely, good times of the month to increase your weekly mileage are during the latter part of the follicular phase (week 2) and the midluteal phase (end of week 3 to the beginning of week 4), when estrogen concentration is high.

If you have one or more of the characteristics of the female athlete triad (osteo-porosis, disordered eating, menstrual irregularities; see chapter 12), do not try to increase the size of your base. With the female athlete triad, the greatest risk of training is to your bones, so trying to increase your weekly mileage may result in a stress fracture. Pregnancy is another condition that precludes you from increasing your base. While exercising during pregnancy will not harm you or your fetus and is even beneficial both during pregnancy and after delivery, pregnancy should be viewed as a time to maintain aerobic fitness rather than a time to increase your training load. Once you have acquired an adequate base to meet your running goals, it's time to integrate other forms of training to address other variables that influence your running performance.

8

Acidosis (Lactate) Threshold Training

A threshold is the point at which change occurs. During sufficiently intense exercise, this point is detected by an inability of the cardiorespiratory system to supply enough oxygen to meet the metabolic demands of the active muscles. In other words, the demand for oxygen is greater than its supply. Thus, stimulation of anaerobic metabolism increases, with a greater reliance on glycolysis and with the accompanying accumulation of lactate in the muscles and blood. The acidosis (lactate) threshold is the slowest running speed above which lactate accumulates and acidosis occurs. It demarcates the transition between running that is almost purely aerobic and running that includes significant oxygen-independent (anaerobic) metabolism. Therefore, the acidosis threshold represents the fastest speed you can sustain aerobically. When you think about it like this, it becomes obvious that it is important to raise the acidosis threshold as part of your training. The benefit to being able to run aerobically at 6:30-mile pace compared to 7:00-mile pace is obvious: It means you'll be running 30 seconds per mile faster before you fatigue.

The acidosis threshold also signifies a change in fuel use. At running speeds slower than acidosis threshold pace, you use a combination of fat and carbohydrate for fuel. As running speed increases, the contribution from fat decreases and the contribution from carbohydrate increases. At speeds faster than the acidosis threshold, you use only carbohydrate (blood glucose and muscle glycogen). Thus, the female-specific trait of a greater reliance on fat and lesser reliance on carbohydrate only comes into play when you run at a pace slower than your acidosis threshold because speeds above the acidosis threshold mandate the use of carbohydrate.

Measuring the Acidosis Threshold

The acidosis threshold is typically measured during a $\dot{V}O_2$max test by taking blood samples from a finger prick or from a catheter placed into a vein in the arm. The blood is then tested for lactate concentration. The acidosis threshold is defined as the speed (or $\dot{V}O_2$) at which the blood lactate concentration begins to increase rapidly. A shift in the lactate curve to the right (see the dotted curve in figure 8.1) represents an increase in the lactate threshold (it now occurs at a faster speed) and an improvement in endurance. Because we are measuring lactate, it is called the lactate threshold, although we prefer to use the term acidosis threshold because it is the acidosis, rather than the lactate, that is of most interest because acidosis contributes to fatigue.

In lieu of taking blood samples during the test, changes in ventilation and respiratory gas samples are often measured to indicate the lactate threshold. A close relationship exists between ventilation and metabolism. As speed increases, a greater reliance on oxygen-independent metabolism increases the production of carbon dioxide, which stimulates ventilation to exhale the carbon dioxide. The ventilatory threshold thus refers to the running speed at which there is a nonlinear increase in ventilation as a result of a rapid increase in carbon dioxide in the blood. Alternatively, the lactate threshold can be measured with a series of steady-state runs at increasing speeds, with blood samples taken at regular intervals during each run. At the slower speeds, lactate increases slightly and plateaus. When acidosis

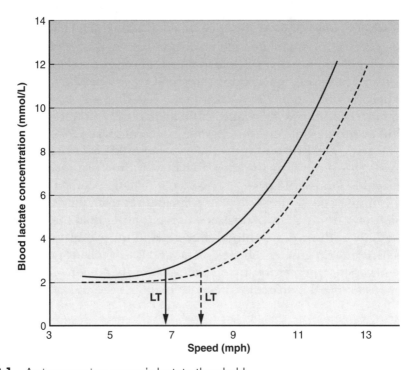

Figure 8.1   An increase in a runner's lactate threshold.

threshold pace is exceeded, however, lactate continues to increase rather than leveling off. The higher the percentage at which the acidosis threshold occurs in relation to your $\dot{V}O_2$max, the better your aerobic fitness and the faster you will run any race.

The longer the race for which you're training, the more important it is to train your acidosis threshold because the closer the race pace will be to your acidosis threshold pace and the more important it becomes to be able to hold a solid pace for an extended time. So, for the half-marathon and marathon, the acidosis threshold should be the focus of your training. This is an unexplored area of training for most recreational runners who want to run a half-marathon or marathon. Most large marathon training groups either completely ignore acidosis threshold training or give it only cursory attention because most of their emphasis is on the weekend long run. However, to successfully run these long races requires getting used to running comfortably hard for a long time. The keys to success for the longer races are getting your acidosis threshold pace as fast as you can and being able to run as close to your acidosis threshold pace as possible for as long as possible. If, however, your goal is only to cross the finish line of a marathon regardless of the time it takes to get there, acidosis threshold training is less important.

Training the acidosis threshold allows elite and recreational runners to increase their acidosis threshold pace so they can run long races faster.

Kyodo via AP Images

Training the acidosis threshold increases the speed at which acidosis occurs, enabling you to run at a higher percentage of $\dot{V}O_2$max for a longer time. Increasing your acidosis threshold pace allows you to run faster before you fatigue because it allows you to run faster before oxygen-independent metabolism (and thus fatigue) begins to play a significant role.

You can target the acidosis threshold by running at or near your acidosis threshold pace. Research has shown that runners who do specific acidosis threshold workouts show significantly greater improvements in their ability to hold a hard pace than those who only do interval training. Unlike interval training, a major advantage to acidosis threshold training is that the workouts remain aerobic, which means you won't fatigue as much. With acidosis threshold training, you get a huge bang for your buck.

Acidosis Threshold Pace

Acidosis threshold workouts are the most difficult workouts to run at the correct pace. Many runners, especially those who are young or inexperienced with these workouts, have a difficult time holding back the pace and finding their fastest sustainable aerobic pace, which requires practice. Acidosis threshold workouts are not all out. They are high-end aerobic.

Acidosis threshold pace is about 10 to 15 seconds per mile slower than 5K race pace (or about 10K race pace) for runners slower than about 40 minutes for 10K. For highly trained and very good runners, acidosis threshold pace is 25 to 30 seconds per mile slower than 5K race pace (or 15 to 20 seconds per mile slower than 10K race pace). Subjectively, the pace should feel comfortably hard.

In the absence of race data, heart rate and blood lactate levels are excellent tools for determining acidosis threshold pace because heart rate and blood lactate levels are closely linked to intensity of effort. Because most runners do not have access to blood lactate analyzers, that leaves heart rate, which has become an easy physiological variable to measure with the broad use of heart rate monitors. For recreational runners, acidosis threshold pace corresponds to about 80 to 85 percent of maximum heart rate, while for very good runners, it corresponds to about 85 to 90 percent of maximum heart rate.

Many runners and coaches miss the nuances of the acidosis threshold when prescribing training paces for workouts. Many magazines and books say that acidosis threshold pace is 25 to 30 seconds per mile slower than 5K race pace, 15 to 20 seconds per mile slower than 10K race pace, and between 10-mile (16K) and half-marathon race pace. However, these guidelines are only true for very good runners. In other words, if a 15-minute 5K runner can run 30 seconds per mile faster than acidosis threshold pace (which equals 110 percent of acidosis threshold pace) for those 15 minutes, certainly a 25-minute 5K runner is not also going to be able to run 30 seconds per mile faster than acidosis threshold pace (which equals 106 percent of acidosis threshold pace) for 25 minutes, 10 minutes (and 66 percent) longer than the good runner. The better your endurance, the longer you can hold your acidosis threshold pace and the better you are at sustaining a high fraction of your acidosis threshold pace.

Someone who runs a 10K in 50 minutes is likely running slower than her acidosis threshold pace for a 10K, not 20 seconds per mile faster. And someone who runs a half-marathon in one hour and 45 minutes is certainly not running anywhere near acidosis threshold pace. What matters is how long it takes to run the distance, not the distance itself. Remember that your body is sensitive to intensity over time; the longer the time, the lower the intensity.

Acidosis Threshold Workouts

Dr. Jason uses five types of acidosis threshold (AT) workouts with the runners he coaches. The key to these workouts is to run at your AT pace. As you progress, add more volume at your AT pace rather than running faster.

AT Run

Run continually at AT pace, starting at about 3 miles (5K; 15 to 20 minutes) and increasing up to 6 miles (9.6K; about 45 minutes). This is the most basic of AT workouts, but it is effective for improving your acidosis threshold. It's important to keep the AT pace as steady as possible during this workout, with little to no fluctuation in pace. The point is to raise your blood lactate level to its threshold value, which indicates the onset of acidosis, and then hold it there for the duration of the workout.

Long AT Run

For marathoners who need to get used to running for longer periods at close to AT pace, this workout is a continuous run slightly slower than AT pace, for 6 to 10 miles (9.6-16K; 45 to 60 minutes) at 10 to 20 seconds per mile slower than AT pace. Sometimes, it's beneficial to run a bit slower than AT pace to accommodate a longer distance, which comes with the psychological demand of holding a comfortably hard pace for an extended time.

AT Intervals

This workout consists of short runs at AT pace with short rest intervals, such as 4 × 1 mile at AT pace with one minute of rest or 8 × 1,000 meters at AT pace with one minute of rest. This interval workout makes the AT run both physically and psychologically easier and increases the distance you can run at AT pace. Although it is tempting to run faster when the work periods are shorter, the purpose of this workout is the same as it is with the continuous AT run—to increase the acidosis threshold. Therefore, make sure you do not run faster when doing AT intervals than when you do AT runs. You must still run at AT pace. Each repetition should be run at exactly the same pace, completing all reps as close as possible to the same time.

AT+ Intervals

Run this version of AT intervals slightly faster than AT pace (hence the plus) with very short rest intervals, such as two sets of 3 or 4 × 800 to 1,000 meters at 5 to 10 seconds per mile faster than AT pace with 45 seconds of rest and two minutes of rest between sets. This workout, performed after you have completed several AT runs and AT intervals, adds slightly more stress to the AT intervals as a way to further stimulate changes in AT pace to reach a faster speed.

AT and LSD Combo Run

As a twist on the 1970s term, long slow distance, this challenging workout for marathoners is a medium-long distance run (12 to 16 miles [19-26K]) with a portion at AT pace, such as the following:

- 4 miles (6.4K) at AT pace + 8 miles (13K) easy,
- 5 miles (8K) easy + 3 miles (5K) at AT pace + 5 miles (8K) easy + 3 miles (5K) at AT pace, or
- 10 miles (16K) easy + 4 miles (6.4K) at AT pace.

As you progress, increase the training load by increasing the volume of a single workout or by adding a second acidosis threshold workout each week or both. Only increase the pace of the workouts once your races have shown that you are indeed faster. Although it is tempting to try to beat your time from last week in the same workout this week, the way you improve your acidosis threshold is by progressively increasing the volume of training you do at acidosis threshold pace, not by trying to force the pace to get faster by running faster workouts. This is a big mistake runners make. Think of your acidosis threshold as the ceiling of steady-state aerobic running; the more you keep running at the ceiling, the more likely you are to make physiological adaptations that will ultimately raise that ceiling. Female runners tend to be very good at and adapt well to these acidosis threshold workouts given their predisposition for aerobic training. So embrace this type of training because it will likely lead to great results.

Aerobic Power Training for $\dot{V}O_2$max

$\dot{V}O_2$max is an important physiological variable for a distance runner because it represents your ability to consume and use oxygen. Although $\dot{V}O_2$max has a large genetic influence, it is still possible to increase it, especially if you are not highly trained. There are a couple of ways to increase your $\dot{V}O_2$max. Initially, increasing your weekly mileage will do the job because running more miles improves your ability to extract and use oxygen by increasing mitochondrial and capillary volumes and aerobic enzyme activity. The more mitochondria and their associated enzymes you have in your muscles, the greater your capacity to use oxygen. The more trained you are, however, the more important the intensity of training becomes to improving $\dot{V}O_2$max.

Measuring $\dot{V}O_2$max

The direct measurement of $\dot{V}O_2$max during a maximum exercise test provides the most accurate assessment of aerobic power. Although the classical definition of $\dot{V}O_2$max is the maximum volume of oxygen that is consumed per minute, many laboratories collect air samples over a shorter time period (sometimes for each breath) and extrapolate to a minute's value.

Typically, the treadmill test starts at a slow speed (about your normal easy running pace) and gets progressively harder with each stage (which is usually two to four minutes), initially by increasing speed and then by increasing grade, until you are completely exhausted and can no longer keep pace with the treadmill. You run while wearing a nose clip to prevent breathing through your nose and breathe through your mouth into a snorkel-like mouthpiece connected to respiratory gas analyzers that measure how much oxygen you inhale and how much carbon dioxide you exhale. $\dot{V}O_2$max is defined as the highest $\dot{V}O_2$ value achieved during the test, usually during the last completed stage. The whole test takes 10 to 15 minutes.

$\dot{V}O_2$max can be measured either in liters of oxygen per minute or in milliliters of oxygen per kilogram of body weight per minute (ml/kg/min). To compare runners of different sizes, it is usually measured relative to body weight. The $\dot{V}O_2$max of elite female distance runners is over 60 ml/kg/min, while that of their elite male counterparts is over 70 ml/kg/min. This is because men's greater cardiac output sends more blood and oxygen to the muscles, meaning that more hemoglobin in the blood transports more oxygen to the muscle mass that consumes oxygen. Even when the difference in muscle mass between men and women is accounted for and $\dot{V}O_2$max is expressed relative to lean body mass, men still have a higher $\dot{V}O_2$max than women. But, as studies on elite female runners have shown, plenty of female distance runners have a higher $\dot{V}O_2$max than men. Some research has shown that both absolute and relative $\dot{V}O_2$max are slightly lower during the luteal phase than during the follicular phase of the menstrual cycle, suggesting that interval workouts and races that are run close to $\dot{V}O_2$max pace (800 meters to 5K) may be more difficult during the luteal phase. (See chapter 2 for an explanation of the follicular and luteal phases.)

A runner can improve her performance by training her $\dot{V}O_2$max, which increases her ability to consume and use oxygen.

$\dot{V}O_2$max Training

The more aerobically trained you are, the more important the training intensity becomes to improving $\dot{V}O_2$max. One of the best methods to improve the capacity of the cardiorespiratory system—specifically, the heart's ability to pump blood and oxygen to the active muscles—is interval training using work periods of three to five minutes and recovery intervals equal to or slightly shorter than the work periods. The cardiorespiratory adaptations associated with interval training, including hypertrophy of the left ventricle, greater stroke volume, and greater cardiac output, increase your $\dot{V}O_2$max and raise your aerobic ceiling.

Because $\dot{V}O_2$max is achieved when maximum stroke volume and heart rate are reached, perform the work periods at an intensity that elicits maximum heart rate during each work period. This type of training, which is very demanding, is one of the best methods for improving cardiorespiratory conditioning. Work periods lasting at least three minutes are necessary for aerobic-power training because it takes time for $\dot{V}O_2$ to reach its maximum value after you start to run. However, shorter work periods can also improve $\dot{V}O_2$max as long as you use very short and active recovery intervals to keep $\dot{V}O_2$ elevated throughout the workout. Five-minute work periods are the longest you should use for $\dot{V}O_2$max training because work periods longer than that necessitate a decrease in speed in order to repeat the work period more than a couple of times.

$\dot{V}O_2$max Pace

$\dot{V}O_2$max pace is the speed at which you reach your $\dot{V}O_2$max. You should be able to hold the pace for 7 to 10 minutes. Therefore, $\dot{V}O_2$max pace falls between 1-mile and 2-mile (1.6-3.2K) race pace for most runners. For highly trained and very good runners, $\dot{V}O_2$max pace corresponds to 3,000-meter or 2-mile race pace (about 15 seconds per mile faster than 5K race pace).

In the absence of race data, you can use heart rate to monitor $\dot{V}O_2$max workouts. Whether you are recreational or elite, you should reach at least 95 percent of your maximum heart rate by the end of each work period because you achieve $\dot{V}O_2$max when you reach maximum stroke volume and heart rate. To determine your maximum heart rate, run 1 mile (four laps of a track) while wearing a heart rate monitor, starting at a comfortable pace and picking it up each lap until you are running as fast as you can over the final lap. Check your heart rate monitor a few times over the final lap. The highest number you see is your maximum heart rate.

$\dot{V}O_2$max Workouts

Following are examples of $\dot{V}O_2$max interval workouts. Make sure you warm up adequately before each workout, completing your warm-up with a few 100-meter strides at $\dot{V}O_2$max pace to get your legs used to faster running and to make a seamless transition into the workout. Be careful of starting out too fast. Subjectively, $\dot{V}O_2$max pace should feel hard but manageable. The rest interval for each example should be equal to or less than the time spent in the work period. For shorter work periods (200 and 400 meters), use a rest interval that is shorter than the work period.

> 5 or 6 × 800 meters at $\dot{V}O_2$max pace
> 4 or 5 × 1,000 meters at $\dot{V}O_2$max pace
> 3 or 4 × 1,200 meters at $\dot{V}O_2$max pace
> 15 to 20 × 400 meters at $\dot{V}O_2$max pace
> 35 to 40 × 200 meters at $\dot{V}O_2$max pace
> $\dot{V}O_2$max ladder: 2 sets of 800, 1,000, and 1,200 meters at $\dot{V}O_2$max pace
> $\dot{V}O_2$max cut-downs: 1 or 2 sets of 1,600, 1,200, 1,000, 800, and 400 meters at slightly slower than $\dot{V}O_2$max pace (about 5K race pace) for the 1,600, $\dot{V}O_2$max pace for the 1,200, 1,000, and 800, and slightly faster than $\dot{V}O_2$max pace for the 400
> $\dot{V}O_2$max pyramid: 800, 1,000, 1,200, 1,000, and 800 meters at $\dot{V}O_2$max pace

If you can run 3,000 meters in 11:15 (or 2 miles in 12:00), the previous workouts would correspond to the following:

> 5 or 6 × 800 meters in 3:00 with 2:30 to 3:00 jog recovery
> 4 or 5 × 1,000 meters in 3:45 with 3:00 to 3:30 jog recovery
> 3 or 4 × 1,200 meters in 4:30 with 3:30 to 4:00 jog recovery
> 15 to 20 × 400 meters in 1:30 with 45 seconds jog recovery
> 35 to 40 × 200 meters in 45 seconds with 22 seconds jog recovery
> 2 sets of 800, 1,000, and 1,200 meters in 3:00, 3:45, and 4:30 with 3:00 to 3:30 jog recovery
> 1 or 2 sets of 1,600, 1,200, 1,000, 800, and 400 meters in 6:15, 4:30, 3:45, 3:00, and 1:26, with 3:00 to 3:30 jog recovery
> 800, 1,000, 1,200, 1,000, and 800 meters in 3:00, 3:45, 4:30, 3:45 and 3:00 with 3:00 to 3:30 jog recovery

Notice that the pace is the same for all of the workouts, despite the different distances run. Most runners run the first couple of repetitions too fast, making subsequent repetitions slower. Make sure you run the correct pace from the beginning of the workout so that you run just as fast at the end of the workout as you did at the beginning. If you run slower than about 12 minutes for 2 miles (3.2K), do the workouts a bit faster than 2-mile (3.2K) race pace. It's important that the recovery periods remain active with light jogging to keep oxygen consumption ($\dot{V}O_2$) elevated throughout the workout. This helps you to reach $\dot{V}O_2$max sooner during the next work period, so that you can spend more time running at $\dot{V}O_2$max. The exact distances you use in the workout are not that important, as long as they take three to five minutes to run (unless you opt for the shorter distances and do many repetitions). What matters is the progression of distance and repetitions over the course of the training program.

Although longer work periods provide a greater load on your cardiorespiratory system, shorter work periods enable you to accumulate a greater distance at

$\dot{V}O_2$max pace in a single workout. Therefore, you can use work periods that are considerably shorter than three minutes as long as you do many repetitions with very short recovery periods. Although it is tempting to run faster when the work periods are shorter, the pace should be the same for all of the workouts because the goal is the same—to improve $\dot{V}O_2$max. Just as you do in acidosis threshold workouts, as you progress through your $\dot{V}O_2$max workouts, increase the training load by adding more repetitions or decreasing the recovery periods rather than by running faster. When you run a faster race, that's the sign to increase the pace of the workouts because that shows that your fitness level has improved. Although it is tempting to run the workouts faster each time, the way you improve your $\dot{V}O_2$max is by increasing the volume of training you do at $\dot{V}O_2$max pace. Don't try to force the pace to get faster by running faster workouts. Repeatedly running at your heart's maximum capability to pump blood is threatening to your cardiorespiratory system. When your body is threatened, it makes physiological adaptations that will assuage the threat and ultimately increase its capability. Therefore, running faster than $\dot{V}O_2$max pace is not any better than running at $\dot{V}O_2$max pace when the purpose is to increase $\dot{V}O_2$max.

Figure 9.1 illustrates what happens to oxygen consumption during an interval workout. During the first work period, $\dot{V}O_2$ initially rises rapidly and then more

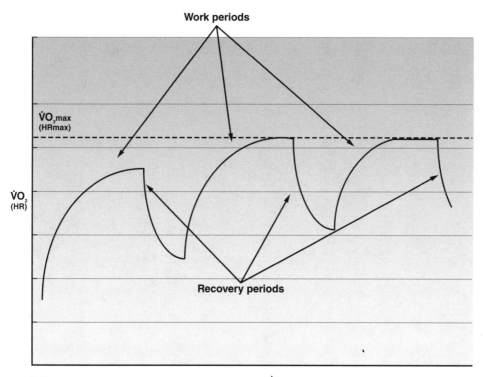

Figure 9.1 The increase in oxygen consumption ($\dot{V}O_2$) and heart rate (HR) during an interval workout.

slowly toward the end of the work period. In the example in figure 9.1, $\dot{V}O_2$max is reached briefly during the second work period and is reached sooner during the third work period because of the elevated $\dot{V}O_2$ at the beginning of the third work period. During the recovery interval, $\dot{V}O_2$ decreases because of the low demand for oxygen from the muscles. If the recovery interval is short (equal to or less than the time spent running), $\dot{V}O_2$ will not decline all that much. This is a good thing because the next work period will then begin with the $\dot{V}O_2$ elevated. $\dot{V}O_2$ will then rise again during the subsequent work period, to a point higher than during the first work period. If planned right, $\dot{V}O_2$ will reach $\dot{V}O_2$max after a couple of work periods, which is the goal of the workout. This type of workout is difficult because not only is oxygen being consumed at its fastest rate, but also because there is considerable involvement from oxygen-independent metabolism.

As with acidosis threshold training, maximize your adaptive response to $\dot{V}O_2$max workouts by running them at times during your menstrual cycle that will maximize them. Although there is a lot of individuality, many women find that high-intensity runs are easier to complete during the days corresponding to low estrogen levels (week one of the menstrual cycle following menses). The lower heart rates and breathing rates during this time contribute to less perceived exertion. In contrast, many women find that hard running during the last two weeks of the menstrual cycle is difficult. Therefore, times of the month when estrogen is low would be best for $\dot{V}O_2$max workouts.

Speed and Strength Training

At first glance, distance running doesn't seem to have much to do with big, strong muscles. Indeed, the best runners in the world are quite small, with slim legs and arms that would make some Hollywood actresses drool. However, although people often associate strength and power with big muscles, they're not always related. It's not what your muscles look like; it's what they do that matters. If trained properly, muscles can do amazing things. Just ask the Kenyan and Ethiopian runners with the slim legs.

After you have performed a large volume of aerobic work, it's time to put the roof on the house with speed training. The best way to improve speed is, unsurprisingly, to train at faster speeds. Many runners shy away from speed training because it can be intimidating. After all, it's physically uncomfortable. It's physically and psychologically easier for people to run long and slow than to run short and fast. But running short and fast provides many benefits. For women in particular, anaerobic training can create stronger, shapelier muscles.

Although speed and strength training are important, it's the combination of the two—power—that's most important. Power, which equals force (strength) times velocity (speed), is the most overlooked trait for distance-running performance. For a muscle to be powerful, it must be strong and it must be fast. Although an increase in speed, strength, or both increases power, the more important characteristic for a runner is speed because your feet are in contact with the ground for only a fraction of a second, not nearly enough time to generate maximum force. It is far more important to increase the rate at which you produce force. A key factor in becoming a better runner is to enhance the steps involved in muscle fiber recruitment and contraction, improving the speed at which muscles produce force. Athletic performance is ultimately limited by the amount of muscular force and power that can be produced and sustained. Several physiological traits influence force and power, including neuromuscular coordination, skeletal muscle mechanics and energetics, efficiency of converting metabolic power into mechanical power, and the skeletal muscles' aerobic and anaerobic metabolic capacities.

When you begin to include speed work, either drop your weekly mileage or maintain your mileage from where it was before adding speed work. Never increase your running volume and intensity at the same time.

Anaerobic-Capacity Training

Anaerobic capacity refers to the ability to regenerate energy (ATP) through the anaerobic-glycolysis energy system. The shorter the race, the greater the reliance on anaerobic glycolysis for energy. However, every distance race from 800 meters to 10K has a significant anaerobic contribution, making anaerobic-capacity training an important training component. To improve your anaerobic capacity, you need to use anaerobic glycolysis as the predominant energy system, which is accomplished by running fast for 45 seconds to two minutes, with recovery intervals one to three times as long as the time spent running. These workouts increase glycolytic enzyme activity in the muscles so that glycolysis can regenerate ATP more quickly for muscle contraction and improve the ability to buffer the muscle acidosis that occurs when there is a large dependence on oxygen-independent (anaerobic) metabolism.

The pace for anaerobic-capacity workouts must be fast enough to rely heavily on anaerobic glycolysis, cause acidosis, and recruit fast-twitch muscle fibers. The appropriate pace is 400- to 800-meter race pace for recreational runners and 800-meter to mile race pace for competitive, trained runners.

Following are examples of anaerobic-capacity workouts. These workouts are fast, but not all out. With anaerobic-capacity training, the exact distances aren't important. What's important is that you're running very fast for at least 45 seconds and not more than two minutes (to maximize the involvement of anaerobic glycolysis and minimize the reliance on the aerobic system). Match the distances to this time frame.

> 6 to 8 × 400 meters at mile race pace with a 1:1 work-to-rest ratio
> 4 or 5 × 600 meters at mile race pace with a 1:1 work-to-rest ratio
> 2 sets of 400, 800, and 400 meters at mile race pace with 1:00 recovery and 5:00 recovery between sets
> 2 sets of 4 × 300 meters at 800-meter race pace with a 1:2 work-to-rest ratio and 5:00 recovery between sets
> Anaerobic capacity ladder: 2 to 4 sets of 300, 400, and 600 meters at mile race pace with a 1:1 1/2 work-to-rest ratio and 3:00 to 5:00 recovery between sets

> Anaerobic capacity pyramid: 1 or 2 sets of 300, 400, 600, 800, 600, 400, and 300 meters at mile race pace, with a 1:1 1/2 work-to-rest ratio and 5:00 recovery between sets

If you can run 1 mile (1.6K) in six minutes, the previous workouts correspond to the following:

> 6 to 8 × 400 meters in 1:30 with 1:30 jog recovery
> 4 or 5 × 600 meters in 2:15 with 2:15 jog recovery
> 2 sets of 400, 800, and 400 meters in 1:30, 3:00, and 1:30 with 1:00 jog recovery and 5:00 recovery between sets
> 2 sets of 4 × 300 meters in 1:00 with 2:00 jog recovery and 5:00 recovery between sets
> 2 to 4 sets of 300, 400, and 600 meters in 1:07, 1:30, and 2:15 with 1:40 to 3:20 jog recovery (choosing the upper end of the recovery range following longer work periods) and 3:00 to 5:00 recovery between sets
> 1 or 2 sets of 300, 400, 600, 800, 600, 400, and 300 meters in 1:07, 1:30, 2:15, 3:00, 2:15, 1:30, and 1:07 with 1:40 to 4:30 jog recovery (choosing the upper end of the recovery range following longer work periods) and 5:00 recovery between sets

If you train with men, which occurs on many high school and college cross country and track teams and in running clubs, you may need to alter your workouts to equate the stress because men typically run faster than women. For example, if you run on a team and the coach gives both the men and women the same workout—400 meters at mile race pace—the men may run 75 seconds (5:00 pace) while the women may run 85 seconds (5:40 pace), which makes the workout more stressful for the women because they are running for a longer time at the same relative intensity. Therefore, instead of running 400 meters like the men do, run 350 meters, which would take 75 seconds.

Anaerobic-Power Training

Anaerobic power refers to the ability to regenerate ATP through the phosphagen (ATP-CP) system. Although most distance runners don't spend much time training anaerobic power, it is important for middle-distance races, such as the 800 meters and mile (and its metric counterpart, 1,500 meters), which require a lot of speed. To improve your anaerobic power, use the phosphagen system as the predominant energy system. You can accomplish this by running 5- to 15-second sprints with three- to five-minute recovery intervals to allow complete replenishment of creatine phosphate in the muscles.

Following are examples of anaerobic power workouts. These workouts increase muscle power, increase the activity of creatine kinase, the enzyme responsible for breaking down creatine phosphate, and increase the activation of fast-twitch motor units by the central nervous system. The speed for anaerobic-capacity workouts is nearly all out; however, they are very short so as not to cause acidosis.

> 6 to 8 × 100 meters at close to top speed with 3:00 rest

> 2 sets of 5 × 50 meters at close to top speed with 3:00 rest and 5:00 to 10:00 rest between sets

> 2 or 3 sets of 100, 50, and 25 meters at close to top speed with 3:00 rest and 5:00 to 10:00 rest between sets

The longer the rest interval, the more creatine phosphate will be restored and the more you can use the phosphagen system as an energy source during subsequent sprints. In contrast to the active-recovery intervals during $\dot{V}O_2max$ and anaerobic-capacity training, the recovery intervals during anaerobic-power training should be passive (standing and only slow walking; no jogging) to allow creatine phosphate to be restored in the muscles.

While the menstrual cycle affects specific aspects of aerobic performance, it does not seem to affect anaerobic capacity and power or high-intensity, intermittent running. Therefore, no specific times of the month are better suited for speed and power training.

Plyometric Training

Plyometric training includes jumping and bounding exercises involving repeated rapid eccentric (lengthening) and concentric (shortening) muscle contractions to improve muscle power. During the stretch-shortening cycle of muscle contraction, muscles produce more force during the concentric contraction if the contraction is immediately preceded by an eccentric contraction. This happens because muscles store elastic energy during the eccentric contraction, which is then used during the subsequent concentric contraction. Plyometric exercises exploit this elastic property of muscles, making the muscles more explosive and powerful.

In addition to their ability to improve muscular power, plyometrics may also improve your running economy through a neuromuscular mechanism by increasing your muscles' rate of force production. When done right, plyometric training is intense and puts a lot of stress on your tendons. Therefore, before undertaking plyometrics, you should have an underlying base of strength.

Because power is developed much quicker than endurance, you only need to do plyometrics for a few weeks. Table 10.1 provides a sample plyometric program and suggests appropriate numbers of sets and repetitions for specific exercises. This six-week program starts off with a couple of exercises and adds several more exercises every week or so. The plyometric exercises that follow can help you improve muscle power, which will make you a smoother, faster runner.

Table 10.1 Sample Plyometric Training Program

Week	Single-leg hop	Bleacher hop	Double-leg bound	Alternating-leg bound	Squat jump	Depth jump	Box jump
1	2 × 10	2 × 10					
2	2 × 10	2 × 10					
3	2 × 10	2 × 10	2 × 10	2 × 10			
4	2 × 10	2 × 10	2 × 10	2 × 10	2 × 10		
5	2 × 10	2 × 10	2 × 10	2 × 10	2 × 10	2 × 10	2 × 10
6	2 × 10	2 × 10	2 × 10	2 × 10	2 × 10	2 × 10	2 × 10

SINGLE-LEG HOP

Stand on one leg with the other leg bent so it doesn't touch the ground and then hop up and down. Repeat with the other leg. The focus of these hops is the ankle joint, with the power coming from the gastrocnemius muscle in the calf. Variations of the single-leg hop include hopping forward and backward on one leg or hopping side to side on one leg.

BLEACHER HOP

Stand at the bottom of the bleacher steps on one leg and then hop up the steps. Walk down and hop up again on the other leg.

DOUBLE-LEG BOUND

Stand with your legs shoulder-width apart and bend your knees in a squat position so your thighs are parallel to the ground (photo a). Jump forward with both legs as far as possible and land in a squat position (photo b), and then repeat.

ALTERNATING-LEG BOUND

In an exaggerated running motion, bound (which looks like a combination of running and jumping) forward from one leg to the other. Extend your back leg and push off forcefully from the ball of the foot. Drive your front leg by raising your knee up.

SQUAT JUMP

With hands on hips in a squat position (photo a), jump straight up as high as you can (photo b). Upon landing with soft knees, lower yourself back into a squat position in one smooth motion, and then immediately jump up again.

DEPTH JUMP

Stand on a one-foot-tall (30 cm) box (photo
a), then jump down to the ground and land in
a squat position (photo *b*). From this squat
position, jump straight up as high as you
can (photo *c*).

BOX JUMP

Stand with feet shoulder-width apart and knees bent in a squat position in front of a box about two feet (61 cm) high (photo *a*). Jump with both feet onto the box (photo *b*). Immediately jump into the air and land back on the ground on the other side of the box in a squat position (photo *c*). As you gain experience with the exercise, try jumping with one foot at a time.

Follow these recommendations for safety and to get the best results from plyo-metric training.

- Always do plyometric exercises on soft surfaces that provide good footing, such as grass, artificial turf, or a rubber mat.
- Begin with just one or two sets of each exercise and allow for full recovery between sets.
- Precede a plyometric workout with a general warm-up that gradually becomes more intense.
- To maximize the use of stored elastic energy, try to spend as little time on the ground as possible between hops, bounds, and jumps. This helps you to concentrically contract your muscles immediately after eccentrically contracting them.
- Include high-intensity plyometric exercises, such as depth jumps and box jumps, only after you have mastered lower-intensity and moderate-intensity exercises (e.g., single-leg hops, leg bounds, and squat jumps).

Strength Training

Much has been written about strength training for runners: lunges while holding dumbbells in your hands, calf raises on the edge of a stair, and endless repetitions of abdominal crunches while balancing on a big, lime-green exercise ball. Have you ever wondered whether these training suggestions will really lead to a new 5K or marathon personal record? As you probably have surmised from the previous chapters of this book, to become a better runner, you must maximize your cardiorespiratory and muscular systems' abilities to transport and use oxygen.

Interestingly, there are no studies showing that strength training, when performed either with a moderate amount of weight for many repetitions per set (a muscular-endurance program) or with a heavy weight for a few repetitions per set (a muscular-strength program), increases oxygen delivery to and use by the muscles. The responsibility of oxygen delivery rests on the shoulders of your cardiorespiratory system, and the responsibility of oxygen use rests on the shoulders of your mitochondria, neither of which are heavily influenced by strength training.

To a large extent, the physiological changes resulting from strength and endurance training are contradictory. For example, when the volume and intensity are high enough, strength training stimulates muscle fiber hypertrophy (growth in muscle fiber size). While it's easier for men to increase muscle mass because of their much higher level of testosterone, women can increase muscle mass, too. This can increase body weight, which increases the metabolic cost of running. In addition, larger muscles may have fewer capillaries and mitochondria per area of muscle, which would be detrimental to endurance. Endurance training causes muscles to respond in an opposite fashion by increasing capillary and mitochondrial volumes and densities to facilitate the diffusion and use of oxygen. Running lots of miles also decreases body weight, which improves running economy. Endurance training also exerts a *volume effect* on the heart, increasing the internal dimensions of the left ventricle so it can maximize its stroke volume and cardiac output, while strength training has a *pressure effect* on the heart, increasing the thickness of the left ventricular wall.

Despite the different physiological adaptations between strength and endurance training, many runners still lift weights, partly in belief that it will prevent injuries or make them faster runners or both. In regard to injury prevention, although there are plenty of popular magazines and coaches and runners that espouse the benefits of strength training to prevent injuries, whether strength training prevents injuries in runners is not totally clear. With some possible exceptions, most running injuries occur because of suboptimal training practices (e.g., increasing mileage too quickly, introducing speed work too quickly, or increasing mileage and intensity concurrently) and not because you're not strong enough. The biggest risk factors of running-related injury are prior injury and weekly running mileage. Although many studies have shown significant increases in bone mineral density in response to strength training, the magnitude of increase in bone mineral density is only 1 to 2 percent. Some studies have even found that strength training has no significant effect on bone mineral density. Whether such a small increase in bone mineral density is enough to prevent running-related bone injuries that are common in female runners has not been determined.

In regard to making you a faster runner, strength training can improve distance running performance in previously untrained people, in young inexperienced runners, and in older runners who have lost some of their muscle mass. This is because it increases their overall fitness level. Because of its ability to maintain or increase bone mineral density and muscle mass, strength training is more important for postmenopausal and older runners than it is for younger, normally menstruating runners. However, more experienced, highly trained runners are less likely to benefit from strength training and may even be hampered by it, especially if it is performed at the expense of increasing running volume or intensity. The question that needs to be answered is, "What's going to give you more bang for your buck: increasing the volume or quality of your running training or strength training?" Well, it depends. For example, a 25-minute 5K runner may improve her running performance by strength training because the overall training stimulus (and thus the improvement in overall fitness) is greater when performing both running and strength training. However, this runner is better served by spending more time running and improving the cardiorespiratory and metabolic traits associated with endurance.

Given that strength training does not improve the cardiorespiratory or metabolic factors associated with distance-running performance and its unresolved ability to significantly reduce the risk of running-related injuries, the question remains, "Do female runners need to strength train to improve performance?" Maybe, depending on your age, if it's done right, and if it's done as a supplement to rather than as a substitute for your running training. As discussed in chapter 5, strength training can have a huge impact on older female runners because one of the significant characteristics of older runners is the loss in muscle mass, specifically the fast-twitch muscle fibers. Because those fibers are responsible for speed and power, strength training can restore some of your strength and power.

When performed on top of a base of aerobic training, strength training can help you get faster if done with a program geared toward increasing muscular strength (the maximum amount of force muscles can produce) rather than muscular endurance (the ability to sustain or repeat a submaximum force). Ironically, the best type of strength training for distance runners is similar to that performed by football players. Research has shown that endurance athletes training with heavy weights can improve their maximum strength and running economy through neural adaptation. To gain strength and become a better runner, it's actually better to lift heavy. Having said that, you shouldn't jump right into lifting heavy weights without first doing muscular endurance training, just as you shouldn't jump into speed work without first doing aerobic-base training. So before you begin to lift heavy, prepare your muscles and connective tissue by using lighter weights and more repetitions for a few weeks.

As a female runner, you may benefit from strength training more than your male counterpart, who already has more muscle mass and therefore a greater capacity to produce force and power. Because men have about 10 times the amount of testosterone as women, it's difficult for women to increase muscle mass to a great extent, so don't worry about getting bulky because it's not going to happen. The key to your strength training is to get stronger solely by improving the neuromuscular characteristics associated with strength. Table 10.2 provides a sample strength-training program using the exercises that follow. As your strength improves, re-assess your 1RM every few weeks and adjust the amount of weight accordingly.

Table 10.2 Sample Strength-Training Program

The first three weeks focus on the strength component of power, and the second three weeks focus on the speed component. Start with two sessions per week. 1RM is 1-repetition maximum. (See chapter 4, page 60, for instructions on determining 1RM.)

Week	Squat	Hamstring curl	Calf raise	Power clean	Dead lift
1	4-6 sets of 3-5 reps at ≥ 90% 1RM w/ 5 min rest	4-6 sets of 3-5 reps at ≥ 90% 1RM w/ 5 min rest	4-6 sets of 3-5 reps at ≥ 90% 1RM w/ 5 min rest	4-6 sets of 3-5 reps at ≥ 90% 1RM w/ 5 min rest	4-6 sets of 3-5 reps at ≥ 90% 1RM w/ 5 min rest
2	4-6 sets of 3-5 reps at ≥ 90% 1RM w/ 5 min rest	4-6 sets of 3-5 reps at ≥ 90% 1RM w/ 5 min rest	4-6 sets of 3-5 reps at ≥ 90% 1RM w/ 5 min rest	4-6 sets of 3-5 reps at ≥ 90% 1RM w/ 5 min rest	4-6 sets of 3-5 reps at ≥ 90% 1RM w/ 5 min rest
3	4-6 sets of 3-5 reps at ≥ 90% 1RM w/ 5 min rest	4-6 sets of 3-5 reps at ≥ 90% 1RM w/ 5 min rest	4-6 sets of 3-5 reps at ≥ 90% 1RM w/ 5 min rest	4-6 sets of 3-5 reps at ≥ 90% 1RM w/ 5 min rest	4-6 sets of 3-5 reps at ≥ 90% 1RM w/ 5 min rest
4	3-5 sets of 20-50 reps at 30-40% 1RM w/ 2-3 min rest	3-5 sets of 20-50 reps at 30-40% 1RM w/ 2-3 min rest	3-5 sets of 20-50 reps at 30-40% 1RM w/ 2-3 min rest	3-5 sets of 20-50 reps at 30-40% 1RM w/ 2-3 min rest	3-5 sets of 20-50 reps at 30-40% 1RM w/ 2-3 min rest
5	3-5 sets of 20-50 reps at 30-40% 1RM w/ 2-3 min rest	3-5 sets of 20-50 reps at 30-40% 1RM w/ 2-3 min rest	3-5 sets of 20-50 reps at 30-40% 1RM w/ 2-3 min rest	3-5 sets of 20-50 reps at 30-40% 1RM w/ 2-3 min rest	3-5 sets of 20-50 reps at 30-40% 1RM w/ 2-3 min rest
6	3-5 sets of 20-50 reps at 30-40% 1RM w/ 2-3 min rest	3-5 sets of 20-50 reps at 30-40% 1RM w/ 2-3 min rest	3-5 sets of 20-50 reps at 30-40% 1RM w/ 2-3 min rest	3-5 sets of 20-50 reps at 30-40% 1RM w/ 2-3 min rest	3-5 sets of 20-50 reps at 30-40% 1RM w/ 2-3 min rest

SQUAT

With feet shoulder-width apart or slightly more, stand in front of a barbell that is sitting on a rack. Place the barbell across the back of your shoulders below your neck and grab the barbell from behind with a grip slightly greater than shoulder width. Lift the barbell off the rack so it rests on your shoulders and upper back (photo *a*). Keeping your back straight, bend your knees and squat until your thighs are parallel to the floor (photo *b*). Move your hips back as if you're attempting to sit in a chair. Straighten your legs and stand up to return to the starting position. A spotter can assist for safety.

HAMSTRING CURL

Lie facedown on the floor with a resistance band looped around your ankle and tethered to an immovable object. Curl your leg toward your butt. You can also use a hamstring curl machine with the pad just below your calves and your hips flat against the bench, adjusting your position so that your knees are in line with the pivot point of the machine.

CALF RAISE

Stand with feet together then lift one foot off the ground. With the other foot, push against the ground with the ball of your foot to raise yourself. To make the exercise more difficult, hold a dumbbell in each hand or rest a barbell or weighted bar across the back of your shoulders and neck. You can also do calf raises on the edge of a stair or platform by hanging your heel over the edge.

POWER CLEAN

Stand with feet hip- to shoulder-width apart. Bend your legs and grab a barbell with an overhand grip at slightly wider than shoulder width (photo *a*). Your thighs should be nearly parallel to the floor, and your shoulders should be square and directly over the bar. To lift the barbell, forcefully extend the hips and knees, keeping your back straight and the bar as close to the body as possible. Your shoulders remain over the bar and your elbows stay fully extended. When the knees and hips reach full extension, shrug your shoulders upward. As the shoulders reach their highest elevation, flex your elbows and pull your hands up to bring the bar to chest height (photo *b*). Your elbows point out to the sides. Then pull your body under the bar, moving the arms around and under the bar and at the same time flexing the hips and knees again. Lift the elbows to the front so that your upper arms are near parallel to the floor with the bar resting in front of your shoulders (photo *c*). After gaining control and balance, stand up by extending the hips and knees to a fully erect position (photo *d*). From the standing position, bend your legs again and drop your arms to lower the bar back to the starting position.

DEAD LIFT

Stand with feet hip- to shoulder-width apart. Squat and grab a barbell with an overhand grip slightly wider than shoulder width (photo *a*). To lift the barbell, stand up, pushing with your legs and keeping your back straight (photo *b*). Lower the bar back to the ground by squatting, keeping your back straight and your knees pointed in the same direction as your feet.

Perform strength training during your speed phase of training rather than during the aerobic-endurance phase because speed, strength, and power are more closely related physiologically than are strength and endurance. Likewise, do your strength and power workouts on the same days that you do speed work rather than on the days you do your aerobic running.

In contrast to the clear physiological effects of estrogen and progesterone that influence endurance performance, it's not as clear whether these hormones affect the development of strength in women. Some research has shown that the phase of the menstrual cycle does not influence muscle strength, while other research has shown that it does.

Although your ability to do speed and strength training is not influenced by sex hormones, estrogen plays a significant role in what happens after high-intensity workouts. Estrogen has a protective effect on muscle tissue, diminishing skeletal muscle damage after a workout and inhibiting inflammation. It also influences the activation and proliferation of satellite cells, which help repair muscle tissue after it has been damaged. Estrogen can therefore help you recover faster, enabling you to do speed and strength workouts more often when your estrogen level is high.

Given estrogen's role in muscle damage and repair and its possible role in the development of muscle strength, female runners with low estrogen levels—those with menstrual irregularities and amenorrhea or who are postmenopausal—may take longer to recover from speed and strength-training workouts and may have a more difficult time increasing muscle strength. In addition to the previously discussed bone protection provided by oral contraceptives and hormone replacement therapy, amenorrheic and postmenopausal runners may want to consider taking oral contraceptives or beginning hormone replacement therapy so they can recover faster. You should discuss these options with your doctor.

Building Your Training Program

Training is more than just a splattering of workouts. Apart from designing your workouts based on science and research so that they cause specific physiological changes that will enable you to run faster, you want to organize all of your workouts into a progressive, systematic training program that takes advantage of your unique physiology as a woman and allows you to achieve your optimum fitness and performance. Largely due to the effects of estrogen, most female runners are suited for and adapt to endurance training. However, you also run the risk of injuries if you undertake large volumes of endurance training in the absence of menstruation or during postmenopause, times when you lack estrogen. So, spend time on your aerobic training, but be systematic about it.

When it comes to designing your training program, there's no secret women's-only formula. To quote a well-known antiperspirant commercial, it's strong enough for a man, but made for a woman. The components of a training program are the same for both sexes: base building, acidosis threshold training, aerobic-power ($\dot{V}O_2$max) training, and speed and strength training. The differences, however, lie in the program's subtleties. Unlike a male runner's training program, which may only need tweaking based on fatigue, rate of adaptation, and circumstances outside of running (work, family, and so on), the female runner's training program incorporates more adjustments based on fluctuations of hormones and other female-specific conditions.

Your training program must always be open to change, moving a workout here or there based on how you feel, or backing off the training load altogether when certain conditions arise, like amenorrhea, pregnancy, or anemia. If you have a bad workout, don't beat yourself up over it. Remember that the physical influences of your menstrual cycle, the emotional influences of hormones, and the psychological stresses of balancing all the demands on your life can contribute to a bad workout. The secret is knowing how and when to manipulate the training variables to optimize the work and maximize the results so you can get the largest return on your investment. So, while you'll still do the same types of workouts as your male counterpart, you'll do them in a way or at a time or even emphasize certain things that allow you to get the most bang for your buck and avoid injury.

Periodization Plan

Traditionally, distance runners use a linear periodization structure of training, in which the training program initially builds in volume before decreasing in volume and increasing in intensity. Although this structure works for women as it does for men, most female runners can benefit from spending more time on the volume and emphasizing the aerobic training over the high-intensity training.

Phase 1: Base Building

Whether you're training for a mile or a marathon, the base-building phase of your training is the first and longest phase. The focus of this phase is the volume of training. Because female runners readily adapt to mileage, this is one area in which you can take advantage of being a woman. Push the endurance work. Run as much as you can physically and psychologically handle without getting injured, but do it systematically. Make sure you consume enough calories to keep pace with your caloric expenditure, and make sure you have adequate iron in your diet so you don't become anemic.

Build your mileage in accordance with your menstrual cycle. In the eight-week training cycle in table 11.1, weeks 1, 3, 5, and 7 are good times to increase your weekly mileage because estrogen is on the rise, coinciding with weeks 2 and 4 of the menstrual cycle. When estrogen is on the downswing—weeks 1 and 3 of the menstrual cycle—either maintain your weekly mileage (weeks 2 and 6 of training cycle) or decrease it (weeks 4 and 8 of training cycle). Notice that the recovery weeks (weeks 4 and 8 of training cycle) occur at the same time that estrogen is low (weeks 1 or 3 of menstrual cycle). Because many runners experience lethargy, cramps, bloating, or other symptoms during menses (first few days of week 1 of the menstrual cycle), you can use that time to back off on the mileage (weeks 4 and 8 of training cycle).

Building on these first eight weeks, the next cycle of your base-building phase, shown in table 11.2, can include hills and fartleks to add more quality aerobic running to your program. If you live in an area that does not have hills, you can do hill workouts on a treadmill using an incline. When doing fartleks in your base-building phase, it's important to keep them aerobic, with the speeds only getting as fast as acidosis threshold pace. You do not want to do anaerobic work while you are building an aerobic base. Save the anaerobic work for later.

Regardless of the race distance for which you're training, the pattern of the base-building phase is similar for all because the purpose is similar—to increase

Table 11.1 Sample Base-Building Program

Week of training cycle	Week of menstrual cycle	MILES PER DAY							
		Mon	Tues	Wed	Thurs	Fri	Sat	Sun	Total
1	4 or 2	3	5	6	4	5	Rest	7	30
2	1 or 3	3	4	6	4	5	Rest	8	30
3	2 or 4	4	5	7	4	6	Rest	9	35
4	3 or 1	2	3	5	3	4	Rest	6	23
5	4 or 2	4	5	7	4	6	Rest	9	35
6	1 or 3	4	5	7	4	6	Rest	9	35
7	2 or 4	5	6	8	5	6	Rest	10	40
8	3 or 1	2	4	5	3	5	Rest	7	26

Table 11.2 Sample Base-Building Program With Hills and Fartleks

Week of training cycle	Week of menstrual cycle	MILES PER DAY							
		Mon	Tues	Wed	Thurs	Fri	Sat	Sun	Total
9	4 or 2	5	Hills • 1-mile warm-up • 4 × 800 m hill at 5K-race-pace effort w/ .5 mile jog down for recovery • 1-mile cool-down	5	8	6	Rest	10	40
10	1 or 3	6	Fartlek 5-mile fartlek w/ speeds up to AT pace*	5	8	6	Rest	10	40
11	2 or 4	5	Hills • 1-mile warm-up • 5 × 800 m hill at 5K-race-pace effort w/ .5 mile jog down for recovery • 1-mile cool-down	4	8	6	Rest	10	40
12	3 or 1	3	Fartlek 4-mile fartlek w/ speeds up to AT pace*	3	5	4	Rest	7	26

*AT pace refers to the pace at your acidosis (lactate) threshold. See chapter 8 for details.

your aerobic capacity. The only differences lie in how high your mileage gets and how long the phase is, with longer races (half-marathon and marathon) requiring higher mileage and a longer phase than shorter races (5K and 10K). However, these differences are not as major as you might think because all races that take longer than three minutes to run are heavily influenced by the aerobic system, so even the 1,500 meters and mile (1.6K) require a large aerobic base. The major differences in training programs come after the aerobic base-building phase is completed. So if you are training for a 5K and one of your friends is training for a marathon, you can train together during your base-building phase.

Phase 2: Acidosis Threshold Training

Progressing from the build-up in mileage takes you to more formal, quality aerobic training in phase 2 with acidosis threshold workouts (see table 11.3). The longer the race for which you're training, the more important acidosis threshold training becomes and the more time you should spend on this physiological variable. Possibly because of its representation as the highest sustainable aerobic intensity, female runners, most of whom have an estrogen-triggered predisposition toward aerobic training, respond very well to acidosis threshold training. Be systematic as you integrate these workouts into your training. Start with one workout per week and, as you progress, add a second workout per week.

As with the base-building part of your training program, try to organize the training weeks around your menstrual cycle so that increases in the training volume coincide with the latter part of the follicular phase, when your estrogen level is high. Avoid running challenging acidosis threshold workouts around menses, especially if you don't feel well at that time or if you feel bloated because of the rapid drop in progesterone as you shift from the luteal phase to the follicular phase. For example, if you have a 28-day cycle starting on Monday, and menses occurs on days one to three (Monday to Wednesday), plan your acidosis threshold workout on Thursday or Friday that week. If you have two workouts planned, you can do them on Thursday and Saturday, or do just one workout the week of menses and two workouts during the other three weeks of your cycle. If your menses lasts five days, do one workout the week of your period and two workouts during the other three weeks of your cycle. If you are not adversely affected by your period and don't experience much discomfort, it's okay to do the workouts and see how you respond.

Phase 3: Aerobic-Power ($\dot{V}O_2$max) Training

The next phase of training brings you to interval training to target improvements in $\dot{V}O_2$max. Although you have been attending to your $\dot{V}O_2$max with the aerobic work because $\dot{V}O_2$max has an important peripheral (muscle) component that includes increases in mitochondrial volume and capillarization that enhance muscle oxygen

Table 11.3 Sample Acidosis Threshold (AT) Training Program

Include a warm-up and cool-down before and after each workout and fill in the other days of the week with runs to meet mileage goals.

Week	AT workout 1	AT workout 2
CYCLE 1		
Week 1	3 × 1 mile (1.6K) at AT pace w/ 1-min rest	
Week 2	3 miles (5K) at AT pace	
Week 3	4 × 1 mile (1.6K) at AT pace w/ 1-min rest	
Week 4 (recovery week)	3 × 1 mile (1.6K) at AT pace w/ 1-min rest	
CYCLE 2		
Week 5	4 × 1 mile (1.6K) at AT pace w/1-min rest	
Week 6	2 × 2 miles (3.2K) at AT pace w/ 2-min rest or 4 miles (6.4K) at AT pace	
Week 7	5 × 1 mile (1.6K) at AT pace w/ 1-min rest	
Week 8 (recovery week)	3 × 1 mile (1.6K) at AT pace w/ 1-min rest	
CYCLE 3		
Week 9	5 × 1 mile (1.6K) at AT pace w/ 1-min rest	4 miles (6.4K) at AT pace
Week 10	2 sets of 3 × 1,000 m at 5 to 10 sec/mile faster than AT pace w/ 45 sec rest and 2-min rest between sets	4 miles (6.4K) at AT pace
Week 11	2 sets of 4 × 1,000 m at 5-10 sec/mile faster than AT pace w/ 45 sec rest and 2-min rest between sets	5 miles (8K) at AT pace
Week 12 (recovery week)	3 × 1 mile (1.6K) at AT pace w/ 1-min rest	

AT pace refers to the pace at your acidosis (lactate) threshold. See chapter 8 for details.

extraction from the blood, the most potent stimulus to improve your $\dot{V}O_2max$ is interval training that attends to your maximum stroke volume and cardiac output. If you have been doing two AT workouts per week, replace one of them with a $\dot{V}O_2max$ workout so that you equally emphasize acidosis threshold and $\dot{V}O_2max$. Over time, add a second $\dot{V}O_2max$ workout each week. See table 11.4 (page 136) for an example of how to incorporate these workouts into your training.

Table 11.4 Sample Aerobic-Power ($\dot{V}O_2$max) Training Program

Include a warm-up and cool-down before and after each workout and fill in the other days of the week with runs to meet mileage goals.

Week	$\dot{V}O_2$max workout 1	$\dot{V}O_2$max workout 2
CYCLE 1		
Week 1	4 × 800 m at $\dot{V}O_2$max pace w/ 1:1 work:rest ratio	
Week 2	5 × 800 m at $\dot{V}O_2$max pace w/ 1:1 work:rest ratio	
Week 3	4 × 1,000 m at $\dot{V}O_2$max pace w/ 1:1 work:rest ratio	
Week 4 (recovery week)	3 × 800 m at $\dot{V}O_2$max pace w/ 1:1 work:rest ratio	
CYCLE 2		
Week 5	4 × 1,000 m at $\dot{V}O_2$max pace w/ 1:1 work:rest ratio	
Week 6	5 × 1,000 m at $\dot{V}O_2$max pace w/ 1:1 work:rest ratio	
Week 7	3-4 × 1,200 m at $\dot{V}O_2$max pace w/ 1:1 work:rest ratio	
Week 8 (recovery week)	3 × 1,000 m at $\dot{V}O_2$max pace w/ 1:1 work:rest ratio	
CYCLE 3		
Week 9	5 × 1,000 m at $\dot{V}O_2$max pace w/ 1:1 work:rest ratio	15 × 400 m at $\dot{V}O_2$max pace w/ 1:1/2 work:rest ratio
Week 10	800, 1,000, 1,200, 1,000, 800 m at $\dot{V}O_2$max pace w/ 1:1 work:rest ratio	17 × 400 m at $\dot{V}O_2$max pace w/ 1:1/2 work:rest ratio
Week 11	4 × 1,200 m at $\dot{V}O_2$max pace w/ 1:1 work:rest ratio	2 sets of 800, 1,000, 1,200 m at $\dot{V}O_2$max pace w/ 1:1 work:rest ratio
Week 12 (recovery week)	4 × 1,000 m at $\dot{V}O_2$max pace w/ 1:1 work:rest ratio	

Phase 4: Speed Training

The final and shortest phase of your program is speed training to develop anaerobic capacity and muscle power. As you did with the $\dot{V}O_2$max training, introduce anaerobic capacity training with one workout per week, then progress to two workouts per week (see table 11.5). If you're going to include power-type

Table 11.5 Sample Anaerobic-Capacity Training Program

Include a warm-up and cool-down before and after each workout and fill in the other days of the week with runs to meet mileage goals.

Week	Anaerobic-capacity workout 1	Anaerobic-capacity workout 2
CYCLE 1		
Week 1	6 × 400 m at mile race pace w/ 1:1 work:rest ratio	
Week 2	7 × 400 m at mile race pace w/ 1:1 work:rest ratio	
Week 3	4 × 600 m at mile race pace w/ 1:1 work:ratio	
Week 4 (recovery week)	4 × 400 m at mile race pace w/ 1:1 work:rest ratio	
CYCLE 2		
Week 5	4 × 600 m at mile race pace w/ 1:1 work:rest ratio	2 sets of 3 × 300 m at 800-m race pace w/ 1:2 work:rest ratio and 5-min recovery between sets
Week 6	1-2 sets of 300, 400, 600, 800, 600, 400, 300 m at mile race pace w/ 1:1 1/2 work:rest ratio and 5-min recovery between sets	2 sets of 4 × 300 m at 800-m race pace w/ 1:2 work:rest ratio and 5-min recovery between sets
Week 7	2 sets of 400, 800, 400 meters at mile race pace w/ 1-min recovery and 5-min recovery between sets	2 sets of 4 × 300 m at 800-m race pace w/ 1:2 work:rest ratio and 5-min recovery between sets
Week 8 (recovery week)	2 sets of 300, 400, 600 m at mile race pace w/ 1:1 1/2 work:rest ratio 5-min recovery between sets	

strength and plyometric training in your program, this is the phase in which to do it because strength and power training are more compatible with speed training than are strength and power training with endurance training. Preface the power-type strength and plyometric training with a base phase of strength training to prevent injuries. Emphasize the strength and power training during your speed-training phase, and do it on your speed-training days.

The amount of emphasis you give to each training component—base building, acidosis threshold training, aerobic-power ($\dot{V}O_2$max) training, and anaerobic-capacity training—depends on several factors, including your strengths and weaknesses, the length of the race for which you're training, and the number of weeks you have until your race. As you progress from one phase of training to another, the secondary emphasis of one training cycle (which includes fewer workouts than what's afforded to the primary emphasis) becomes the primary emphasis of the next. For example, as you shift from acidosis threshold training to $\dot{V}O_2$max training, progress from one AT workout per week to two AT workouts per week, then to one AT workout and one $\dot{V}O_2$max workout per week, and finally to two $\dot{V}O_2$max workouts per week. Follow this same pattern as you move from $\dot{V}O_2$max training to anaerobic-capacity and speed training. In this way, the training program is seamless, devoid of abrupt changes in intensity.

Recovery

An important component of a training program is recovery, perhaps even more important than the training itself because all of the adaptations to training that you're striving to accomplish occur during recovery. So to become a better runner, you must factor recovery into your program, especially when you are running high mileage or performing high-intensity training. Plan your training in three- to five-week cycles, using the first two to four weeks to push the training and introduce the stress. Use the final week of the cycle as a recovery week to absorb the training you've just done, make the necessary adaptations, and recover so you can handle the upcoming training load. Think of the training process as taking two steps forward, one step back, two steps forward, one step back. Make your training polarized—run easy on your easy days so you can truly recover and hard on your hard days to provide stress. When designed this way, with both stress and recovery given equal attention and diligence, it is an elegant system that works.

Several factors affect how quickly and completely you recover from your workouts, including age, training intensity, nutrition, environment, stress, and level of cardiorespiratory fitness. The most significant of these factors is age. As discussed in chapter 5, younger runners recover faster between workouts, enabling them to perform hard workouts more often. Workout intensity is the next biggest factor; higher-intensity workouts require longer recovery time. Your environment also plays a role in recovery, with altitude and cold weather slowing recovery. Because recovery is an aerobic process, a high level of cardiorespiratory fitness speeds recovery because of the quicker delivery of nutrients and removal of metabolic waste by the circulatory system. Nutrition and hydration are also big factors influencing recovery, with carbohydrate and protein being the most important nutrients (see chapter 14).

In addition to estrogen's effects during exercise, it may also affect your recovery. Research has shown that estrogen inhibits inflammation and plays a significant role in stimulating muscle repair and regeneration following strenuous exercise. Although the exact mechanisms by which estrogen influences skeletal muscle damage, inflammation, and repair are not totally clear, scientists believe that estrogen may exert its protective effects in at least three ways: by acting as an antioxidant, by stabilizing the muscles' membranes, and by governing the regulation of genes.

Racing During the Menstrual Cycle

Racing across the menstrual cycle is a complicated matter. Although several studies have found that performance during endurance exercise varies between phases of the menstrual cycle, an equal number of studies have shown no difference in endurance performance between phases. Variations in endurance performance across menstrual phases may largely be a consequence of changes to exercise metabolism that are stimulated by the fluctuations in the concentrations of estrogen and progesterone. Anecdotally, many women claim that they don't run well in the few days surrounding their periods. If you've run a race during *that time of the month*, you know how bad of an experience it can be. It's pretty clear that you should try to avoid racing during your period. The amount of menstrual flow and, therefore, the amount of blood and iron you lose, will also affect how you feel the week following your period. Women who bleed a lot may feel sluggish following their periods, which would make that a difficult time to race.

If endurance performance is indeed better at certain times of the month, it seems that, in general, it is better during the late follicular phase of the menstrual cycle prior to ovulation, which is characterized by the preovulatory surge in estrogen and suppressed progesterone concentrations. Performance may also be better during the middle part of the luteal phase (a week after ovulation), which is also characterized by rising estrogen accompanying a high level of progesterone. Since progesterone exerts some negative influences on body temperature, fluid balance, and breathing, endurance performance may only be improved in the mid-luteal phase compared with the follicular phase when the ratio of estrogen to progesterone is high (i.e., the increase in estrogen concentration is high relative to the increase in progesterone concentration).

Estrogen promotes a greater use of fat for energy and spares muscle glycogen, which can improve women's performance in long races.

Estrogen promotes a greater use of fat for energy as your limited store of glycogen is spared and stimulates a greater storage of muscle glycogen, both of which are important factors for long races. If you're planning to run a marathon or ultramarathon, races that are greatly influenced by the amount of glycogen stored in skeletal muscles, try to plan it to coincide with the midluteal phase of your menstrual cycle. A study published in *International Journal of Sport Nutrition and Exercise Metabolism* in 2007 compared muscle glycogen content in women during different phases of the menstrual cycle after eating either a normal diet for three days (2.4 grams of carbohydrate per pound of body weight per day) or a high-carbohydrate diet for three days (3.8 grams of carbohydrate per pound of body weight per day). Women had the greatest muscle glycogen content during the midluteal phase of the menstrual cycle after both the normal and high-carbohydrate diets. Muscle glycogen was lowest during the midfollicular phase; however, the amount of muscle glycogen in this phase was greater after the high-carbohydrate diet.

While the high concentration of estrogen during the luteal phase can improve your endurance performance because of its effects on metabolism and glycogen storage, the high concentration of progesterone during the luteal phase increases body temperature and negatively affects fluid balance, causing a loss of water and electrolytes. This can be bad news for long races like the marathon because both increased body temperature and dehydration, through their effects on stroke volume and cardiac output, cause fatigue in the marathon. Therefore, if the date of your marathon falls during your luteal phase, when progesterone is high, using optimal body-cooling and hydration strategies will be even more important for you than they normally are. Progesterone also increases breathing rate, which can increase the perception of effort since runners often link their breathing to how hard they're working. Taken together, all of these issues suggest that, for running performance to be improved during the midluteal phase, the effects of the rising estrogen would have to outweigh the effects of the rising progesterone.

Part III
Health and Wellness

Female Athlete Triad

12

Body composition influences the performance of many physical activities, running among them. Propelling yourself forward requires strength and endurance. A high ratio of lean body mass to fat in female distance runners, therefore, is an important determinant of successful running performance. While endurance training can decrease body fat, will a recreational runner with 20 percent body fat improve her performance by reducing her body fat percentage to the 12 to 14 percent typically seen in elite runners? This is a difficult question to answer.

In an attempt to manipulate body composition and enhance performance, female runners mistakenly correlate weight loss with a reduction in body fat. Coaches and the running community further propagate this misconception that low body weight enhances success. However, little or no evidence exists that weight loss improves performance in already lean athletes. Endurance athletes such as runners and cross-country skiers may average 12 to 18 percent body fat, whereas some marathon runners have 6 to 8 percent body fat. As you can appreciate, there are large variations and these measurements are only one aspect of a runner's physiological profile. Although it is true that weight loss in women runners who are carrying extra weight will improve their running, both in terms of performance and joint health, weight loss in relatively lean women runners can result in a loss of lean body tissue, lead to worsened performance, and is detrimental to their health. Despite these negative consequences, the desire to attain the ideal body composition to improve performance is a primary factor contributing to the female athlete triad in endurance runners. (If you are trying to shed some extra pounds, see the Weight Loss and Caloric Intake Section in Chapter 14.)

Defining the Female Athlete Triad

The female athlete triad is a serious health condition that can lead to irreversible health consequences if left undetected and untreated. When it was first described in 1992, the three components consisted of disordered eating, amenorrhea, and osteoporosis. Recognizing that many more female athletes were at risk of developing this syndrome than was previously thought, the definition was broadened in 2007 to include reduced energy availability from consuming fewer calories than expended, menstrual disorders, and low bone mineral density. Bone mineral density (BMD) is a measurement that reflects the amount of calcium in your bones and is usually calculated as grams per centimeter. Low BMD is defined as bone density that is below the expected range for your age.

Each component of the triad is interrelated and exists on a continuum of severity between health and disease (see figure 12.1). Imagine at the healthy end of the spectrum a female runner with adequate energy (calorie) intake, normal monthly menstrual cycles, and optimal bone health. Conversely, at the unhealthy end of the spectrum is a runner with persistent energy deficiency, with or without disordered eating, an absence of menstrual cycles (amenorrhea) or other types of menstrual dysfunction, and bone loss which, if left untreated, progresses to osteoporosis. Osteoporosis is a disease characterized by low bone mass and compromised bone strength, making a woman more susceptible to fractures caused by minor trauma.

Health problems associated with the female athlete triad can occur without being on the extreme end of the spectrum. For example, even subtle changes in the menstrual cycle can affect bone mineral density, leading to stress fractures. Progression along the continuum occurs at different rates, although the cycle begins with inadequate nutrition for the level of physical activity. Thus, reduced energy availability is the central component. Female distance runners have a higher incidence of both amenorrhea (absence of menstrual cycles) and reduced energy intake than other athletes, increasing the likelihood that the triad will be present. In the sections that follow, we will discuss in more detail each aspect of the female athlete triad.

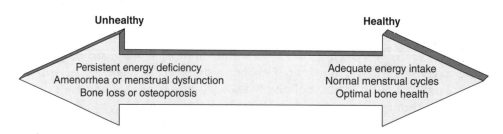

Figure 12.1 Continuum of the female athlete triad.

Reduced Energy Availability

Low energy availability results from insufficient dietary energy intake or increased exercise energy expenditure. In either instance, an energy deficit occurs in which caloric intake does not match energy expenditure. Too few calories are consumed to meet the energy needs of daily living plus those needed for exercise. For example, say you run 30 miles (48K) per week. Depending on your speed and effort level, you would need to consume an additional 2,000 to 3,000 calories per week to account for the increased energy needs of your weekly running mileage. As your mileage increases, your caloric intake also needs to increase. If you are running 80 miles (129K) per week, you require an additional 5,000 to 8,000 calories per week, depending on your speed and effort level.

Failing to meet these additional energy needs of exercise will result in an energy deficit. If the energy deficit is too great, the body responds by suppressing certain physiological functions that are essential for health, such as altering the regular secretion of luteinizing hormone (LH) from the pituitary gland. This, in turn, leads to decreased estrogen production, causing menstrual dysfunction. Decreased estrogen levels affect bone resorption and bone accumulation. While the suppres-

sion of these physiological functions may reduce or even eliminate the energy deficit, it does not increase energy availability. If the condition of low energy availability persists, running performance suffers, a deficiency of important nutrients (e.g., calcium, vitamin D, iron, and zinc) develops, and reproductive and bone health are jeopardized.

Low energy availability can occur from an unconscious or conscious decision. It is not uncommon for female runners to inadvertently eat too little to adequately fuel their physical activity and everyday living needs. Dieting in an effort to become thinner or leaner is the primary intentional cause of inadequate energy intake. Dieting and other abnormal eating behaviors can include restricting dietary energy intake or limiting types of food eaten, fasting, frequently skipping meals, and using diet pills. Sometimes the drive to become thin can develop into an eating disorder.

Clinical eating disorders, including anorexia nervosa (often referred to as anorexia) and bulimia nervosa (often referred to as bulimia), are illnesses with serious health consequences. A woman with anorexia has a distorted view of her body image and an intense fear of gaining weight or becoming fat even though markedly underweight. A person with anorexia severely restricts calories and often exercises

Runners must maintain proper caloric intake to avoid the negative health effects of low energy availability.

McPHOTO/Blickwinkel/age fotostock

obsessively. Bulimia is characterized by episodes of binge eating during which the person consumes large quantities of food in a single sitting. Overcome with guilt, the bulimic compensates with inappropriate behaviors (including self-induced vomiting; the use of diuretics, laxatives, or enemas; fasting; and excessive exercise) in an effort to prevent weight gain. Regardless of why too few calories are consumed, your eating behaviors do not have to be to the point of a clinical eating disorder to place you at risk for the other two components of the triad.

Caloric restriction is independently associated with both irregular menstruation and low bone mineral density. You could have normal menstruation and still have low bone mineral density if your dietary habits are inadequate to meet your caloric needs. Given the large number of calories expended from many miles of running, you need to make sure you consume enough calories to offset your high caloric expenditure. Many runners simply don't eat enough to meet their needs for specific nutrients, such as calcium and vitamin D, which can put your bones at risk for injury. Low energy availability is the key risk factor for stress fractures among female runners. You need to consume at least 1,500 milligrams of calcium per day and 400 to 800 International Units (IU) of vitamin D per day.

Vitamin D is sometimes called the sunshine vitamin because it can be synthesized in the body through the interaction of sunlight with your skin. Although adequate production of vitamin D requires that you spend only 15 minutes in direct sunlight (between 10 a.m. and 3 p.m.) each day, circumstances such as where you live, where you run, what time of day you run, and sunscreen use will affect your vitamin D needs. Most women runners will meet at least some of their vitamin D needs through exposure to sunlight. However, you may not get enough sun exposure to produce the required amounts of vitamin D if, for example, you live in the northern part of the United States between October and March, run early in the morning or late in the evening, train indoors, or use sunscreen with an SPF of 8 or greater. In these instances, you can acquire adequate vitamin D by using a vitamin supplement.

Menstrual Disorders

The spectrum of menstrual disorders progresses from eumenorrhea, or normal menstruation with normal estrogen levels, to amenorrhea, or loss of three or more menstrual cycles in a row and markedly decreased estrogen levels. In between are conditions that involve low estrogen levels with resulting menstrual irregularities. These conditions include luteal-phase deficiency, anovulation (absence of ovulation), and oligomenorrhea (irregular and less frequent cycles). Women runners have a high incidence of menstrual irregularities. Notwithstanding this incidence, irregular cycles or cessation of menstrual cycles is the body's way of communicating that something is wrong. Despite what you may hear from other women runners and coaches, anything other than normal menstruation is abnormal in a female runner and puts you at risk for bone complications as a result of the persistent low levels of estrogen.

Luteal-phase deficiency refers to a shorter luteal phase (ovulation to menses) that produces inadequate progesterone and a prolonged follicular phase (see chapter 2). Because the overall cycle length usually does not change, many women are unaware of this problem until their childbearing years when they try to become pregnant and infertility problems are discovered.

Anovulation, or absence of ovulation, is caused by decreased estrogen and progesterone levels. As a result, menstrual bleeding becomes unpredictable. Cycles can become short (less than 21 days) or more commonly occur at intervals greater than 35 days, a condition known as oligomenorrhea. These irregular and less frequent cycles are common in women runners. Female distance runners with a history of stress fractures are more likely to have a history of oligomenorrhea.

Not long ago, the prevailing belief was that amenorrhea and other menstrual irregularities were a benign consequence of strenuous exercise. Runners still often view weight loss and losing their menstrual cycles as precursors to improved performance. In fact, it was once proposed that maintenance of normal menstrual function required a body fat content of at least 22 percent of body weight. However, numerous studies of eumenorrheic runners have shown body fat levels of less than 22 percent. That being said, it is likely that a specific body fat percentage is necessary for normal menstrual function, but this percentage varies widely from woman to woman. We now know that exercise alone does not cause menstrual disorders, nor is low body weight alone sufficient to explain the onset of menstrual disorders. Women with similar body mass indexes (BMI) vary in their menstrual response to exercise.

Menstrual disorders occur when too few calories are consumed for the amount of energy expended. Studies have shown that 30 kilocalories per kilogram of lean body mass per day is a crucial threshold for maintaining menstrual function. Lean body mass is an estimation of how much the nonfat parts of your body, including bones, organs, muscles, blood, and water weigh. To calculate your lean body mass, you need an estimation of your body fat percentage. Two simple methods to estimate body fat percentage include skin fold thickness and girth measurements. Both methods should be performed by someone trained in body composition assessment. Check your local YMCAs, health clubs, university recreational facilities, and professional trainers to see whether they offer these services.

Once you have an estimation of your body fat percentage, you also need your total body weight in kilograms. If you know your weight in pounds, divide that number by 2.2 to determine your body weight in kilograms. Then, use the following formulas to calculate your lean body mass:

Total body weight in kilograms × (% body fat ÷ 100) = body fat in kilograms

Total body weight in kilograms – body fat in kilograms =
lean body mass in kilograms

Then multiply your total lean body mass by 30 kilocalories to determine how many calories you need per day (although kilocalorie is the commonly used unit of measurement, the value is referred to as calories). As an example, if a runner weighs 125 pounds, or about 57 kilograms (2.2 lbs = 1 kg) and has 45 kilograms of lean body mass, she would need to eat a minimum of 1,350 calories (30 kcal × 45 kg) per day to maintain menstrual function. Recognize that the caloric threshold described here only takes into account the number of calories needed to maintain menstrual function. Additional daily calories need to be consumed to account for the energy expenditure of running.

As noted in chapter 2, the normal menstrual cycle depends on a coordinated feedback system of sex hormones. A negative energy balance disrupts this system by suppressing hormone production, which can cause menstrual abnormalities because the body adapts by conserving energy at the expense of ovulation and the menstrual cycle. Therefore, if your training is accompanied by dietary restriction, your menstrual cycle may be disrupted. Fortunately, you can restore your menstrual cycle with adequate nutrition and caloric consumption.

Bone Health

The final component of the triad focuses on bone health. The continuum proceeds from optimal bone strength to low bone mineral density (BMD) and osteoporosis if low BMD is left untreated. BMD refers to the density of minerals (for example, calcium) in your bones and, as noted in chapter 4, can be measured by DXA scans. Osteoporosis is characterized by the loss of bone mass and deterioration of the microarchitecture of the bone tissue that predisposes you to an increased risk of fracture. Osteoporosis can also be defined as a reduction in bone mineral density equal to 2.5 standard deviations below the average for women at the age of peak bone mineral density. Low estrogen levels and inadequate nutrition affect bone mineral density.

When circulating estrogen levels are normal, bone removal and formation are in balance and maintain skeletal strength and integrity. Bone remodeling is an active, lifelong process consisting of two distinct stages: bone resorption (breakdown and removal) and bone formation (building). In the presence of low levels of estrogen, bone resorption increases. Bone formation is unable to compensate. The end result is a loss of bone mineral density. Inadequate caloric consumption, including inadequate calcium intake, contributes to the problem by further promoting bone resorption and suppressing formation. After approximately age 30 in women, bone resorption may begin to outpace bone formation. When women reach menopause—usually between the ages of 45 and 55—bone resorption significantly exceeds formation and women begin to lose bone more rapidly. This places them at increased risk for developing osteoporosis and suffering fractures.

The majority of peak bone mass is achieved during childhood and the remaining during adolescence and early adulthood. Bone mineral density begins to decline around age 30 at a rate of 0.3 percent per year unless you become amenorrheic, oligomenorrheic, or menopausal, at which point bone mineral density declines up to 2 percent per year, although case reports in marathon runners with menstrual dysfunction have noted bone mineral losses as high as 7 percent per year.

Are You at Risk for the Female Athlete Triad?

To determine whether you are at risk, ask yourself the following questions. If your responses indicate a possible abnormality based on the criteria provided, you should adjust your training, increase your caloric intake, and seek advice from your health care provider.

Menstrual History

- *When was your most recent period?* A normal cycle length is 21 to 35 days; the average is 28 days. Your most recent period should fall within this range.

- *How much time usually passes from the start of one period to the start of another?* Menstrual cycles that occur at intervals greater than 35 days are abnormal.

- *How many periods have you had in the last year?* Women should have 10 to 13 menstrual cycles in 12 months.

- *What was the longest time between periods in the last year?* An absence of a menstrual cycle for three months or longer indicates low estrogen levels and puts your bones at risk.

Dietary History

- *Do you limit the amount of food you eat and restrict certain food groups?* Female athletes need to consume calories from all food groups and enough to support their daily needs. Restricting what you eat puts you at risk for nutrient and caloric deficiencies.

- *Do you frequently skip meals?* Skipping meals puts you at risk of consuming too few daily calories.

- *Do you worry about your weight or body composition?* Excessive worry suggests you are dissatisfied with your body image. This could be a symptom of a more severe problem.

- *Do you use diet pills, make yourself vomit, or use laxatives?* These are abnormal strategies to lose weight and suggest an underlying problem with body image.

Musculoskeletal History

- *Have you ever had a stress fracture?* Low bone mineral density is a key contributor to stress fractures.

- *Do you have a family history of osteoporosis?* A family history of osteoporosis increases your risk for osteoporosis. Be proactive with strategies to increase your bone mineral density.

The most important determinant of BMD in women, therefore, is the circulating concentration of estrogen. Any condition that reduces estrogen concentration negatively affects bone remodeling, which explains why your risk for osteoporosis and fractures increases dramatically with amenorrhea and after menopause, when there is a lack of estrogen. Indeed, estrogen deficiency caused by amenorrhea is the most significant risk factor for osteoporosis in active women. Several studies have found a significant loss in BMD, particularly at the lumbar spine, in amenorrheic athletes. Follow-up studies in these same runners noted that lumbar spine BMD increased in the runners who resumed normal menses, whereas runners with persistent menstrual irregularities experienced further loss of bone mineral density.

Weight-bearing exercise like running is good for your bones. Research has shown that females who participate in sports involving running and jumping, such as soccer, distance running, basketball, gymnastics, and volleyball, have greater BMD than nonactive people and even more than athletes in nonimpact sports, such as swimming, cycling, cross-country skiing, and rowing. However, although athletes in weight-bearing sports have greater BMD, it's difficult to say that exercise by itself is its cause because bone density is also influenced by heredity. More long-term research needs to be done to determine the effect of participation in weight-bearing sports on BMD. Typically, eumenorrheic female runners have 5 to 15 percent greater bone mineral density than women who don't run. To have the greatest impact on your bone health, you should run before you reach skeletal maturity, which occurs by age 30. As you age, the capacity of bone to respond to stress decreases. Therefore, running in adolescence maximizes bone health as females age. The gains in adolescence are maintained into adulthood.

Although no bone mineral density value can accurately predict fracture risk, bone density in female runners that is below the expected range for age is worrisome. Combined with a history of nutritional deficiencies and low estrogen from menstrual dysfunction, the stage is set for the development of stress fractures. Studies have revealed that amenorrheic athletes are two to four times more likely to sustain stress fractures than eumenorrheic athletes. These fractures tend to be multiple and occur in sites that often result in a poor and prolonged recovery, including fractures of the hip, spine, and pelvis. (See chapter 13 for more discussion of stress fractures.)

Although some running is good for the bones, more running is not necessarily better. Cross-sectional research examining the effects of different amounts of running on BMD in women has shown a negative association between running mileage and BMD; however, this issue is complicated in women by the negative effect of training volume on menstruation and associated estrogen levels, which itself affects BMD. A cross-sectional study on female distance runners aged 18 to 44 years found slightly negative correlations between BMD of the lumbar spine and femur and weekly running distance. Specifically, runners who ran 10K per week more than other runners had a 1 percent lower lumbar spine BMD and a 2 percent lower femoral neck BMD. A long-term study found that BMD of the lumbar spine and proximal part of the femur of female college cross country runners tended to decrease over a six-month training period during which they ran more than 40 miles (64K) per week.

Oral contraceptives have been used to treat runners with low bone mineral density and stress fractures. Oral contraceptives may normalize menstrual periods and provide estrogen, but they will not necessarily improve bone health in runners

Increasing BMD and Maintaining Bone Health

Use the following exercise strategies to maintain bone health:

- Perform high-intensity strength training.
- Perform strength training that focuses on the muscles of the lumbar spine and anterior and posterior hip (including the exercises in this chapter and in chapter 10).
- Perform plyometric exercises, such as box jumps, depth jumps, and bounding (see chapter 10).
- Emphasize movement in various directions.
- Perform weight-bearing exercise during adolescence and before skeletal maturity is reached.

Nutrition strategies include the following:

- Consume 1,500 milligrams of calcium per day.
- Consume 400 to 800 IU of vitamin D per day.
- Consume as many calories each day as you expend.
- Eliminate excessive alcohol consumption (no more than one drink per day for women and two drinks per day for men).

with low bone mineral density. Research on oral contraceptives and their effect on the bones has shown mixed results. While some studies have demonstrated an increase in BMD from oral contraceptive use, others have found no effect on BMD. Studies have even demonstrated a worsening of BMD, especially when taken during late adolescence or early adulthood. It seems that oral contraceptive use may result in increased BMD only if taken at the onset of menopause. In premenopausal women with normal menstrual cycles and normal bone mineral density, oral contraceptive use does not seem to benefit bone health. To be safe, consult with your health care provider before taking oral contraceptives.

Studies in amenorrheic runners have noted increases in BMD of 5 percent per year when subsequent increases in body weight occurred. While 30 kilocalories per kilogram of lean body mass per day is necessary to restore menstrual function, increases in BMD and subsequent weight gain requires more than 45 kilocalories per kilogram of lean body mass per day. To continue the earlier example, the runner who weighs 57 kilograms with 45 kilograms of lean body mass would need to eat a minimum of 2,025 calories (45 kcal × 45 kilograms) per day to increase BMD. More research is needed to determine whether increases in body weight are necessary to increase BMD.

You can effectively restore menstruation and improve your BMD by increasing your energy availability. This can be done through a simple reduction in training coupled with an increased caloric intake. A registered dietician can help you estimate your energy needs. Adequate amounts of bone-building nutrients such as calcium (1,500 mg per day) and vitamin D (400 to 800 IU per day) are essential. Calcium carbonate and calcium citrate supplements are well absorbed and tolerated. Although most runners do not smoke, treatment of low BMD should include cessation of smoking and a reduction in alcohol consumption. Women runners with low BMD should consume no more than two drinks per day. Too much alcohol inhibits the cells responsible for bone formation. Heavy drinkers (more than three drinks per day) will sustain further losses in bone, hastening the development of osteoporosis.

Despite the uncertainty regarding how much running is too much, exercise (both weight bearing and strength training) combined with adequate nutrition is one of the most important ways to improve BMD. Incorporate movements that result in high loads at high rates (i.e., a lot of force directed to the bone quickly, as in plyometric exercises) and load the bone from multiple directions, using movements that incorporate varying angles, such as forward and back movements, side to side movements, and so on. Exercise can work against gravity, such as in hopping, or against resistance by using weights or resistance bands. However, exercises must target the specific bones in which you want to increase BMD. In addition to the exercises found in chapter 10, the following exercises are also effective.

HIP FLEXION WITH RESISTANCE

Hook one end of a strength band (or elastic tubing) around a solid structure. Stand facing away from the secured end of the elastic tubing at a distance that creates resistance in the band. Loop the other end of the band or tubing around one ankle. Shift your weight to the foot without the band. This single-leg stance requires you to bend your knee slightly while maintaining a level pelvis. Once in this position, tighten the muscles of the front thigh on the leg with the band or tubing to move the leg forward while keeping the knee straight. Return to the starting position. Do three sets of 10 then repeat with the other leg.

RESISTED HIP EXTENSION WITH RESISTANCE

Hook one end of a strength band (or elastic tubing) around a solid structure. Stand facing the secured end of the band or tubing at a distance that creates resistance in the band. Loop the other end of the band or tubing around one ankle. Stand on the foot without the band so your knees are slightly bent and your pelvis is level. Pull your other leg straight back, keeping your knee straight. Do not lean forward. Return to the starting position. Do three sets of 10 then repeat with the other leg.

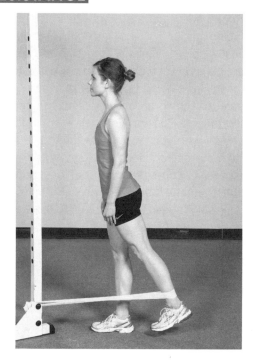

HIP ABDUCTION WITH RESISTANCE

Hook one end of a strength band (or elastic tubing) around a solid structure or object. Stand perpendicular to the secured end of the band and at a distance that creates resistance in the band. Loop the other end of the band or tubing around the ankle farthest from the object. Position yourself in a single-leg stance with your weight on the leg closest to the object. Extend the leg with the band out to the side, keeping your knee straight. Return to the starting position. Do three sets of 10 then repeat with the opposite leg.

HIP ADDUCTION WITH RESISTANCE

Hook one end of a strength band (or elastic tubing) around a solid structure or object. Stand perpendicular to the secured end of the band and at a distance that creates resistance in the band. Loop the other end of the band or tubing around the ankle closest to the object. Position yourself in a single-leg stance with your weight on the leg farthest from the object. Bring the leg with the band across your body, keeping your knee straight, stretching the tubing, and crossing in front of your weight-bearing leg. Return to the starting position. Do three sets of 10 then repeat with the opposite leg.

LOWER-EXTREMITY LOADING

Create a plus sign on the ground with two pieces of masking tape, both 12 inches long (30 cm). Stand in one of the quadrants created by the plus sign, with your feet together but not touching. Bend your knees slightly, keeping your back straight and a slight forward bend at the waist. Keep your arms at your sides. Taking off from and landing on the balls of your feet, take very quick, low hops back and forth over the horizontal line in front of you (see photo a). Emphasize quick, controlled movements just high enough to clear the tape line. Hop for 15 seconds and repeat three times with a 15-second rest between. Repeat the exercise by taking quick, low hops sideways over the vertical line (photo b). Do three sets of 15 seconds with a 15-second rest between each set.

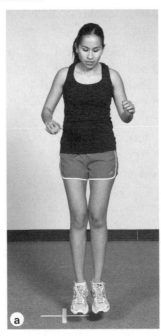

Forward and back.   **Side to side.**

LOWER-EXTREMITY LOADING PROGRESSION

After approximately one week of forward and back and side to side hops, add diagonal hops. Imagine diagonal lines drawn through the intersection of the plus sign. Keeping your hips level and hops low, hop quickly back and forth between the upper left and lower right quadrants (see photo *a*). After three sets of 15 seconds, repeat hopping to the upper right and lower left quadrants. Add time weekly in increments of 5 seconds with the goal of attaining three sets of 30 seconds in all directions while hopping on both feet (see table 12.1). After mastering this, repeat the progression as single-leg hops on each leg (photo *b*). Imagine stopping midstride in your run. This is the position of the single-leg stance: knee bent, forward hip flexion, and level pelvis.

Diagonal hop.

Forward and back single-leg hop.

Table 12.1   Sample Lower-Extremity Loading Plan

Week	Horizontal hop	Vertical hop	Diagonal hop	Rest interval between each set
1	3 × 15 sec	3 × 15 sec		15 sec
2	3 × 15 sec	3 × 15 sec	3 × 15 sec	15 sec
3	3 × 20 sec	3 × 20 sec		15 sec
4	3 × 20 sec	3 × 20 sec	3 × 20 sec	15 sec
5	3 × 25 sec	3 × 25 sec		15 sec
6	3 × 25 sec	3 × 25 sec	3 × 25 sec	15 sec
7	3 × 30 sec	3 × 30 sec		15 sec
8	3 × 30 sec	3 × 30 sec	3 × 30 sec	15 sec

After completing the first eight weeks, repeat the entire progression using a single-leg stance.

Health and Performance Effects

It is not uncommon for runners with components of the triad to perform well, sometimes for long periods. However, eventually, the physical and psychological consequences of the triad affect performance and well-being. As the energy deficit continues, power, muscle strength, and stamina decrease. Performance improvements gained through a well-designed training plan stop. Running times over the same distance slow and it becomes difficult completing what used to be an effortless workout.

Inadequate intake of important vitamins and minerals such as calcium, vitamin D, zinc, magnesium, iron, and B complex vitamins result in anemia, suppressed immune function, and suboptimal healing. Runners begin to tire more quickly, get sick more easily, and take longer to recover between workouts. Mental fatigue from the energy drain also occurs. Runners experiencing components of the triad find it difficult to concentrate, their coordination is impaired, and they are more irritable. Running activities are less pleasurable and runners may lack motivation.

Continued bone loss leading to irreversible osteoporosis is the most worrisome effect of the triad. Resulting stress fractures are slow to heal because of the negative nutritional balance. Multiple fractures can lead to increased incidence of osteoarthritis depending on the site of the fractures. Frequent stress fractures curtail running activities and, if severe, could permanently end a running career. Prolonged low energy availability, with or without disordered eating, can also impair health. Although eating disorders are beyond the scope of this book, recognize that they are associated with psychological problems and profound medical complications that require a team of specialists for treatment.

Decreasing your weight can improve performance, especially in long races, but you must modify your body composition in a healthy manner. Keeping records of body weight, menstrual function, and miles run per week will help you find the body weight that is ideal for health and performance. If you have had a stress fracture, if your menstrual cycle has changed, or if you notice more frequent illnesses or injury, seek evaluation by your health care provider. You are the best line of defense for preventing the female athlete triad.

13

Injuries and Female Runners

As a runner, your performance depends on a delicate balance between periods of intensive training and periods of recovery. This balance allows for optimal musculoskeletal adaptations. Failure to allow for adequate recovery between training sessions can lead to a breakdown of the body's ability to repair itself and eventually to overuse injury. Injuries result from repeatedly applying a stress to a particular body part over time. Overuse injuries of the lower extremity are by far the most common injuries seen in distance runners. These injuries include patellofemoral pain syndrome (pain under and around the kneecap), iliotibial band syndrome (also known as iliotibial band friction syndrome and occurs as pain on the outside of the knee caused by inflammation of a band of tissue that extends from the hip to the knee), medial tibial stress syndrome (commonly known as shin splints), Achilles tendon problems, plantar fasciitis (heel or arch pain caused by irritation of the tissue on the bottom of the foot), and stress fractures.

Unlike your male counterparts, female runners are further predisposed to injury because of the unique relationship between mechanical, hormonal, and nutritional factors. As noted throughout this book, the defining physiological characteristic of women is estrogen. Adequate circulating estrogen is critical to menstruation and bone health. When this is disrupted, as is the case with menstrual dysfunction and poor energy intake, your risk of injury increases. Smaller bones and less muscle mass are gender-specific factors beyond your control that further predispose you to injury. Indeed, they contribute to the two injuries that occur commonly in female distance runners: stress fractures of the lower extremity and patellofemoral pain syndrome.

Potential for Injury

The longer you are a runner, the more likely you are to sustain an injury. The statistics on running injuries are quite dramatic. Studies demonstrate up to four injuries per 1,000 hours of running. Therefore, if you run 5 to 10 hours per week throughout the year, you will accumulate 250 to 500 hours of running. At this rate, you could develop one or two injuries per year. As a group, at least half of all runners, both male and female, experience injury annually, and 25 percent are injured at any given time.

When broken down by specific injury type, the knee is the most common site for running-related injury, with patellofemoral pain syndrome accounting for approximately 25 percent and iliotibial band syndrome accounting for 12 percent of all running-related injuries. Achilles tendon problems cause 16 percent of runners to stop running indefinitely. Stress fractures account for 4 to 15 percent of all injuries to runners. The incidence of stress fracture varies in runners because of gender, age, and site of the stress fracture.

While much of the running injury data suggest that lower-extremity injuries are a result of participation in the sport rather than the sex of the runner, females are at greater risk for injuries when certain factors such as menstrual dysfunction develop. Numerous studies have confirmed that female runners are more likely to develop a stress fracture in the absence of regular menstrual cycles. In a study of a group of collegiate runners, stress fractures occurred in 49 percent of women who had fewer than five periods per year. Of the women who had regular menses (10-13 menses per year), 29 percent developed stress fractures.

Risk Factors for Running Injury

Several intrinsic and extrinsic factors can cause running injuries. Intrinsic factors are characteristics of the individual and include sex, age, bone density, hormonal factors, and anatomical factors such as foot type (highly arched feet or flat feet) and leg-length discrepancy. Extrinsic factors are characteristics of the environment and include training variables such as mileage, pace, training surface, and equipment such as orthotics and shoes. Despite our awareness of these potential risk factors, only a few firm conclusions can be drawn from existing studies as to which risk factors are major contributors to running injuries.

Miles run per week has been identified as the greatest predictor of injury risk in most studies. Yet, the threshold of training volume above which the risk of injury increases has been poorly defined, especially for female runners. The data for women are limited and inconsistent. Male runners who train more than 40 miles (64K) per week experience two to three times more injuries than males who run fewer than 40 miles per week. Other studies have suggested a threshold as low as 20 miles (32K) per week for both men and women. Daily running, length of the long run, and changes in running routine such as a sudden increase in weekly distance or a change in the type of training, such as hills or interval training, have also been associated with an increase in running injuries. However, many of these conclusions have been drawn from work with military recruits, a group that is probably different from the recreational runner. Regardless, the main cause of running injuries appears to be the amount of stress applied to the tissues.

As noted throughout this book, large volumes of endurance training are a key to running success. Yet, total running mileage is an important predictor of running injury. Finding a training schedule that allows you to achieve your running goals while remaining injury free requires a delicate balance that is individualized. One woman may be able to tolerate 40 miles (64K) per week, and another may be able to tolerate only 25 miles (40K) per week to stay injury free. Training adaptations can't occur when you constantly exert yourself. Adaptations occur during recovery. An imbalance between training and recovery will lead to tissue breakdown and eventual injury. Consistency in your training is one of the keys to success. Incorporating hard and easy days, increasing your running volume gradually, and organizing your training into cycles as noted in chapter 11 decrease your risk of injury, allowing you to achieve consistency in your training and success as a runner.

Evidence also confirms that a history of previous lower-extremity injury predisposes you to subsequent injury. Studies demonstrate that if you have suffered an injury in the past year, your likelihood of suffering another injury is one and a half times greater than if you had never suffered an injury. To prevent another injury, you must allow an injury to heal before you resume training, and you must address all factors that may have contributed to your injury. Because most overuse injuries can be traced to training errors such as too much weekly mileage or increasing your weekly mileage too quickly, you should focus on this variable.

Table 13.1 (page 160) provides a summary of the common injuries experienced by female runners and the symptoms, causes, and treatments for those injuries. The following sections discuss each injury in further detail.

Stress Fractures

Despite an incomplete understanding of the role of all potential risk factors, it is possible that intrinsic and extrinsic risk factors interact with each other and contribute to certain types of injuries differently. This is particularly apparent when we look at factors that influence the development of stress fractures in female runners. Stress fractures were first described more than 150 years ago in military recruits and were referred to as *march fractures* because of their association with marching. It wasn't until the running boom in the 1960s that similar fractures were recognized in runners and the term *stress fracture* came into general use.

A *fracture* refers to the breaking of a bone and is the result of a single traumatic event. Conversely, a *stress fracture* refers to a bone that breaks after being exposed to repeated stresses, rather than a single traumatic episode. In both types of fractures, the bone is broken; the difference between the two injuries is the cause. Stress fractures occur when abnormal stress is applied to normal bone, such as increased mileage in preparation for a long-distance race or when a normal

Table 13.1 Common Running Injuries

Injuries	Symptoms	Causes	Treatment
Stress fractures	Localized pain at fracture site	Training overload	Cessation of running
		Menstrual disturbances	Ice
	Gradual onset of pain, increasing in intensity and duration	Low bone mineral density	Walking boot
			Muscle strengthening
	Possible swelling	Insufficient caloric intake	Gradual return to training
Patellofemoral pain syndrome	Pain behind, under, or around the patella	Training errors	Activity modification
		Muscle imbalance and weakness	Lower-extremity and core strengthening
	Pain increases with running and stair use	Excessive or insufficient foot pronation	Orthotics
Iliotibial band syndrome	Pain and tightness on the outside of the knee, usually worse when running downhill	Training errors	Activity modification
		Running on cambered surfaces	Ice
		Stiff shoes that limit pronation	Strengthening of hip and gluteal muscles
			Foam roller
		Highly arched feet	
		Weakness of the lateral gluteal muscles	
Achilles tendinitis and tendinosis	Pain in posterior heel or Achilles tendon	Training errors	Activity modification
		Highly arched foot	Eccentric calf muscle strengthening
	Swelling	Calf muscle inflexibility or weakness or both	
	Gradual onset that grows worse with activity		Heel lift with or without orthotics
Plantar fasciitis	Pain on the bottom of the heel, sometimes extending to arch	Foot abnormalities	Activity modification
		Tight calf muscle	Calf muscle stretching
	Pain worse with first steps in morning or after prolonged periods of rest	Weak foot muscles	Foot muscle strengthening
			Night splint
			Orthotics

stress is applied to weakened bone. This latter scenario is seen in people with low bone mineral density (BMD), such as runners with the female athlete triad. (See chapter 12.)

Stress fractures are classified as low risk and high risk based on the fracture site and the risk of complications. Most stress fractures in runners are low risk. The most common stress fracture site in both male and female runners is the medial (inside) or posterior (back) portion of the tibia (the larger of the two lower-leg bones; see figure 13.1). The next most common site is the metatarsal bones (the long bones in the foot; see figure 13.2), especially the second, third, and fourth metatarsals. Stress fractures in the neck of the femur (thighbone; see figure 13.3, page 162) and pelvis are more common in female runners than in male runners. In fact, stress fractures of the femoral neck are seen predominantly in women and carry a high risk of serious complications if not properly cared for.

Maintaining bone health is the greatest defense against developing stress fractures. Ensuring that your daily caloric consumption meets your daily energy needs plus running needs will prevent the development of menstrual disorders and maintain circulating estrogen levels. Often this requires an additional 3,000

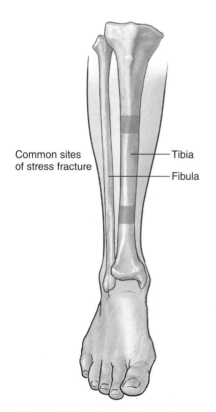

Figure 13.1 The inside and back of the tibia bone are common sites for stress fractures in all runners.

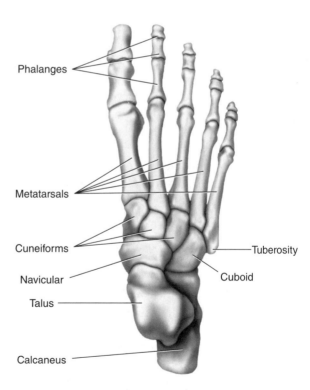

Figure 13.2 The metatarsal bones are common sites for stress fractures.

to 5,000 calories per week depending on the pace and volume of running. Adequate amounts of calcium
and vitamin D are essential. Daily
supplementation with calcium
(2,000 mg) and vitamin D (800 IU)
has been reported to decrease the
stress fracture rate by as much as
27 percent in female navy recruits.

Runners who develop stress
fractures typically sense a gradual
onset of pain that is not present at
the beginning of a run but develops
toward the end of the run. Stress
fractures are characterized by a
sharp pain at a specific point on the
bone that you can feel when pressing on it. Sometimes swelling over
the fracture site occurs. With continued running, the pain increases
and develops earlier during the run.
If left untreated, pain occurs with
walking and even at rest without
any pressure applied to the site.
In the case of a stress fracture of
the femoral neck, the pain usually
occurs in the groin and is often
confused with a groin strain.

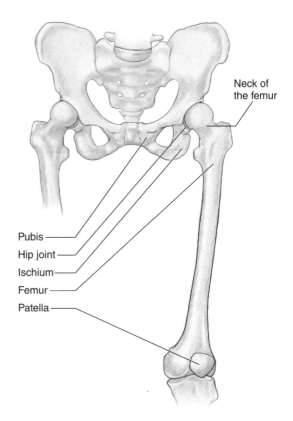

Figure 13.3 The neck of the thigh bone and the
pelvis are common sites for stress fractures in
female runners.

Rest is the cornerstone of treatment for stress fractures along with adequate
caloric consumption and intake of calcium and vitamin D. The severity of the
fracture dictates how quickly you can return to running. If you think you have a
stress fracture, seek evaluation promptly.

Causes of Stress Fractures

Normal bone reacts to both the stress of weight bearing and the stress of muscle
forces by an adaptation referred to as Wolff's law. Under this adaptation, bone
strength increases in response to increased demand by a process called bone
remodeling. As you learned in chapter 4, bone remodeling is an active, lifelong
process of bone resorption and formation. A stress fracture results from an imbalance in the bone remodeling process and the inability of the bone to adequately
adapt to the repetitive stress of running. Bone weakens and a stress fracture
occurs. Too much stress on the bone with insufficient recovery between training
sessions, an accelerated bone remodeling process, premature bone loss, lower

bone mineral density, or some combination of these factors contribute to stress fractures in female runners.

When circulating estrogen levels are normal, bone removal and formation are in balance and skeletal strength and integrity are maintained. However, bone loss occurs when estrogen levels are low, as occurs with menstrual disorders. The loss of estrogen reduces bone mass in two ways. First, calcium excretion increases, resulting in disruption in calcium balance and a need for more calcium. Second, bone resorption accelerates without an increase in bone formation to compensate.

Significant contributors to the development of stress fractures in women runners include menstrual disturbances, low bone mineral density (BMD), and insufficient intake of calories and nutrients. A 12-month study of track athletes identified history of menstrual disturbance, lower bone mineral density, and a low-fat diet as risk factors for stress fractures in women. No predictive risk factors for men were identified in this study. In general, if you have a menstrual disturbance, your risk for developing a stress fracture is two to four times greater than it is for your counterparts with normal menstrual cycles. Additionally, your risk for stress fracture recurrence increases. A study comparing amenorrheic runners with normally menstruating runners found that 50 percent of amenorrheic runners had had more than one stress fracture compared with only 9 percent of runners who regularly menstruate. While the female athlete triad or any of its components is a significant contributor to stress fracture development in females who participate in weight-bearing exercise, other risk factors have been identified as well.

The amount of muscle mass in the lower extremities has received much attention as a structural explanation for the increased incidence of stress fractures in women runners. A major role of muscles is to absorb energy. If less mass is present or muscles are fatigued, energy absorption is compromised and bone stress increases. One study has identified less lean mass in the lower limb as a risk factor for stress fractures in women runners, independent of any other risk factors. For every 0.4 inch (1 cm) decrease in calf muscle circumference, a fourfold greater risk of stress fracture was noted. Additional studies are needed to better define how much muscle mass is needed to reduce stress fracture risk.

Finally, while no running surface has been clearly identified as more likely to cause injury, several studies of runners who run on concrete have noted higher rates of stress fractures in women than in men. An explanation for the apparent sex difference is unclear but is likely caused by multiple factors. Further study is warranted.

Treatment of Stress Fractures

If you receive a diagnosis of a stress fracture from your doctor, the most important treatment is complete rest from your running activities. Depending on the stress fracture site, your health care provider may put you in a walking boot. Icing early in the injury, 15 to 20 minutes up to three times a day, is beneficial and can be continued throughout the healing period. To maintain your cardiorespiratory fitness, cross-train with activities such as cycling, swimming, and deep-water running with a flotation device. Strengthening the muscle groups surrounding the joints above and below the fracture site should be part of your treatment plan as long as it does not cause pain at the stress fracture site. Using resistance bands is a good method for these exercises. Although frequently used by runners, avoid anti-inflammatory medication like ibuprofen. These medications may hinder the bone-healing process. Recovery from uncomplicated stress fractures often takes three to four weeks, although it can take longer. Once your injury is fully healed, you can resume running. Return to training in a slow and gradual manner to minimize the risk of reinjury.

Patellofemoral Pain Syndrome

Patellofemoral pain syndrome is the most common cause of knee pain in runners and is particularly prevalent in female runners. In a seven-year review of patients seen at a sports medicine clinic, the ratio of women diagnosed with patellofemoral pain syndrome compared to men was nearly two to one. Typical symptoms include pain behind, under, or around the patella (kneecap) that increases with running or climbing or descending stairs. It usually comes on gradually and can affect both knees simultaneously.

The knee is referred to as a hinge joint because its motion is back and forth like a hinged door. Its primary movements are flexion and extension of the leg. Because of the knee joint's structure, it depends on the surrounding ligaments (which connect bone to bone) and tendons (which connect muscle to bone) for support and function. In front of the knee is the patella, which lies within the quadriceps tendon. When the knee extends (straightens) and flexes (bends), the patella glides back and forth within the trochlea, a groove in the end of the femur. The patella and femoral trochlea comprise the patellofemoral joint.

The patellofemoral joint is stabilized by soft tissue that controls the movement of the patella within the trochlea, also known as *patellar tracking*. Alterations in patellar tracking can result in patellofemoral pain syndrome.

Causes of Patellofemoral Pain Syndrome

Several factors cause patellofemoral pain syndrome, including an imbalance in the stabilizing muscles, altered biomechanics of the lower extremity, increased stress across the patellofemoral joint, and anatomical factors. Abnormalities in the anatomical alignment of the lower extremities, particularly in women, are believed to be the primary contributors to patellofemoral pain syndrome. These anatomical abnormalities include leg-length discrepancy and foot-plant irregularities, such as excessive or insufficient pronation during running. The use of orthotics for these issues has shown reduction in knee pain. The Q-angle (angle at which the femur meets the tibia; see chapter 1) is also suspected to cause patellofemoral pain. A larger angle increases the force the quadriceps muscle exerts on the patella, which may predispose the patella to abnormal tracking. The research, however, is inconclusive.

Orthotics

Orthotics are shoe inserts that replace the removable shoe insole and are commonly used by runners. They are designed to correct biomechanical problems in order to prevent or treat lower-extremity injuries. Orthotics can be custom molded or prefabricated and purchased off the shelf. Cushioned insoles (flat, thin layers of foam that are either full or partial length) differ from orthotics because they aim to reduce pressure on a specific area on the foot by providing additional cushioning and comfort.

Widespread use of orthotics for a multitude of foot, leg, and knee ailments has occurred for decades despite a lack of evidence supporting their effectiveness for injury treatment and prevention. The last several years has brought a better understanding of their use for injury treatment. In fact, several studies have demonstrated the effectiveness of custom-molded orthotics for the treatment of patellofemoral syndrome in women and the treatment of plantar fasciitis in both men and women. The benefits of orthotic use in the treatment of Achilles tendonitis are inconclusive. And while treating certain injuries with orthotics has been shown to be effective, the use of orthotics for injury prevention in runners needs further study. Because the evidence for orthotic use in injury prevention is inconclusive, we do not recommend that you use orthotics unless you are recovering from an injury.

While training errors such as changes in training frequency, duration, and intensity can contribute to patellofemoral pain syndrome, other risk factors have also been identified. Multiple studies have shown that hip muscle weakness contributes to patellofemoral pain syndrome and that pain decreases and function improves following hip muscle strengthening. These findings, along with evidence that core muscle weakness is a risk factor for patellofemoral pain syndrome, have dispelled the long-held belief that weakness in the quadriceps muscle is the primary contributor. As a result, treatment and preventive strategies have changed.

Treatment of Patellofemoral Pain Syndrome

Once you have been diagnosed with patellofemoral pain syndrome, treatment focuses on pain control, exercises to increase strength, and in some women runners, orthotics. Because overload plays an important role in the development of patellofemoral pain syndrome, reducing your running volume, discontinuing hill running, and even curtailing your running activities may be necessary. Substituting cross-training activities that do not cause pain can help you maintain cardiorespiratory fitness. Exercises to strengthen your hip and gluteal muscles, hamstrings, core muscles, and quadriceps, such as those described later in this chapter, are an effective treatment. If your symptoms do not improve with a home exercise program, rehabilitation under the guidance of a physical therapist or a comparable professional familiar with women's running injuries is beneficial.

Orthotics help stabilize the foot when running and reduce impact. Evidence supports their use to treat patellofemoral pain syndrome, particularly in women runners who overpronate (foot rolls inward excessively upon landing) or

For patellofemoral pain, knee braces and straps can provide some relief of symptoms but for long-term relief runners should use a rehabilitation program.

underpronate (foot doesn't roll inward enough upon landing to adequately absorb shock). Although a variety of knee braces, knee sleeves, and patellar straps (commonly advertised as Cho-Pat straps) are often used to treat patellofemoral pain syndrome, the effectiveness of their use is inconclusive. While they may provide symptomatic relief, focusing on a comprehensive rehabilitation program that addresses the muscles and other structures that move the lower extremity offer the best long-term relief.

Common Overuse Injuries

Although stress fractures and patellofemoral pain syndrome are the most common running-related injuries among women, other overuse injuries can occur in female runners, including iliotibial band syndrome, plantar fasciitis, and Achilles tendonitis. These injuries are common in both recreational and experienced runners who increase their training load too quickly.

Iliotibial Band Syndrome

Iliotibial band syndrome (ITBS) is the most common cause of pain on the outside of the knee among runners and occurs from repetitive friction of the iliotibial band against the outside of the knee. The iliotibial band is a sheath of connective tissue that runs down the thigh from the hip to just below the knee (see figure 13.4). The main functions of the iliotibial band are to assist with outward movement of the thigh and to stabilize the outside of the knee. Symptoms are typically progressive and often begin with a sensation of tightness on the outside of the knee. Pressing on the outside of the knee while flexing it usually reproduces the pain. With time and continued activity, the tightness progresses into a localized pain or burning sensation on the outside of the knee. Some runners experience a clicking sensation caused by the iliotibial band tightening and snapping across the joint when the knee flexes and extends. The symptoms are often worse when running downhill.

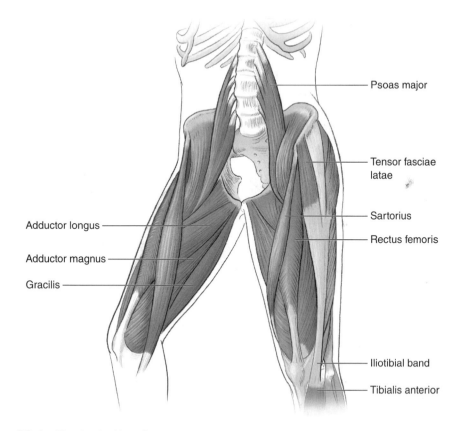

Psoas major

Tensor fasciae latae

Sartorius

Rectus femoris

Adductor longus

Adductor magnus

Gracilis

Iliotibial band

Tibialis anterior

Figure 13.4 The iliotibial band.

Excessive or abrupt increases in mileage, preexisting iliotibial band tightness, running downhill, too much running around a track in one direction, too much running on cambered road surfaces, stiff shoes that limit pronation, highly arched feet that don't adequately pronate (which transfers the shock of landing to other parts of the leg), and hip and gluteal muscle weakness contribute to this injury. Running mechanics, specifically internal rotation of the leg and changes in knee flexion as the heel strikes the ground, also appear to contribute to ITBS. Runners who have ITBS have greater knee flexion at heel-strike, a greater strain in the iliotibial band while the leg is on the ground during the running motion, and greater internal knee rotation at the end of a long, exhausting run than runners who don't have ITBS.

Traditional treatment of ITBS has focused mainly on stretching and pain reduction. Rest from running may be necessary, along with ice and stretching. Cross-training that does not aggravate the condition can be done to maintain fitness. Using a foam roller can help mobilize, or loosen, the iliotibial band and surrounding tissues. A foam roller is a firm foam log about 6 inches in diameter available in various lengths. To use a foam roller effectively, lie on your side with the affected iliotibial band on top of the foam roller. Roll forward and back so that the foam roller moves between your knee and hip bones, using your body weight to apply pressure. Foam rollers can be purchased at sporting goods stores or ordered online. Massage also works well. Strengthening the hip and gluteal muscles, which improves control of the leg when it first lands on the ground can also alleviate symptoms. As with most injuries, the longer you experience symptoms the longer it may take to recover.

Achilles Tendinitis and Tendinosis

Achilles tendinitis and tendinosis are the most common forms of tendon injuries in runners. Runners, male and female alike, have a 30 times greater risk of developing Achilles tendon problems than nonrunners do. The Achilles tendon attaches the two calf muscles (gastrocnemius and soleus) to the heel and is the thickest and strongest tendon in the body. While inflammation (tendinitis) may contribute to your symptoms in the first few days, the symptoms are the result of a degenerative process (tendinosis) in the collagen fibers that make up the tissue. Over time, the fibers may weaken, leading to tearing of the tendon, although this occurs more commonly in males.

Regardless of the distinction, the symptoms are the same: a gradual onset of pain over the Achilles tendon. In mild cases, pain may occur only when running. As it becomes more severe, pain may be present during your normal daily activities or even at rest. The tendon area will become tender to your touch and visibly swollen. Pinching the tendon between your thumb and forefinger usually reproduces the pain.

Injury to the Achilles tendon occurs when the amount of stress on the tendon exceeds the ability of the tendon to adapt to the load. Factors that contribute to Achilles tendon problems include training errors such as too rapid of an increase in mileage, too much interval training or hill running, inadequate recovery between sessions, highly arched feet, calf weakness, and inflexible calf muscles.

Similar to treatment of other overuse injuries, initial treatment includes rest and activity modification. Activities that do not load the tendon, such as swimming or cycling, are alternatives while your tendon recovers. Evidence suggests that the most effective treatment for Achilles tendinosis is calf strength training with eccentric contractions (lengthening the muscle fibers as a load is applied) because it helps form new collagen, which is the main component of the tendon. Eccentric training can be done by performing a heel-drop exercise on a stair or step (see page 176). This exercise lengthens the muscle fibers as a load (your body weight) is applied. Heel lifts and orthotics are widely used despite limited evidence of their effectiveness. Interestingly, since the introduction of shoes that control pronation, an increase in Achilles tendon injuries has occurred. A recent review of research failed to identify any controlled, clinical trials to support their use in treating Achilles tendonitis.

Plantar Fasciitis

Plantar fasciitis can be a debilitating injury for runners. A band of connective tissue on the bottom of the foot that runs from the heel to the toes, the plantar fascia acts like a ligament that helps support the arch of the foot when you run. Similar to

Achilles tendinitis, plantar fasciitis is a degenerative condition. As a result of this degeneration, microscopic tears occur with overload and the plantar fascia loses its ability to support the arch. The result is heel pain, frequently on the inside edge of the heel, or pain along the arch. The pain is often worse during the first steps in the morning or after prolonged sitting, but it decreases with activity and then aches afterward. As the condition becomes more severe, the pain may be present all the time when walking and running. Both flat feet and highly arched feet can be risk factors, although research is divided on this issue. Tight calf muscles and weakness in the muscles in the sole of the foot can also increase your risk of plantar fasciitis.

Plantar fasciitis can be a stubborn injury. Numerous treatments have been used with limited evidence of their effectiveness. Once believed to be beneficial, current evidence no longer supports shockwave therapy. Avoiding the aggravating activity, stretching and strengthening the calf muscles, and strengthening the muscles of the foot can improve symptoms. Tension night splints, which hold the foot in a flexed position while you sleep, may be helpful. Orthotics may also help to reduce symptoms by decreasing tension in the plantar fascia. Studies have found no difference between the effectiveness of prefabricated or custom-molded orthotics. Although it is not something that runners like to hear, rest may be the best option. Of people with plantar fasciitis, 80 to 85 percent of them will experience a significant decrease in pain within the first six months regardless of the treatment used.

Training, Surfaces, and Shoes

While the number of miles or the amount of time you run each week is the most important component of your training, it also can lead to injury. The main cause of running injuries is an increase in training volume or intensity. To prevent overuse injury, you must control the amount of stress applied to the tissues. If the amount of stress does not exceed the body's ability to adapt, overuse injury is less likely to occur. The frequency and intensity of your training must be increased in small, incremental steps. Avoid erratic changes in your training schedule and incorporate rest.

Increase your training volume or intensity gradually and systematically and avoid hard workouts two days in a row. For example, if you are scheduled to do an interval workout one day and a hill workout another day, be sure to have a rest day or easy run sandwiched between. While it is frequently recommended to increase your training volume by no more than 10 percent per week, your running ability and experience will dictate the amount and the rate at which you can increase your training volume without risking injury. For example, if you have been running 25 miles (40K) per week for several weeks, you should be able to increase to 30 miles (48K) per week without problem (a 20% increase) as long as the stress is spread out over the whole week. A well-planned training program will allow you to run for a long time without injury.

Your weekly long run should not exceed the longest run in your training cycle by more than 2 miles (3.2K). For example, if during the third week of your training

Practical Tips for Designing a Training Program

- Combine walking with running if you're a new or recreational runner.
- Add nonimpact cross-training activities to boost cardiorespiratory fitness.
- Increase interval and hill training gradually. Generally, this is the addition of one hill or one interval per week.
- Incorporate rest or easy days between hard workouts.
- Warm up before interval training.
- Organize your training into three- to four-week cycles with two to three weeks of progressive build-up, followed by one week of less-intense training.
- Keep a training log and record your mileage, the rate of change from week to week, types and intensity of workouts, and how you felt during the run. Documenting the details of your training provides insight into the relationship between training and injury.
- Refer to your training log at the first sign of pain and make adjustments.

cycle you ran 10 miles (16K) and your long run in the recovery week that followed was 7 miles (11K), your long run to start the next build-up cycle should be no longer than 12 miles (19K). To minimize your risk of injury, your weekly long run should never be more than double the length of any other run during the week. That being said, marathon training programs for recreational runners may exceed this recommendation. While risky, the rationale for programs that work up to a 20-mile (32K) run on only 30 to 35 miles (48-56K) per week is that several full rest days during the week allow time for your body to recover between workouts. If you're going to do 20-mile runs on only 30 to 35 miles per week, try to include a midweek medium-long run that is half to two-thirds the distance of your long run so you avoid making the long run too physically stressful.

Training surface has frequently been blamed as a contributor to injury. Yet, no surface has been clearly identified as more likely to cause injury. All surfaces present a similar risk if you are adapted to that surface. And each surface requires different adaptations. For example, running on concrete requires your body to absorb the stress of impact. Running on soft surfaces, such as grass, requires your body to learn how to stabilize and balance itself because of the unevenness. Uphill running stresses your Achilles tendon and plantar fascia, whereas running downhill increases impact and braking. It is only when you make a rapid change in surface without allowing your body to adapt that your risk of injury increases. Training on a variety of surfaces is good for you. However, you should incorporate different surfaces gradually into your training plan.

Over the last 20 years, new shoe technologies have been designed to offer cushioning, support, and stability. Shoe companies have led us to believe that fitting foot type to shoe type decreases the risk of injury. Very few published studies and no solid evidence shows that this practice makes a difference. Despite all the technological advances, runners continue to experience injury.

The size, width, and shape of the shoe should match the shape of your foot and should not cause pressure points or deform or squeeze your toes. Women have much narrower heels than men do, so select a shoe that has adequate heel support and fit. The weight of the shoe is also important because it can affect oxygen consumption. A 1 percent increase in the weight of a shoe can cause a 3 percent increase in oxygen consumption. If you are a competitive runner, consider experimenting with a lightweight shoe to conserve your energy and prevent fatigue. Because shoes have a limited lifespan, monitor the wear of your shoes. Change your running shoes every 350 to 500 miles (560-800K). Another option to preserve wear is to alternate two pairs of shoes.

Minimalist shoes with very thin soles are becoming increasingly popular, the idea being that they decrease the risk of injury by altering your foot-strike pattern and reducing your contact time with the ground. While current thinking is based on anthropology and theory, rigorous scientific studies are needed before conclusions can be drawn. Barefoot running shoes, designed to simulate barefoot running, are another type of minimalist shoe. While some studies suggest that barefoot running shoes may improve

Runners should change surfaces, such as asphalt to trails, gradually to allow their bodies to adapt and to avoid injury.

running mechanics, other studies have shown unfavorable or inconsistent results. Clearly, further research is needed. If you are intrigued by barefoot running shoes, make a smooth and progressive transition. Start with one minute of running in minimalist shoes and increase the time by a minute with each successive run, putting on traditional shoes for the remainder of your training. Throughout this transition, listen to your body. Any new symptom of pain in your calf, Achilles tendon, plantar fascia, or metatarsal bones—tissues that are being stressed with barefoot running shoes—suggests that you are progressing too quickly.

Helpful Tips for Buying Shoes

- Make sure the shoe fits the shape of your foot. It should feel comfortable immediately.
- Buy shoes later in the day when your feet are slightly swollen.
- Try on both shoes, and wear the same type of sock that you would run in.
- Practice running in the shoe while you are still in the store.
- Wiggle your toes in the shoes. Your toes should be able to move around. A finger-width between the toes and the end of the shoe is usually adequate.
- Do not consider the price or the look of the shoe as an indication of quality.
- Buy a shoe that is breathable. The shoe's upper (the part of the shoe above the sole) should be made of fabric such as nylon mesh, which allows airflow.

Strength Training for Injury Prevention

Having a strong core and lower-extremities can help prevent injuries. Incorporate exercises that strengthen the hip muscles (especially the hip abductors, the muscles on the outside of the thigh), gluteal muscles, quadriceps, foot muscles, and calf muscles two or three times per week.

SIDE-LYING LEG LIFTS

Target muscles: Hip abductors and gluteal muscles

Lie on your side with the bottom leg flexed at the hip and at the knee. Keeping your back perpendicular to the floor, straighten the top leg, pull it back (extend at the hip) three inches (7.5 cm), and lift it approximately eight inches (20 cm). Keep the leg straight and point the toes inward and toward the ground. Perform 2 to 3 sets of 15 to 20 repetitions. Complete the exercise on both sides.

CLAMSHELLS

Target muscles: Hip abductors and gluteal muscles

Lie on your side with your spine straight and the legs stacked. Bend your hips to 45 degrees and your knees to 90 degrees. Keeping the feet together, lift the top knee (like a clam) two to three inches (5-7.5 cm), hold for two seconds, then return to the start position. Perform 2 to 3 sets of 15 to 20 repetitions. Complete the exercise on both sides.

MONSTER WALKS

Target muscles: Hip abductors and gluteal muscles

Place a resistance band either around the ankles or right below the kneecaps. Begin the exercise with the knees and hips slightly flexed and feet shoulder-width apart so there is tension on the band. Step to the side. Each step to the side increases tension on the band. Repeat the exercise walking in the other direction, leading with the other leg. Walk 30 to 60 seconds in each direction. Perform 2 to 3 sets.

WALL SITS

Target muscles: Quadriceps

Stand about two feet (0.6 m) away from a wall, facing away from it. Lean back so your back and the back of your hips touch the wall. Slide down until your knees are at a 90-degree angle. Keeping the abs contracted, hold for 20 to 60 seconds. Return to the start and repeat the sequence. Perform 2 to 3 sets of 15 to 20 repetitions.

STEP-UPS

Target muscles: Quadriceps

Stand facing a step or box four to eight inches (10-20 cm) high. Step onto the box, placing the foot of the lead leg completely on top of the box. Shift your weight to this leg and straighten your knee to lift the body and the other leg off the ground. Do not push off the ground with the foot of the trailing leg. Return to the starting position. Perform 2 to 3 sets of 15 to 20 repetitions. Switch the lead leg and repeat.

WALKING LUNGES

Target muscles: Quadriceps, gluteal muscles

Stand with the feet together. Keeping the abdominals tightened and the back straight, take a large but controlled step forward on one leg. Lower the hips toward the floor and bend both knees almost to 90 degrees. Do not let the back knee touch the ground. The front knee should be over the ankle and should not move forward past the toes. Push off with the foot on the trail leg and step forward to bring the feet together again. Perform another lunge, leading with the other leg. Walk for 30 to 60 seconds. Perform 2 to 3 sets.

STEP-DOWNS

Target muscles: Quadriceps, gluteal muscles

Stand on one leg near the edge of a step four to eight inches (10-20 cm) high. Your foot should be completely on the box and your toes should be near the edge. Bend the knee, lowering the nonweight-bearing leg in front of the step toward the ground. Touch the heel to the ground but do not place your weight on the foot. Keep the pelvis level. Return to the start position by lifting your body backward. Do not push off with the foot that is touching the ground. Perform 2 to 3 sets of 15 to 20 repetitions. Then complete the exercise on the other leg.

HEEL DROPS

Target muscles: Calf muscles

Stand on your toes on the edge of a step with your heels elevated and your legs straight. Lower the heels so they are slightly lower than the toes. Raise back onto the toes. Complete the exercise with knees straight and with knees bent. Hold your hands against a wall or other solid structure for balance as needed. You can also do the exercise on one leg at a time. Perform 2 to 3 sets of 15 to 20 repetitions per leg.

ARCH RAISERS

Target muscles: Foot muscles

Stand barefoot on one leg. Place one hand against a wall or other solid structure for balance. Imagine your foot is a tripod and place even pressure on your big toe, pinkie toe, and heel. Ground these three points as you lift up your arch. Repeat the exercise with the other foot. Perform 2 to 3 sets of 15 to 20 repetitions with each foot.

TOWEL ROLL

Target muscles: Foot muscles

Sit on a chair and place a towel on the floor in front of you under your bare foot. Use your toes to pull the towel toward you. Your hip and knee should not move. Repeat with the other foot. Add resistance by placing a weight or a heavy book at the end of the towel. Perform the exercise for 30 seconds per foot. Complete 2 to 3 times.

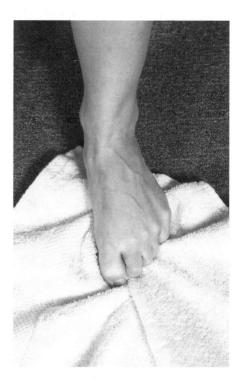

Flexibility for Injury Prevention

Flexibility generally describes the range of motion present in a joint. It varies among people, decreases with age, adapts to the demands you make on it, and can be modified through training. Several types of stretching can increase flexibility. The type that runners may be most familiar with is static stretching, which is lengthening a muscle by holding a position for 15 to 60 seconds. Dynamic stretching incorporates more running-specific movements and is gaining popularity. Dynamic stretching uses the speed of movement to bring about a stretch. Unlike in static stretching, the end position is not held.

The prevailing belief among runners is that static stretching will reduce your risk of injury. Unfortunately, evidence does not support this belief. In fact, most studies suggest that static stretching before exercise does not reduce the incidence of injury and may even increase it. Recent scientific studies suggest that dynamic stretching before exercise may be preferable. The effect of stretching on running performance is equally confusing. While some research suggests that better flexibility leads to better running performance, other research suggests that stretching can negatively affect running performance. Several studies have shown that among runners, those who are less flexible in their hamstrings are more economical with a lower rate of oxygen consumption when covering the same distance at the same speed as more flexible runners.

Studies have evaluated different types of stretches and different timing of stretching in runners of different ages, different sex, and different ability. Although comparing studies is difficult, we can draw conclusions. It may seem surprising that static stretching immediately before exercise has no effect on injury prevention and has a negative impact on speed and endurance, and that stretching done at other times may or may not be beneficial. One study raises the possibility that stretching after activity may decrease injury risk, while another study has suggested that injury severity rather than risk of injury is decreased. And no study has demonstrated improved race performance if you stretch after or outside of periods of running. If you want to stretch before you run, use dynamic stretches, which improve the mobility of prime muscles through their full range of motion, which is important for runners. Use static stretches separate from your running rather than before or after a run.

Dynamic Stretches

For each exercise, move actively through the range of motion, contracting the muscle group opposing the one being stretched. When using a strap, use it only for light assistance at the end of the range of motion.

GLUTEAL STRETCH

Lie on your back and bend the knee of one leg, placing your hands behind your knee and thigh. Keep the other leg straight and on the ground. Using the abdominals and hip flexors, lift the exercising leg toward your chest. Gently assist your leg at the end of the stretch with your hands. Hold the stretch for one to two seconds, return to starting position, and repeat. Repeat the sequence with the other leg.

BENT-LEG HAMSTRING STRETCH

Lie on your back with both knees bent and your feet flat on the ground. Make a loop with a strap, lift one foot off the ground, and place it into the loop. Grasp the ends of the strap and lift your leg until your thigh is perpendicular to the ground and your lower leg is parallel with the ground (photo *a*). Gradually extend your knee by contracting your quadriceps, causing your foot to rise toward the ceiling (photo *b*). Lock your knee and point your foot straight up. Use the strap for gentle assistance at the end of the stretch, but do not pull your leg. Hold the stretch for one to two seconds, return to starting position, and repeat. Repeat the sequence with the other leg.

STRAIGHT-LEG HAMSTRING STRETCH

Lie on your back with one knee bent and the foot of that leg flat on the ground. Make a loop with a strap and place your other foot into the loop, locking your knee so the leg is fully extended (photo *a*). While keeping your leg straight, lift it toward your chest, aiming your foot toward the ceiling. Grasp the ends of the strap with both hands and slightly pull the strap toward your chest to assist at the end of the stretch, but do not pull your leg (photo *b*). Hold the stretch for one to two seconds, return to the starting position, and repeat. Repeat the sequence with the other leg.

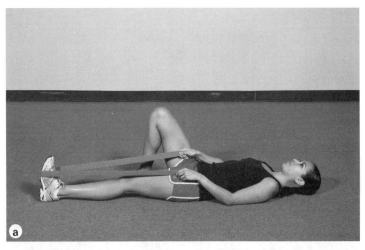

QUADRICEPS STRETCH

Lie on your side with your knees bent, as in a fetal position. Place your bottom arm under the thigh of your bottom leg. Reach down with your upper hand and grab the shin, ankle, or forefoot of your top leg. Keeping your leg parallel to the ground, contract your hamstrings and glutes, and move your thigh back as far as you can, using your hand or the strap to give a gentle assist at the end of the stretch. Keep your head lifted off the floor to avoid putting any strain on your neck. Hold stretch for one to two seconds, return to starting position, and repeat. Repeat the sequence with the other leg.

ADDUCTOR STRETCH

Lie on your back with both legs extended. Loop a strap around the back of the lower leg (just above the ankle), across the ankle, and under your foot, so the ends of the strap are on the outside. Lock that knee and slightly rotate the other leg inward. Using your abductors (the muscles on the outside of your thigh), extend your exercising leg out from the side of your body. Keep slight tension on the strap and use it for gentle assistance at the end of the stretch, but do not pull your leg. Hold stretch for one to two seconds, return to starting position, and repeat. Repeat the sequence with the other leg.

DYNAMIC CALF STRETCH

Sit with both legs extended in front of you. Loop a strap around one foot. Flex your foot back toward your ankle, using the strap for a gentle assist at the end of the movement. Hold stretch for one to two seconds, return to starting position, and repeat. Repeat with the other foot.

Static Stretches

Static stretches should be slow and progressive. Hold each stretch for 30 seconds. You should feel a stretch, but if you experience pain, you are pushing the stretch too far.

HIP FLEXOR STRETCH

Stand in a position similar to a lunge, with the rear knee resting on the ground and the front knee at a 90-degree angle. Place your hands on the front knee. Keep your pelvis level and your back straight. Slowly lean forward until you feel a stretch in the front of the hip of the rear leg. Repeat the stretch with the other leg.

HAMSTRING STRETCH

While lying on your back, keep one leg straight on the ground. Flex the hip of the other leg and bend it to 90 degrees and clasp your hands behind your knee. Straighten your knee until you feel a stretch. Repeat the stretch with the other leg.

QUADRICEPS STRETCH

While standing and keeping the trunk, hips, and knees in alignment, bend one knee and grasp the foot of that leg with the hand on the same side. Pull the heel toward the butt to increase the stretch. Be sure the knee of the stretching leg does not move ahead of the other knee or move out to the side. If needed, place the free hand on a chair or wall for balance. Repeat the stretch with the other leg.

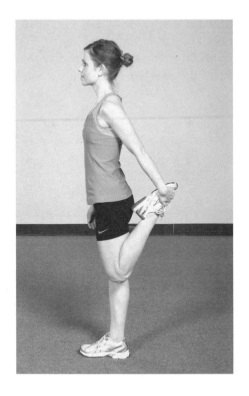

ILIOTIBIAL BAND STRETCH

Stand upright, using a wall or chair for balance if needed. Extend your leg and bring it behind the other leg. Bend at the waist to the opposite side until you feel a stretch on the outside of the hip.

GLUTEAL STRETCH

While sitting, extend one leg in front of you. Bend the knee of the other leg and place the foot of that leg on the other side of the straight leg. Grasp the bent knee with opposite hand, place the other hand on the floor for support, and pull your knee toward your torso. Be sure to keep your back straight and chest lifted.

CALF STRETCH

Stand facing a wall. Position one leg a foot or two (30-60 cm) ahead of the other. Bend the front knee and keep the back leg straight. Lean into the wall, keeping the back leg straight and the heel on the floor. Repeat the stretch and bend the back knee. Switch lead legs and repeat both stretches.

Performance Nutrition and Female Runners

A nutritionally sound diet, including both macronutrients (carbohydrate, protein, and fat) and micronutrients (vitamins and minerals), is important for attaining and maintaining a healthy weight, reducing the risk of chronic disease, and promoting overall health. For runners, good nutrition is also essential for optimal performance. Adequate nutrition provides fuel for your training and races, helps you avoid injuries and illness, maximizes your performance, and helps you recover from workouts. Eating well may not guarantee athletic success, but an unbalanced diet will most certainly undermine your training and competitive performance.

Energy Requirements

Performing your best in training and competition requires the proper amount and mix of carbohydrate, protein, and fat. These nutrients provide the fuel for exercise. As you learned in chapter 1, the energy systems used during exercise include the phosphagen and glycolytic (both anaerobic) pathways and the oxidative (aerobic) pathway. The choice of fuel your muscles use depends on the duration and intensity of your exercise, your level of training, and the composition of your diet. The energy requirements to support your training as a runner are largely met by oxidation of fat and carbohydrate. While protein contributes to the energy pool, the contribution is generally small unless carbohydrate supplies are limited. Higher-intensity exercise increases carbohydrate contribution, while fat contributes to energy when exercise is of a lower intensity. The response is similar in men and women, although estrogen influences metabolism in women, causing women to use more fat and less carbohydrate while running at the same pace.

Weight Loss and Caloric Intake

Many women begin a running program to lose weight. Running burns an average of 100 calories per mile. Combined with proper nutrition, it's understandable why women find it to be an effective weight-loss strategy. However, severely restricting your calories while running won't lead to successful weight loss. In fact, it could have the opposite effect by causing your metabolism to slow. While weight loss can only occur when energy output exceeds energy input, it must be done in a safe and healthful manner. A daily deficit of 300 to 500 calories per day achieved by simultaneously increasing daily energy expenditure and decreasing daily caloric intake is a reasonable and achievable goal and will result in a loss of one-half to one pound (0.23-0.45 kg) per week. The percentage of macronutrients you take in remains the same, you just take in fewer total calories and make wise food choices. As is necessary in all runners' diets, your meals and snacks should focus on complex carbohydrate foods like fresh fruits, vegetables, legumes, and whole grains. This will provide fiber and abundant vitamins and minerals.

Meeting energy requirements must be a nutritional priority for female runners. A challenge for many women runners is consuming enough calories to meet their energy needs. Runners' needs are significantly higher than those of people who do not participate in sports. Restricting intake is never the way to become a better runner. To best fuel your body for training and racing, you must have adequate stores of the macronutrients used for energy. To ensure that your body has adequate stores, you must eat and drink an adequate number of calories each day. Your age, weight, activity level, training conditions, and nontraining activity level (also known as your resting metabolic rate) all play a role in your daily needs.

Runners generally have higher caloric needs than nonendurance athletes because of the amount of energy expended in training and competition. Energy balance, therefore, is critical not only for running success, but also for overall health. You are in energy balance when the amount of energy from food, fluids, and supplements taken in equals the amount of energy expended through resting metabolic rate, physical activity, and the thermic effect of food. The thermic effect of food is the amount of energy used by the body to consume and process food. Failure to maintain adequate dietary intake can quickly result in chronic fatigue, dehydration, increased risk for illness and injuries, menstrual disturbances, and bone and muscle loss.

An estimation of your energy needs can be made using a variety of equations. Sport dieticians who work with runners typically use the Harris–Benedict equation. This equation will only estimate your energy expenditure and provide you with a range of caloric needs. A registered dietician can help you individualize your results. The Harris–Benedict equation follows:

$$RMR \times activity\ factor = daily\ energy\ requirement$$

To determine your energy intake requirements using this equation, calculate your resting metabolic rate (RMR) and then multiply it by the appropriate physical activity level. To determine your RMR, you need to know your weight in kilograms and your height in centimeters. If you know your weight in pounds, divide that number by 2.2 to determine your weight in kilograms. If you know your height in inches, multiply that number by 2.54 to find your height in centimeters. Then, you can use the following equation to estimate your RMR:

$$655 + (9.6 \times \text{weight in kilograms}) + (1.8 \times \text{height in centimeters}) - (4.7 \times 30) = \text{RMR}$$

Physical activity levels range from low to high, and the activity factor reflects this difference. Table 14.1 defines activity factors and the corresponding level of exercise. The range allows you to adjust your intake based on your daily volume of running. Use lower values when you perform less-strenuous activity. Higher values represent more intense or prolonged activity, such as high mileage or an interval workout.

To better understand how to use this equation to estimate your daily needs, let's walk through an example for a 30-year-old, 125-pound female runner who is 64 inches tall and is doing a 10-mile (16K) run at 7:30 pace. The first step is to convert the English measurements to metric measurements:

$$64 \text{ inches} \times 2.54 = 162.6 \text{ centimeters}$$

$$125 \text{ pounds} \div 2.2 = 56.8 \text{ kilograms}$$

The next step is to calculate her RMR:

$$655 + (9.6 \times 56.8) + (1.8 \times 162.6) - (4.7 \times 30) = \text{RMR}$$

$$655 + 545.3 + 292.7 - 141 = 1,352$$

Finally, she needs to multiply her RMR by the appropriate activity factor. Based on the length and pace of her run, the activity factor is 1.7:

$$1,352 \times 1.7 = 2,298 \text{ calories to meet energy demands}$$

Table 14.1   Descriptions of Activity Factors

Activity factor	Physical activity level
1.2	No exercise
1.3	Light exercise Running or cross-training 30 min per session
1.5	Moderate exercise Running 60-74 min per session (7:30-8:30 pace)
1.7	Prolonged or strenuous exercise Running 75-89 min per session at 6:30-7:30 pace, includes hills, fartlek, AT-pace runs, long intervals
1.9	Prolonged or intense exercise Running 90-120 min per session or longer, includes intervals, AT pace (5:30-6:30 pace)

Macronutrients

While your caloric needs will increase more than they do for other types of athletes, the macronutrient composition of your diet will be similar. Carbohydrate plays a key role. Because fat provides more than twice as many calories per gram than carbohydrate (9 kcal/g versus 4 kcal/g), fat will be valuable for providing extra calories in a smaller volume. As a consequence of your higher caloric demand, protein will be used for energy production, contributing up to 15 percent of the calories required during long-distance running. Figure 14.1 provides a basic breakdown of the percentage that each macronutrient should compose in your overall diet. The sections that follow provide specific recommendations and guidelines for carbohydrate, protein, and fat intake for female runners.

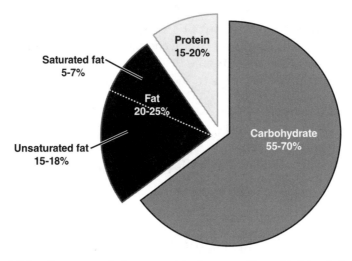

Figure 14.1 Recommended macronutrient composition of total caloric intake.

Carbohydrate

The many proponents of diets like Atkins and South Beach would have the public believe that carbohydrate is some kind of poison. Don't listen to them. As a runner, carbohydrate is your friend. Carbohydrate is the nutritional workhorse because it easily converts into glucose (sugar), which is used by your working muscles and brain. If you eat more carbohydrate than your body needs, the excess glucose is either stored as glycogen in your muscles and liver or as body fat. Glycogen stores are essential for use as fuel when you exercise for long periods, with muscle glycogen depletion becoming the decisive factor that limits prolonged exercise. If your glycogen stores get too low during exercise, you will start to feel fatigued. As you train, your muscles will be able to store more glycogen, allowing you to run longer. Well-trained runners can store 20 to 50 percent more glycogen than untrained individuals can.

Achieving and maintaining optimal carbohydrate intake is important for training intensity, preventing hypoglycemia (low blood sugar) during your run, serving as a fuel source for working muscles, and assisting in postexercise recovery. When the blood sugar of nondiabetic runners gets too low, their muscles rely on fat for energy, which makes completing a workout at a desired pace or intensity difficult because it takes longer to get energy from fat than from carbohydrate. Other common symptoms of low blood sugar include headache, nausea, and irritability.

Carbohydrate use increases as exercise intensity increases, but decreases as exercise duration increases. The goal of carbohydrate ingestion is to fill carbohydrate stores in the muscles and liver. The higher the initial glycogen level, the longer you can run at a given intensity. Because eating increases glycogen stores and exercise depletes them, runners who do not optimally fuel experience prolonged glycogen depletion that ultimately decreases endurance and performance. Current recommendations for daily carbohydrate requirements in runners range from 2.7 to 4.5 grams per pound of body weight, but can be as high as 5.9 grams per pound of body weight depending on the length of the training sessions. (A kilogram equals 2.2 pounds.) You can estimate your carbohydrate needs based on your body weight and the number of hours you train as shown in table 14.2.

Foods that are rich in carbohydrate include grains, beans, fruits, vegetables, dairy products, and sweets. Although all carbohydrate can fuel the body, not all carbohydrate contributes equally to a nutritional diet. Simple carbohydrate, or simple sugar, is digested quickly and includes fruits, fruit juice, honey, molasses, dairy products, and sweets. It will provide energy, but sweets such as soda, candy, and cookies are often low in essential vitamins and minerals and, in the case of cookies and candy, often high in fat. Nutrient-dense carbohydrate can include simple and complex carbohydrate, such as whole-grain breads and cereals, rice, pasta, fruits, vegetables, legumes, and low-fat dairy products such as yogurt. These foods not only provide carbohydrate, they also contain important vitamins, minerals, and fiber. Fiber is important to maintaining a healthy gut.

During training, building up and maintaining glycogen stores requires a carbohydrate-rich diet. Although many runners know the benefits of increasing their muscle glycogen stores before an endurance event, few pay attention to the carbohydrate content of their diet during training. Glycogen depletion can occur over repeated

Table 14.2 Estimation of Daily Carbohydrate Needs

Number of hours of running per day	Grams of carbohydrate per pound (0.45 kg) of body weight*
1	2.7-3
2	3.6
3	4.5
4	5.4-5.9

*1 g of carbohydrate equals 4 cal

days of heavy training when carbohydrate consumption is inadequate. The feeling of sluggishness (sometimes referred to as staleness) associated with muscle glycogen depletion is often blamed on overtraining. Eating a high-carbohydrate diet during training is necessary for maintaining carbohydrate reserves. Carbohydrate should supply about 55 to 70 percent of your total daily calorie intake. As noted in table 14.2, one gram of carbohydrate equals four calories, so you can multiply your recommended daily intake of carbohydrate (in grams) by four to determine how many of your daily calories should be from carbohydrate. When choosing foods, be sure to read the nutrition labels, which will indicate the total amount of carbohydrate in each serving, including the contribution from simple sugars, which is listed as sugar on a nutrition label.

Carbohydrate needs during exercise are divided into three time periods: preexercise, during, and postexercise. Research has demonstrated that consuming carbohydrate in the hours leading up to a training session or a competitive road race is critical for optimal performance, especially if your run will exceed two hours. Preexercise carbohydrate will elevate blood glucose levels to provide energy for the exercising muscles and maximize glycogen stores. Following digestion, carbohydrate enters the circulation as glucose where it can be taken into muscle cells and used for fuel or stored for later use. Using your preexercise carbohydrate initially will spare existing muscle and liver glycogen stores, prevent fatigue, and enhance performance. Many runners, male and female alike, forego consuming carbohydrate before a training run or race, especially if the session or event is scheduled for the morning. This habit can result in premature fatigue. After an overnight fast, liver glycogen stores are markedly depleted. Without the benefits of preexercise carbohydrate, you will have less energy to draw from and your performance will suffer. (See the Fueling Before Training or Races section, page 205, for specific recommendations.)

Consuming carbohydrate during endurance exercise lasting longer than 90 minutes enhances endurance by providing glucose for the muscles to use when their glycogen stores have dropped to low levels. As the muscles run out of glycogen, they rely on blood glucose for fuel. To maintain blood glucose and energy production, you need to ingest carbohydrate while exercising. This does not have to be a large volume of food. Energy bars, gels, or sport drinks that contain 60 to 80 calories from carbohydrate per one cup (240 ml), are often consumed because of their convenience, but other foods, such as fig bars, dried fruit, and crackers, also can provide the needed carbohydrate. Runners should consume 30 to 60 grams of carbohydrate every hour during training and competition to improve endurance.

Do not ingest too much carbohydrate during exercise because this can lead to stomach cramping and diarrhea and hinder performance. Determine your individual needs by experimenting during training with foods that are convenient, easy to eat, and do not cause gastrointestinal distress. While consuming carbohydrate during prolonged exercise is clearly advantageous, it will not replace the need for a preexercise meal.

Runners exercising longer than 90 minutes need to replenish their glycogen stores by consuming small amounts of carbohydrate.

Postexercise fueling is vital for optimal recovery, and timing is important. This is particularly important for runners who train exhaustively on successive days or who run high mileage. Exercise depletes muscle and liver glycogen stores, making carbohydrate the most important nutrient to replenish. Your body responds rather elegantly to situations that threaten or deplete its supply of fuel. Because your muscles prefer carbohydrate as fuel, a metabolic priority of recovering muscle is to replenish muscle glycogen stores. Eating or drinking carbohydrate-rich foods postexercise can replace muscle and liver glycogen stores. Glycogen can be restored within 24 hours when using an optimal dietary strategy.

Glycogen synthesis is a complex biochemical process largely controlled by the hormone insulin and the availability of blood glucose in the circulation. Muscles are picky when it comes to the time for synthesizing and storing glycogen. Although glycogen will continue to be synthesized until storage in your muscles is complete, the process is most rapid if you consume carbohydrate no later than 60 minutes after you run. Indeed, delaying carbohydrate ingestion for two hours after a workout significantly reduces the rate of glycogen resynthesis within the first few hours and slows your recovery rate. Refueling should be a priority after workouts and races.

Because quick delivery of carbohydrate to your muscles following exercise is important, several strategies to enhance glycogen resynthesis after exercise have been suggested, including consumption of foods with a high glycemic index, liquid forms of carbohydrate, and beverages combining carbohydrate and protein. All of these strategies have proven effective in runners.

The glycemic index (GI) is used to classify carbohydrate and refers to how quickly carbohydrate foods raise blood glucose levels. The more quickly blood sugar rises after ingestion, the higher the glycemic index. It makes sense, therefore, that eating foods with a high glycemic index immediately following exercise can replenish your carbohydrate stores quickly. Examples of high-GI foods include watermelon, cornflakes, mashed potatoes, raisins, and white bread. Commercial sport drinks are a good source of liquid carbohydrate to use for initial recovery as is any beverage that contains a large amount of carbohydrate (and protein). For example, research has shown that chocolate milk, which has a high carbohydrate and protein content, is an effective alternative to commercial sport drinks for recovery from exhausting endurance exercise. If your recovery beverage contains carbohydrate and protein, be sure it contains more carbohydrate than protein.

Regardless of how you replenish your carbohydrate stores within 15 minutes of your run, follow this with a small snack of 200 to 300 calories within an hour of your run. This snack should also contain primarily carbohydrate, although adding a small amount of protein will enhance your recovery process. Snack options include a bagel with peanut butter, half a sandwich, cereal with milk, a bowl of oatmeal, or a smoothie with yogurt and fresh fruit. This snack is then followed by a more substantial meal within the next one to two hours, supplying more calories, macronutrients, micronutrients, and fluids.

Protein

Most runners are aware of the need for carbohydrate as part of a good training diet, but their understanding of protein needs is often lacking. Both competitive and recreational runners require more protein than do inactive people. While a nonathlete requires 0.4 gram of protein per pound (0.45 kg) of body weight per day, a recreational runner requires 0.5 to 0.7 gram of protein per pound of body weight per day. A competitive runner requires even more: 0.6 to 0.9 gram of protein per pound of body weight per day.

Protein is important for muscle growth and aids in recovery and repair following muscle damage. Protein is also needed for red blood cell development, antibody production, and the synthesis of new structures that improve running, such as mitochondria and enzymes. As a fuel source, protein provides up to 15 percent of the fuel during activity when muscle glycogen stores are low, but only 5 percent when muscle glycogen stores are adequate. Because protein is important for muscle maintenance and recovery, runners need to consume adequate quantities of protein after daily training and competition.

Runners who do not meet their protein needs are more likely to experience decreased muscle mass, a suppressed immune system, increased risk of injury, and chronic fatigue. Women at risk of insufficient protein intake include those on a low-calorie diet or those on a vegetarian diet, because plant protein is not as well digested as animal protein. Conversely, athletes who routinely exceed protein needs may experience increased risk of dehydration, increased body fat stores, calcium loss, and an unbalanced diet that is often deficient in carbohydrate. Protein should supply 15 to 20 percent of your daily calories.

Ideally, athletes can meet their protein needs through diet. Some runners are drawn to protein powders or amino acid supplements as a means to increase protein intake. Studies have not shown the benefits of protein or amino acid supplements, and gastrointestinal distress can often result from intake of these supplements.

Good protein sources include meats, poultry, fish, eggs, dairy products, nuts, seeds, peanut butter, soy foods, and beans. To limit extra fat, choose lean cuts of meat, skinless chicken and turkey, water-packed tuna, baked or grilled fish, and low-fat or nonfat dairy products. A well-balanced vegetarian diet can easily supply enough protein as long as the protein sources are varied and you eat enough calories during the day. However, if you are vegan and avoid all animal proteins such as milk and meat, you should increase your protein intake by an additional 10 percent. When runners fulfill their caloric requirements, they generally take in enough protein.

Much of the research surrounding fueling before exercise has focused on carbohydrate. While small amounts of protein can be consumed one to three hours before exercise, carbohydrate-rich foods should predominate. Preactivity protein can provide a sense of fullness and can slow digestion of carbohydrate to sustain energy levels. Too much protein before exercise can cause nausea and diarrhea, which will hinder performance.

Unlike carbohydrate, which demonstrates clear performance benefits when ingested during exercise lasting more than 60 minutes, the majority of evidence fails to support a benefit to performance when consuming protein during exercise. Although not as critical as carbohydrate consumption, consuming protein after endurance exercise aids recovery. Along with carbohydrate, protein-rich foods should be consumed 15 to 30 minutes after exercising. Runners should try to consume 6 to 20 grams of complete protein during this time.

Complete protein contains all the essential amino acids in high amounts. These include animal proteins such as eggs, dairy products, meat, and fish. Incomplete proteins do not contain all the essential amino acids in adequate amounts. All plant products, with the exception of soy, are classified as incomplete proteins.

Soy is classified as a complete protein. Continuing to consume protein in subsequent meals from a variety of food sources to meet total daily requirements will ensure that your diet contains all the essential amino acids and will contribute to further tissue repair.

Fat

Typically, Americans eat 35 to 40 percent of their calories as fat, an amount that has been linked to cardiovascular disease, cancer, and the current epidemic of obesity. Despite its bad rap, fat does play a role in a runner's diet. Because it supplies more than twice the number of calories per gram compared to carbohydrate and protein (9 kcal/g versus 4 kcal/g for either carbohydrate or protein), it provides a concentrated calorie source to furnish energy. Fat supplies essential fatty acids that supply energy, help to produce hormones, contribute to nerve function, and carry the fat-soluble vitamins A, D, E, and K into your body. While carbohydrate is the preferred fuel source for running, your body uses fat during low- to moderate-intensity exercise. However, you do not need that much fat for your body to perform well. Fat should supply 20 to 25 percent of your daily calories.

A diet too low in fat may limit your running performance by inhibiting the storage of intramuscular triglyceride, thereby resulting in earlier fatigue during your run. Remember from chapter 1 that intramuscular triglyceride is the major source of fat used when you run because it is physically closer to the muscles' mitochondria. Excess fat intake can increase fat stores and cause gastrointestinal discomfort before and during exercise. High-fat foods take longer to digest, leaving you feeling sluggish. Most of us have plenty of body fat stored for energy during prolonged exercise, so fat loading is not useful. Running does not eliminate the potential adverse health effects of a high-fat diet.

There are three kinds of fat: saturated, polyunsaturated, and monounsaturated. Saturated fat (also known as the artery-clogging fat) tends to have a negative effect on blood cholesterol and may increase your chances of developing heart disease. Trans fat, which is the result of the commercial process of hydrogenation, behaves just like saturated fat in your body, increasing your risk for heart disease. Limit the amount of saturated fat and trans fat that you eat. All animal products, such as meat, poultry, cheese, and whole milk, contain saturated fat. Butter, lard, tropical oils such as palm, coconut, and palm kernel oil, and hydrogenated fat found in margarine, commercial baked goods, and snack foods also contain saturated and trans fats. You can easily identify saturated fat because it is solid at room temperature.

Polyunsaturated fats, such as soybean oil and sunflower oil, and monounsaturated fats, such as peanut oil and olive oil, have a positive effect on blood cholesterol and heart health. These types of fat are found in plant oils and are liquid at room temperature. Choose polyunsaturated or monounsaturated fat over saturated fat whenever possible.

Most studies have failed to find a benefit to eating a high-fat meal before exercise. Consuming a high-fat meal before you run will lead to an upset stomach. With the exception of ultrarunning events lasting four to six hours or longer, fats should not be consumed during exercise. No improvements in performance have been demonstrated, and significant gastrointestinal distress can result. Nor is it necessary to replace certain quantities or types of fat following training or competition. Because even the leanest of runners still has plenty of stored body fat, fat will not be depleted by endurance exercise. Your priority following training and competition should be to ingest adequate amounts of carbohydrate and protein as previously discussed.

Fluids

Despite the occasional compliment you may get as a runner about your well-defined muscles, water, not muscle, is the major component of your body. So when you lose water, there are consequences. Water is vital for many chemical reactions that occur inside your cells, including the production of energy for muscle contraction. The importance of proper hydration for your overall health is well established. It is critical to your success as a runner because of its role in regulating body temperature and maintaining blood plasma volume. Maintaining proper fluid balance ensures peak performance, while failing to adequately rehydrate during and after exercise leads to dehydration. When dehydration occurs, your body temperature increases, your performance suffers, and serious medical problems can occur.

Running causes you to generate heat from muscular contraction. Sweating and the evaporation of this sweat from your skin is the primary method the body uses to cool itself. While weather conditions such as temperature and humidity, the duration and intensity of your run, and your fitness level affect the sweating mechanism, it is only effective if your body is adequately supplied with fluids. Sweat rates can range from 0.8 to 1.4 liters per hour during slower-paced running to 1.4 to 2 liters per hour during intense running in hot weather. However, your gastrointestinal system can absorb only about 0.8 to 1.2 liters of fluid per hour, making it difficult to prevent dehydration, especially while running in the heat. Women generally have lower sweating rates than men. In addition to water, sweat contains sodium and smaller amounts of potassium.

As fluid and electrolyte losses add up, your blood plasma volume decreases. This reduces your ability to provide adequate circulation of blood and oxygen to both your muscles for energy and your body surface to help keep you cool. Fluid loss of 2 to 3 percent of your body weight can cause fatigue and impair performance. As dehydration worsens, muscle cramps may develop. If dehydration becomes severe, cardiac output further decreases and body temperature increases to dangerous levels. This ultimately results in heat exhaustion or heat stroke. The following are warning signs of dehydration:

- Headache
- Muscle cramps
- Dry mouth and thirst
- Fatigue and weakness
- General discomfort and achiness
- Nausea
- Irritability
- Dizziness

Replenishing fluids is essential for high-intensity efforts or for extreme environments.
AP Photo/Jasper Juinen

Because of the decrease in exercise performance and the potential health danger of dehydration, plenty of research on strategies to overcome or at least blunt the effects of dehydration has been done (and an onslaught of sport drinks has been marketed). Beginning a workout fully hydrated or even *hyperhydrating* before a workout can delay dehydration during a run, maintain performance, and decrease the risk of heat-related illnesses. Hyperhydration refers to increasing hydration to a greater level than normal in preparation for the loss of water that will occur when you run in the heat. This can result in the need to urinate during your run. Preexercise fluid intake enhances your ability to control body temperature and increases plasma volume to maintain cardiac output. Drink fluids before every run so that you begin every workout fully hydrated.

At rest, a female runner needs at least 72 ounces (approximately 9 cups [2 L]) of fluid daily to meet basic needs. For female runners, water, 100 percent fruit juice, and low-fat milk are good sources of fluid to meet your daily basic needs. If you are a high-mileage or competitive runner, you may also want to include a sport drink as a fluid source, which will provide additional calories and electrolytes. Carbonated beverages should not be a primary source of hydration because they will cause you to feel full before you have met your fluid needs.

If you have taken in insufficient fluid since your last workout, drink 12 to 20 ounces (360-600 ml) of water or a sport drink at least four hours before exercise. For female runners who weigh 120 to 150 pounds (54-68 kg), 10 to 16 ounces (300-480 ml) is usually sufficient. You can drink another 12 to 20 ounces (360-600 ml) two hours before your workout if you have not urinated or your urine is dark. For both recreational and competitive runners, if you are meeting your basic daily fluid needs and replacing those lost during exercise, preexercise hydration is often not necessary.

In addition to your requirements for daily fluid maintenance, running requires fluid replacement during and after working out. The goal of drinking during exercise is to avoid losing excessive fluid and electrolytes. How much and how often you should drink depend on environmental conditions and the intensity and duration of your run. Unless the environment is extreme or the intensity high, consuming fluids is probably not necessary for runs of 60 minutes or less at moderate intensity. However, consuming sport drinks will benefit runs lasting longer than 60 minutes, especially in hot, humid weather.

Sport drinks not only provide fluid, they also provide carbohydrate for the working muscles and sodium for electrolyte balance. Sport drinks that provide 60 to 80 calories from carbohydrate per cup (240 ml), as well as electrolytes like sodium and potassium, optimize fluid absorption. While opinions vary about quantity, consuming 4 to 10 ounces (120-300 ml) every 15 to 20 minutes is sufficient for most runners. Rehydrating while you run means you need to plan a way to drink during prolonged runs in the heat, whether that means carrying fluids with you, setting them out before you run, or running loops so you can stop at home or at a friend's house.

After exercising it is important to replace your lost fluid and electrolytes. Body weight is the best indicator of your hydration status. If possible, weigh yourself before and after exercise to determine how much you need to drink in order to rehydrate. You also should check the color and volume of your urine. Urine should be plentiful and clear or pale yellow. It should look like lemonade rather than apple juice. Some vitamins tend to turn urine a dark color, so if you take vitamins, rely on urine volume as an indicator of hydration status. For every pound (0.45 kg) of body weight lost during exercise, drink 16 to 24 ounces (480-710 ml) of fluid. You can accomplish this with water or a sport drink, which will also provide sodium and carbohydrate. Other watery foods, such as watermelon and popsicles,

What Should You Drink?

Fluid

- Before running: Drink 16 ounces (480 ml) two hours before exercise.
- During running: Drink about 8 ounces (240 ml) every 15 to 20 minutes. If you sweat heavily, drink more.
- After running: Drink 16 ounces per pound of body weight (0.47 L/0.45 kg) lost during your run.

Sodium

- If your run lasts more than 60 minutes or if you have a documented sodium deficiency, then before, during, and after running consume 0.5 to 0.7 gram (about one-tenth of a teaspoon of salt) per liter of fluid. Most commercial sport drinks already contain adequate sodium.
- If you do not have a sodium deficiency, your regular diet provides sufficient amounts of sodium and you do not need to consume extra.

also count toward fluid replacement. Fruit, such as bananas and oranges, is a good source of potassium. Pretzels, vegetable juice, and dill pickles are excellent sources of sodium. Replace fluids within two hours after exercise.

In certain circumstances you can drink too much water, which causes a sodium imbalance, leading to hyponatremia, the condition in which body fluids become very low in sodium content. This can occur if a runner only consumes plain water during long endurance events like a marathon. Consuming beverages containing sodium during prolonged exercise reduces the risk of hyponatremia. Avoiding overhydration will also reduce your risk. For reasons not completely understood, women are at higher risk than men of developing hyponatremia. Symptoms can include nausea, vomiting, headache, muscle weakness, and confusion. If the condition is not recognized or treated, it can progress to seizures and coma. Despite the recent attention the popular media has given to hyponatremia, the opposite problem—dehydration—is a much bigger issue. At the end of a marathon, many runners may be dehydrated, but only a few at most will develop hyponatremia. So don't be afraid to drink.

Micronutrients

Eating a balanced, nutrient-rich diet provides you with the vitamins and minerals (micronutrients) you require. However, exercise stresses many of the metabolic pathways that require micronutrients. Female distance runners, in particular, are athletes at a high risk of vitamin and mineral deficiencies.

Micronutrients play an important role in energy production, hemoglobin synthesis, maintenance of bone heath, adequate immune function, and protection of the body against oxidative damage. They assist in repair of muscle tissue during recovery from exercise and injury. Routine exercise increases the turnover and loss of micronutrients from the body. As a result, greater intake of micronutrients may be required.

Calcium and Vitamin D

Calcium builds strong bones and teeth and aids in muscle contraction and proper blood clotting. As you learned earlier in the book, adequate intake of calcium, along with vitamin D, is essential for a woman's bone health. Calcium enhances the effects of exercise on bone mineral density, a factor in preventing bone loss and reducing fracture risk. Calcium deficiency is a contributing factor in the development of osteoporosis (see chapter 4). Women ages 19 to 50 should consume 1,000 milligrams of calcium per day. Women older than 50 years should aim for 1,200 milligrams per day. Estimate your dietary calcium intake by multiplying the number of servings of dairy per day by 300 milligrams. The upper daily limit for calcium is 2,500 milligrams. While toxicity is typically not a problem with food intake, it can be a concern in women taking high-dose calcium supplements.

Calcium availability depends on the amount of calcium you ingest. Female distance runners are among the athletes most prone to inadequate calcium intake. When calcium intake does not offset the calcium needs of the body, calcium is withdrawn from the bones to maintain the calcium level in the blood. That's why dietary calcium is so important. If it's insufficient, calcium will be *stolen* from bone to maintain its level in the blood. Furthermore, the efficiency of calcium absorption decreases with age, beginning at about 45 years in females, just at the time that calcium is most needed. The decline in efficiency of calcium absorption with age may be due to declining vitamin D metabolism, making it more likely that you need supplementation of both calcium and vitamin D.

While calcium can be obtained through supplements, dietary sources are best because your body absorbs calcium better when it is obtained through food. Dairy products such as milk, yogurt, and cheese are excellent calcium sources. A one-cup (240 g) serving of most dairy products contains 200 to 300 milligrams of calcium. Other good sources are canned salmon with bones and dark, leafy, green vegetables, such as spinach, kale, and broccoli, as well as fortified foods like orange juice, breads, and cereals.

To determine whether using a supplement is appropriate, you must look at factors such as diet, menstrual cycle, and current bone mass. Calcium supplements include calcium carbonate and calcium citrate. Studies have found few differences between the two products, but it is important to take calcium supplements in doses of 500 milligrams or less throughout the day to achieve maximal absorption. Taking supplements with meals also helps absorption and minimizes side effects.

Although calcium is vital to bone health, it needs vitamin D to be absorbed in the gut. Vitamin D also increases bone resorption to provide calcium from *old* bone to make *new* bone. Some scientific research also has suggested relationships between vitamin D intake and cancer prevention, increased immunity, and possible roles in preventing diabetes. These studies continue to be reviewed, and your health care professional is the best one to advise you on these issues.

Vitamin D is produced when skin is directly exposed to the sun. Using sunscreen blocks the chemical reaction of the sun on the skin, and, as noted in chapter 12, your age, where you live, the time of year, and how much time you spend in the sun all affect skin production of vitamin D. Older women have higher requirements of vitamin D because the skin is less able to synthesize vitamin D from the sun.

Unfortunately, dietary sources of vitamin D are limited to fortified foods and fatty fish. Therefore, the use of a vitamin D supplement is the best way to ensure adequate vitamin D. Vitamin D$_3$ is the preferred supplement for adults. As with calcium, sex, age, diet, and health affect the amount of vitamin D you need. Women aged 19 through 50 years require 600 International Units (IU) a day of vitamin D, and menopausal women and women older than 50 need 800 to 1,000 IU per day of vitamin D.

Iron

Iron is essential for forming the oxygen-carrying proteins in blood (hemoglobin) and muscle (myoglobin). Oxygen-carrying capacity is essential for distance running. Without enough iron to produce red blood cells, a person can develop anemia, a condition in which the body does not have enough red blood cells. Anemia in runners can result in fatigue, poor recovery, and subpar performance. Iron deficiency is caused by diminished dietary iron intake, excessive iron losses, or both. Iron deficiency typically affects women up to the age of 50 because women lose iron every month during their periods.

Women with anemia commonly experience symptoms of weakness, headache, irritability, and poor tolerance to the cold. Female runners with mild anemia may feel normal at rest but note fatigue and decreased stamina with strenuous exertion. In women runners with mild anemia, difficulty performing strenuous exercise like interval training may be the only indication that there is a problem. As anemia progresses, loss of stamina and decreased exercise tolerance occur at easier running intensities. Muscles fatigue faster, heart rate is elevated at lower intensities, shortness of breath occurs, and the ability to sustain even mild exercise is reduced. You may feel sluggish and light headed and experience a loss of appetite. Your friends may tell you that you look pale.

Although other types of anemia exist, iron deficiency anemia is one of the most prevalent nutrient deficiencies in female athletes. The reasons for this include menstrual blood losses, inadequate iron intake, and a higher likelihood of a vegetarian diet. Women runners are at an even greater risk of iron deficiency anemia. Running and endurance training contribute to iron deficiency through losses in sweat and through breakdown of red blood cells. This breakdown is also known

Sensible Nutritional Advice

- Eat a wide variety of foods to ensure that you get the carbohydrate, protein, essential fats, vitamins, and minerals you need.
- Maintain your healthy weight.
- Avoid saturated fat and cholesterol.
- Eat carbohydrate foods that do not contain too much sugar.
- Eat calcium-rich foods.
- Enjoy the sun.
- Don't assume that vitamin supplements are necessary, especially megadoses and megavitamins.
- Drink plenty of water.
- Be critical of advertisements and the promotion of miracle foods, supplements, and energy aids.

as hemolysis, and it occurs from the repeated landing of the feet on hard surfaces, an increased speed of red blood cell movement through the bloodstream, and acidosis from high-intensity training. In addition to iron losses, the high demands by the muscles to make myoglobin further contribute to iron deficiency.

It is estimated that iron-deficiency anemia affects 3 to 5 percent of all women in the United States. Twenty-six to 60 percent of female athletes are affected by iron deficiency. Runners at risk for iron deficiency should check their iron status routinely. A blood test will easily reveal a deficiency. A complete blood count (CBC) is a group of tests that includes a red blood cell (RBC) count, hemoglobin, and hematocrit (the percentage of blood composed of red blood cells). Ferritin is a measure of your body's iron reserves. In iron deficiency anemia, the RBC count, hemoglobin, hematocrit, and ferritin are often lower than normal. To prevent iron deficiency, monitor your iron status, especially during periods of hard training or high mileage.

The treatment for iron deficiency anemia is an iron supplement along with an adequate diet. Because excessive iron can cause iron overload, speak with your health care provider before beginning iron supplementation. If you need to take supplements, you may start to feel better as early as a week after beginning supplementation. Symptoms are frequently resolved by eight weeks.

The two types of iron are heme and nonheme. Heme iron is found in animal foods, such as red meat and dark poultry. These are the most readily absorbable forms of iron. Nonheme iron, which is primarily found in plant foods and is less well absorbed, can be found in dried fruit, dark greens, beans, whole grains, and soy foods. Focus on consuming iron-rich foods daily. The following suggestions will help you increase your iron intake:

- Eat lean red meat or the dark meat of poultry several times per week.
- Add orange juice or other foods containing vitamin C to meals. This aids in iron absorption.
- Consider a cast-iron skillet for cooking acidic foods such as spaghetti sauce.
- Eat meals containing both protein and carbohydrate instead of just a bagel or just a salad.
- Cook foods for a short amount of time in a minimal amount of water to minimize losing iron from the food.
- Choose breads, cereals, and pastas that are iron enriched or fortified.
- If you are vegetarian, consume plenty of fortified cereals, legumes, nuts, and seeds and include foods rich in vitamin C with each meal.

B Vitamins

The B-complex vitamins, specifically thiamine, riboflavin, B_6, and niacin, are involved in energy production pathways and therefore are important in a runner's diet. Folate and vitamin B_{12} are required for the production of red blood cells, for protein synthesis, and for tissue repair and maintenance. Folate and vitamin B_{12} are frequently low in female athletes' diets.

Limited research has examined whether exercise increases the need for the B-complex vitamins. Some data suggest that exercise may slightly increase the need for these vitamins. However, these increased needs can generally be met with a higher caloric intake. Good sources of B-complex vitamins include fortified cereals, pork, ham, tuna, yogurt, milk, chicken, salmon, turkey, bananas, and ground beef.

Severe deficiency of vitamin B_{12}, folate, or both may result in anemia and reduced endurance. Clams, oysters, beef liver, and chicken liver are exceptionally good dietary sources of B_{12}. Salmon, ground beef, tuna, and yogurt are also good sources. Fortified cereals, broccoli, spinach, pinto and black beans, and enriched spaghetti are good sources of folate. Consume enough of these micronutrients to support your training for optimal performance and health.

Antioxidants

Vitamins C and E, the antioxidant nutrients, protect cell membranes in muscles from oxidative damage. Because running can increase oxygen consumption 10 to 20 times higher than it is at rest, it has been suggested that long-term running (daily or almost daily running for several years) produces a constant *oxidative stress* on the muscles and other cells, predisposing them to damage.

Whether exercise increases the need for antioxidant nutrients remains controversial. So far, little evidence shows that antioxidant supplements enhance physical performance. Supplements of vitamins C and E are often marketed to endurance athletes, proclaiming enhanced recovery from intense workouts. While some evidence indicates that vitamin E may enhance recovery, more research is needed. For now, the best nutrition advice is to incorporate plenty of foods containing antioxidants into your daily diet. Athletes at the greatest risk for poor antioxidant intake are those following a low-fat diet, restricting calories, or limiting their fruits, vegetables, and whole grains.

Nuts and seeds, vegetable oil, and products made from vegetable oil, such as margarine and salad dressing, are among the best sources of vitamin E. Animal sources, such as meat, chicken, and fish also contain vitamin E. The richest sources of vitamin C include citrus fruits and their juices, tomatoes and tomato juice, potatoes, green peppers, and green leafy vegetables.

Fueling Before Training or Races

Timing of meals and snacks should be individualized, taking into consideration your gastrointestinal tolerance as well as the duration and intensity of the training session or race. Because most runners do not like to compete on a full stomach, runners generally eat smaller meals as the race nears to allow for gastric emptying. Carbohydrate provides the quickest and most efficient source of energy and is rapidly digested. Some runners, however, consume and enjoy a substantial meal before training or races; others may experience severe gastrointestinal distress after such a meal and rely on a carbohydrate snack, a sport drink, or an energy gel.

Commercially formulated liquid meals are also a good choice for prerace fueling. They are high in carbohydrate, are palatable, and contribute to both caloric intake and hydration. To know what works best for you, experiment with new foods and fluids during training and plan ahead to ensure you will have access to these foods before your races.

As it is in training, the primary food for a prerace meal should be rich in carbohydrate to supply the muscles with glucose for energy, but protein can play a supporting role, too. Protein-rich foods consumed before endurance activities can be beneficial if consumed several hours before exercise. Protein contributes to a feeling of fullness and slows digestion, thus maintaining energy levels for a longer time. Performance can be negatively affected when protein is consumed close to the time of exercise. Limit fat in the prerace meal because it slows digestion. You may need to limit fiber to avoid interrupting your race for a bathroom stop. Above all, choose familiar, well-tolerated foods.

The following tips can guide your fueling practice before training or races. Choose the option that works best for you based on how much time you have for

Carbohydrate Loading

Carbohydrate loading, in which a runner rests the muscles by cutting back on training while also supersaturating them with glycogen in anticipation of a race, has proven effective for half-marathon and marathon races. You should carbohydrate load the week before competition to maximize glycogen levels.

Gradually increase the percentage of carbohydrate consumed up to 70 percent of your total caloric intake and simultaneously decrease the volume and intensity of your training, also known as tapering. This allows for maximum carbohydrate storage in the muscles. A carbohydrate intake of approximately 500 to 600 grams per day is necessary to maximize glycogen stores. Decreased volume and intensity of training results in a decrease in calorie needs. However, to obtain the same glycogen-loading benefit as men, women seem to need to increase their total caloric intake as well, so you'll need extra calories even while you're tapering. Don't worry if those extra calories cause weight gain during your taper. You will lose it all during the marathon. Think of the extra glycogen as your jet fuel—you want to store as much as you can before the marathon and use it all as you run the race. If you want to reduce calories to avoid weight gain while you are tapering, decrease your fat consumption. This will allow you to maintain both your protein and carbohydrate intake without sacrificing your overall nutrition.

Carbohydrate loading before a 10K race and shorter is not helpful and may actually make you feel heavy and stiff. Performance for races that take less than one and a half hours is not limited by the amount of stored glycogen. You already have enough stored carbohydrate to get you through them. If you're training for a 5K or 10K, simply maintaining a high-carbohydrate diet all the time will ensure you have an adequate amount of muscle glycogen.

digestion before the training run or race and your individual tolerance to eating prior to running.

- Three to four hours before training or racing, drink fluids and eat a regular-size meal that is high in carbohydrate, moderate in protein, and low in fat and fiber. Meal ideas include pasta with meat sauce or brown rice with chicken, salad with low-fat dressing, bread, orange juice, and water. Breakfast could include eggs and toast, potatoes, yogurt, and fruit.
- Two to three hours before training or racing, eat a small meal and drink fluids. Meal ideas include half a turkey sandwich or bagel and peanut butter, banana, sport drink, and water.
- One to two hours before a race, eat a small snack and drink fluids. Ideas include apple sauce, oatmeal, yogurt, dry cereal, energy bar, sport drink, and water.
- Thirty minutes to an hour before a race, consume sport drink and water.

For races that occur in the morning, many runners find a 200-400 calorie breakfast, such as a bowl of cereal with low-fat milk or yogurt, to be adequate and easily digestible if consumed two hours before the start of the race.

Appendix
Evolution of Women's Competitive Running

The first female runner of note goes all the way back to ancient Greece. Atalanta, the Greek goddess of travel and adventure, was known for her athletic prowess that rivaled that of most men. Warned against marriage by an oracle, Atalanta came up with a plan to marry only a suitor who could beat her in a race, killing those who failed to outrun her. "I am not to be won till I be conquered first in speed. Wife and couch shall be given as prize unto the swift, but death shall be the reward of those who lag behind," she exclaimed in the Roman poet Ovid's *Metamorphoses*.

Many would-be suitors were beaten until Hippomenes fell in love with Atalanta and wanted to marry her. When hearing of the challenge, he was skeptical, but when Atalanta took off her outer garments for her next race, that was all he needed to send in his race entry. There was one problem, however. He knew he could not beat Atalanta, so he asked for help from—who else?—Aphrodite, the goddess of love. Aphrodite provided Hippomenes with three golden apples to drop on the race course to distract Atalanta. During the race, whenever Atalanta pulled ahead of Hippomenes, he rolled one of the golden apples off of the course, forcing a curious Atalanta to stop and pick up the apple. Atalanta's frequent stops to fetch the apples was just enough for Hippomenes to win the race and Atalanta's hand in marriage.

As successful as Atalanta was in outrunning men, it would be many years before history recorded the first victory by a woman over a man. While men have been running for as long as physical labor has been deemed masculine and heroic, for most of the 20th century running was not considered an activity appropriate for women. Despite how many women run today, women have not been running competitively for very long. The first female runner to try to run competitively may have been the young Greek woman Melpomene, who asked if she could participate in the marathon at the first modern Olympic Games in 1896. Her request denied, she unofficially ran the course a few days earlier in four and a half hours.

After repeatedly petitioning to participate in the Olympic Games, women were finally granted an experimental program of five track and field events in the 1928

Olympic Games in Amsterdam, where American Betty Robinson became the first woman to win an Olympic gold medal in track and field in the 100 meters. However, the visible exhaustion of some of the women at the end of the 800 meters was taken as affirmation that distance running was too dangerous for women, and the event was dropped, not to be seen again until the 1960 Olympics in Rome.

The decades following the 1928 Olympics offered few opportunities for women to compete in long distances. But the lure of running long distances kept women coming to the starting line, if only unofficially. In the early part of the 20th century, much of the attention on distance running centered on the marathon, primarily as a result of the growth and popularity of the Boston Marathon, which had been run for the first time in 1897, a year after the first modern Olympic Games.

Although women were starting to show that they could successfully run long distances, it wasn't until the mid-1960s with the efforts of two women that the world took notice. Denied entry into the 1966 Boston Marathon, 23-year-old Roberta Gibb made history as the first woman to run the Boston Marathon. Hiding in the bushes near the start, she jumped into the race and finished in 3:21:40 as the unofficial women's winner, an accomplishment she repeated in 1967 and 1968.

As important as Roberta Gibb's three unofficial wins were for women's running, it was another woman in the 1967 Boston Marathon who became the pioneer. Not to be denied an official place on the starting line, Kathrine Switzer, who entered the race under the name K.V. Switzer to fool race organizers, became the first woman to complete a marathon as an official entrant. The story of how she was nearly thrown out of the race by marathon official Jock Semple of the Boston Athletic Association, who attempted to push her to the side of the road, received national publicity.

The year 1971 proved to be pivotal for women distance runners. The women's world record for the marathon was lowered four times, both the 3:00 and 2:50 barriers were broken, and the Amateur Athletic Union (now USA Track & Field) permitted women to officially enter its sanctioned marathons. For the first time, the marathon's two biggest stages—Boston and New York—were officially open to women.

Meanwhile, shorter races were becoming popular among women as well. American Mary Decker ran a mile (1.6K) in a world record time of 4:17 to become the first woman to run the distance in under 4:20, showing that women could run fast in addition to running long. Growing pressure from the world athletic community prompted track and field's world governing body to add the women's 3,000 meters to the Olympic Games, establish the 5,000 and 10,000 meters as world record distances for women as they had been for men for a long time, and mandate that any international event that includes a marathon must also include a women's race.

In 1981, the International Olympic Committee voted to add a women's marathon to the 1984 Olympics in Los Angeles, but left out two other distance events that the men had in their program—the 5,000 and 10,000 meters—a controversial decision that prompted the American Civil Liberties Union in the United States to file a lawsuit in Los Angeles on behalf of U.S. women distance runners. In 1984, Joan

Benoit became the first women's Olympic marathon champion in 2:24:52 for all the world to see. The 1984 Olympics also included a controversial women's 3,000 meters, placing even more attention on women's running, as South Africa's Zola Budd, running barefoot, tangled with American gold medal favorite Mary Decker, with Decker falling to the track and out of the race. Following the Olympics, the International Olympic Committee approved the inclusion of the women's 10,000 meters at the 1988 Olympics in Seoul, South Korea, and replaced the women's 3,000 meters with the 5,000 meters at the 1996 Olympics, setting the slate of running events to equal that of the men.

By the late 1990s, distance running was nearly as global for women as it was for men. Countries such as Russia, Japan, New Zealand, Great Britain, and the East African countries of Kenya and Ethiopia that had been dominating men's distance running since the late 1960s were showing that they also had great female runners. In 2003, England's Paula Radcliffe set the current marathon world record of 2:15:25, an average pace of 5:10 per mile and only 9.5 percent slower than the current men's world record of 2:03:38, held by Kenya's Patrick Makau. As Radcliffe's and others' performances have shown, the best women distance runners can outperform all but the very best men.

Index

Note: The italicized *f* and *t* following page numbers refer to figures and tables, respectively.

A

Achilles tendon problems 157, 158, 160*t*, 165, 168
acidosis 6, 87
acidosis threshold (AT) training
    benefits of 103
        menstrual cycle and 134
        pace in 104
        performance and 12-13
        in periodized plan 134, 135*t*
        threshold defined 101
        threshold measurement 102-103, 102*f*
        as training component 84-85
        workout types in 105-106
actin 9, 10*f*
activity factors 189*t*
adductor stretch 181
adenosine diphosphate (ADP) 3-4, 4*f*
adenosine triphosphate (ATP) 3-6, 4*f*
adipose tissue 17. *See also* fat percentage
ADP 3-4, 4*f*
aerobic-capacity training 80-84, 93-98, 94*f*
aerobic-power training. *See* $\dot{V}O_2$max training
aerobic system 6
aging. *See* older runners
alcohol intake 152
alternating-leg bound 119
amenorrhea
    bone health and 14-15, 26, 149-150
    in female athlete triad 147
    stress fractures and 83, 158, 163
anaerobic-capacity training 87-88, 114-115, 136-137, 137*t*
anaerobic glycolysis 4-6, 8, 114
anaerobic-power training 115-116
anemia 202-203
anorexia nervosa 145-146
anovulation 147
anti-inflammatory medications 164
antioxidants 204-205
arch raisers 176
asthma 31
Åstrand, Per-Olof 86
Atalanta (Greek goddess) 207
AT and LSD combo run 106
athlete's heart 7
AT intervals 105
ATP 3-6, 4*f*

ATP-CP system 4, 115
AT run 105

B

Badwater Ultramarathon 21
barefoot running shoes 171
base building
    female athlete triad and 100
    menstrual cycle and 99, 132
    in periodized plan 132-134, 133*t*
    during pregnancy 100
    volume in 93-98, 94*f*
    workout types in 98-99
B-complex vitamins 76, 204
Benoit, Joan 208-209
birth control pills 32-33, 130, 150-151
bleacher hop 118
blood volume
    menstrual cycle and 28
    in pregnancy 41, 43, 45
    sex differences in 18
    training adaptation 81
body composition 17-18, 68-69, 83-84, 143
body temperature 27-28, 33, 40-41, 69
body weight 17, 33, 39, 199
bone mineral density
    aging and 69
    caloric restriction and 146
    in female athlete triad 148-152, 156
    hormone replacement therapy and 57-58
    hormones and 14-15
    increasing and maintaining 69, 151-152, 161-162
    measuring 54
    menopause and 53-55
    menstrual irregularity and 26
    nutrition and 58, 146, 162, 201-202
    oral contraceptives and 32-33, 150-151
    strength training for 60, 123, 152-155, 155*t*
    as stress fracture risk 150, 156, 163
    training volume and 150
bone remodeling 15-16, 162-163
Borg rating of perceived exertion (RPE) 40
Boston Marathon 208
box jump 121
breastfeeding 47-48
breathing 30-31

Budd, Zola 209
bulimia nervosa 145-146

C
calcium 58, 146, 162, 201-202
calf raise 127
calf stretches 182, 185
caloric intake
    amenorrhea and 26
    calculating needs 147-148, 188-189, 189*t*
    role in stress fractures 161-162, 163
    while breastfeeding 47-48
caloric restriction 146
carbohydrate
    glycemic index of 194
    intake of 190-194, 190*f*, 191*t*, 205-206
    metabolism of 20-21, 101
carbohydrate loading 206
cardiac drift 28
cardiac output 7, 41, 43
cardiorespiratory system
    aging and 66, 70-71
    menstrual cycle and 28
    in pregnancy 39-40
cardiovascular system
    performance and 7
    in pregnancy 41, 43
    sex differences in 18-19
    training adaptations 123
cholesterol 53
Cho-Pat straps 166
clamshells 173
consistency of training 83-84
CP 4
creatine kinase 116
creatine phosphate (CP) 4
cross-training
    during injury recovery 164, 165, 167
    for older runners 61*f*, 62*f*, 74
    during pregnancy 36
    in training plan 170

D
dead lift 129
Decker, Mary 208, 209
dehydration. *See also* hydration
    aging and 69
    heart rate and 28
    vs. hyponatremia 200
    pregnancy and 42
    preventing 198
    risks and warning signs 197-198
denervation 67-68
depth jump 120
Dill, David 9
double-leg bound 118
downhill running 90, 166, 170

dynamic stretches 178-182

E
eating disorders 145-146
eccentric contractions 90
electrolytes 199
endurance performance. *See* performance
energy balance 188
energy deficit 144-146
energy production 3-6, 4*f*
energy requirements 147-148, 187-189
estrogen
    in hormone replacement therapy 56
    in menopause 51-53
    men's need for 55
    in menstrual cycle phases 24-26
    in oral contraceptives 32-33
    performance and 28-29, 32, 130, 140
    role in recovery 138
    role in running injuries 157, 163
    as sex difference 13-15, 21
    strength training and 130

F
fall risks 59, 69
fartleks 91, 99
fast-twitch (type II) muscle fibers 11, 84
fat
    intake of 190*f*, 196-197, 205
    metabolism of 13, 21, 88-89
fatigue 5, 21, 29-30
fat percentage 17-18, 22, 143, 147
female athlete triad
    base building and 100
    bone mineral density in 148-152, 156
    component overview 143-144
    continuum of 144*f*
    menstrual disorders in 146-148
    performance effects of 156
    reduced energy availability in 144-146
    risk factors 149
flexibility in training routines 59, 131-132
flexibility training
    dynamic stretches 178-182
    for injury prevention 177-178
    for older runners 68, 75
    static stretches 182-185
foam rollers 167-168
follicle-stimulating hormone 15
follicular phase, of menstrual cycle 24, 27, 31, 99
fracture risks. *See* osteoporotic fractures; stress
    fractures
fueling during exercise 192, 195, 196-197. *See also*
    postexercise fueling; preexercise fueling

G
Gerschler, Waldemar 86-87

GI 194
Gibb, Roberta 208
gluteal stretches 178, 185
glycemic index (GI) 194
glycogen stores
    carbohydrate for 20-21, 190-194, 191t
    menstrual cycle and 28-29, 140
    training adaptation 81, 84
group training 88

H
hamstring curl 127
hamstring stretches 179-180, 183
Harris–Benedict equation 188-189, 189t
heart, enlarged 7
heart disease 53, 57
heart rate, in pregnancy 39-40, 41, 43
heat tolerance 27
heel drops 176
hill training 89-90, 99, 170
hip abduction with resistance 153
hip adduction with resistance 154
hip extension with resistance 153
hip flexion with resistance 152
hip flexor stretch 183
Holmér, Gösta 91
hormone replacement therapy 56-58, 130
hormones
    in menopause 51-53
    in menstrual cycle phases 23-26, 24f
    in oral contraceptives 32-33
    performance and 27-30, 32, 130, 139-140
    role in recovery 138
    role in running injuries 157, 163
    sex differences in 13-15, 21, 55
hot flashes 52, 57
Huxley, Andrew 9
hydration 76, 199-200. *See also* dehydration
hyperhydration 198
hyponatremia 200

I
iliotibial band 166, 167f
iliotibial band stretch 184
iliotibial band syndrome (ITBS) 157, 158, 160t, 166-168
injuries, common. *See also* specific types
    incidence of 158
    risk factors 158-159
    role of estrogen in 157
    types of 157, 160t
injury prevention
    flexibility training for 177-185
    strength training for 123, 172-177
    training volume and 82
intensity 40, 71, 74, 95
interval training

acidosis threshold workouts 105
    in periodized plan 134-135, 136t
    as training component 86-89
    for $\dot{V}O_2$max training 108-109
intramuscular triglyceride 17. *See also* fat percentage
iron 202-204
ITBS 157, 158, 160t, 166-168

J
joint pain, during pregnancy 39

K
knee braces and straps 166
knee pain and injuries
    iliotibial band syndrome 157, 158, 160t, 166-168
    patellofemoral pain syndrome 157, 158, 160t, 164-166
    risk factors 16

L
lactate 5, 29
lactate threshold training. *See* acidosis threshold (AT) training
lactic acid 5, 48
leg lifts, side-lying 172
long AT run 105
long runs 84, 98-99
low blood sugar 40, 191
lower-extremity loading 154-155, 155t
lung function 30-31
luteal phase, of menstrual cycle 25, 27-31, 99, 139-140
luteal-phase deficiency 147
luteinizing hormone 15, 24

M
macronutrients
    carbohydrate 20-21, 101, 190-194, 190f, 191t, 205-206
    in diet composition 190, 190f
    fat 13, 21, 88-89, 190f, 196-197, 205
    protein 22, 190f, 194-196, 205
marathons
    acidosis threshold workout for 106
    group training 88, 98, 103
    women's admission to 207-209
medial tibial stress syndrome 157
Melpomene (Greek runner) 207
menopause
    defined 49-51
    heart disease risk in 53
    hormone replacement therapy for 56-58
    osteoporosis and 53-56
    physiology and symptoms of 51-53
    running and 56
    stress fracture risk in 83

menopause *(continued)*
    training guidelines for 59-60
    training plans for 61-63*f*
menstrual cycle
    acidosis threshold (AT) training and 134
    anaerobic training and 116
    base building and 99, 132
    performance and 31-32
    phases of 23-26, 24*f*
    physiology of 27-31
    racing during 139-140
    strength training and 31, 130
    $\dot{V}O_2$max and 108, 112
menstrual disorders 26, 146-148. *See also* amenorrhea
metabolism
    aging and 68
    menstrual cycle and 28-29
    as performance factor 12-13
    in pregnancy 40
    sex differences in 19-22
micronutrients
    antioxidants 204-205
    B vitamins 76, 204
    calcium 58, 146, 162, 201-202
    exercise effects on 200-201
    iron 202-204
    vitamin D 58, 146, 162, 201-202
mileage. *See* volume of training
mitochondria 7, 8, 10, 81
monster walks 173
mood swings, menopausal 53
motherhood, balancing with training 85
motor learning 79
motor unit remodeling 68
motor units 11-12, 67-68
muscles
    aging and 66-68, 71
    blood flow to 7
    contractions of 9, 10*f*, 90
    fiber types 10-12
    menstrual cycle and 31
    oxygen use 8-9
    in pregnancy 39
    sex differences in 19
muscle soreness 5
muscle weakness 165
myosin 9, 10*f*

N
neuromuscular memory 79
night sweats, menopausal 52, 57
nutrition. *See also* dehydration; specific nutrients
    for bone health 58
    during exercise 192, 195, 196-197
    fluids 197-200
    macronutrients 190, 190*f*, 191*t*, 197
    micronutrients 200-205

    for older runners 76
    postexercise 20-21, 193, 195, 197
    preexercise 192, 195, 196, 205-206
    sensible advice 203

O
older runners
    nutrition and hydration for 76
    physiology of aging 65-69
    training adaptations in 69-71
    training recommendations for 71-75, 72-73*t*
oligomenorrhea 146-147
Olympic athletes 81, 82
Olympic Games 207-209
oral contraceptives 32-33, 130, 150-151
orthotics 165-166
osteoporosis. *See also* bone mineral density
    amenorrhea and 14-15, 26, 149-150
    defined 54, 148
    exercise for 56, 69
    hormone replacement therapy and 57-58
    menopause and 53-55
osteoporotic fractures 55. *See also* stress fractures
overuse injuries. *See* injuries, common
oxidative stress 204

P
pace 93-94, 95, 104
patellar tracking 164
patellofemoral pain syndrome 157, 158, 160*t*, 164-166
performance
    cardiovascular factors 7
    energy production and 3-6, 4*f*
    female athlete triad and 156
    hormones and 28-29, 32, 130, 139-140
    menstrual cycle and 27-32
    metabolic factors 12-13
    muscular factors 8-12
perimopause 50
periodized training phases. *See also* specific phases
    acidosis threshold (AT) training 134, 135*t*
    base building 132-134, 133*t*
    component emphasis in 137-138
    speed training 136-137, 137*t*
    $\dot{V}O_2$max training 134-135, 136*t*
phosphagen system 4, 115
plantar fasciitis 157, 160*t*, 165, 168-169
plyometric training
    benefits of 116
    exercises 117-121
    safety guidelines 122
    sample program 117*t*
PMS 25
polyunsaturated fat 196
postexercise fueling 20-21, 193, 195, 197
postmenopause 51

postpartum depression 47
postpartum exercise 46-47
postural stability 69
power 113-114
power clean 128
preexercise fueling 192, 195, 196, 205-206
pregnancy
     base building during 100
     exercise benefits during 36-37
     exercise contraindications during 37-39, 38*t*
     exercise goals during 42
     exercise guidelines for 35-36, 44
     physiology of 39-41
     postpartum exercise 46-47
     running during 41-46
premature menopause 50
premenstrual syndrome (PMS) 25
pressure effect on heart 123
progesterone
     in hormone replacement therapy 56
     in menstrual cycle phases 24-26
     in oral contraceptives 32-33
     performance and 27, 28-30, 32, 139-140
     as sex difference 15
pronation 164, 165-166, 168
protein 22, 190*f*, 194-196, 205

Q
Q-angle 16, 164
quadriceps stretches 181, 184

R
Radcliffe, Paula 209
rating of perceived exertion (RPE) 40
recovery
     for injury prevention 157
     in interval training 86-87
     for older runners 71, 74, 99
     postexercise fueling 20-21, 193, 195, 197
     from strength training 130
     training adaptations and 99, 159
     as training component 138
reduced energy availability 144-146
Reed, Pam 21
Reindell, Hans 86-87
respiratory alkalosis 30
rest, for injury treatment 163, 168, 169
Road Runners Club of America 88
Robinson, Betty 208
RPE 40
running bras 96
running economy 9, 31, 82

S
sarcopenia 67-68
saturated fat 196
Semple, Jock 208

sex chromosomes 13
sex differences
     anatomical 15-17
     body weight, composition 17-18
     cardiovascular 18-19
     hormonal 13-15
     metabolic 19-22
     muscular 19
     summary of 14*t*
shoes 168, 170-172
single-leg hop 117
size principle 12
sleep disturbances, menopausal 52, 57
slow-twitch (type I) muscle fibers 10-11
smoking 152
specificity of training 79-80
speed training
     anaerobic-capacity training 114-115
     anaerobic-power training 115-116
     in periodized plan 136-137, 137*t*
     plyometrics 116-122, 117*t*
     power and 113-114
     training volume and 83, 114
sport drinks 40, 192, 194, 199
sports bras 96
squat 126
squat jump 119
static stretches 182-185
step-downs 175
step-ups 174
strength training
     for bone mineral density 60, 123, 152-155, 155*t*
     exercises 126-129, 152-155, 172-177
     for injury prevention 123, 172-177
     for injury treatment 165, 168
     menstrual cycle and 31, 130
     for older runners 60, 61*f*, 62*f*, 68, 71, 74-75
     recovery from 130
     training adaptations 122-123
     as training component 124-130, 125*t*
stress fractures. *See also* osteoporotic fractures
     causes of 162-163
     described 159-161, 160*t*, 161*f*, 162*f*
     incidence of 158
     prevention of 161-162
     risk factors 26, 83, 150, 156, 157
     symptoms of 162
     treatment of 163-164
stretching. *See* flexibility training
stride mechanics 16-17
stroke volume 7, 28, 41, 43
surfaces 170
sweat rates 197
Switzer, Katherine 208

T
talk test 40

tapering 91, 206
Team in Training 88
testosterone 13-15
thermic effect of food 188
thermoregulation. *See* body temperature
towel roll (exercise) 177
training adaptations
    cardiovascular 7
    heat tolerance 27
    limits to 81-82
    in older runners 69-71
    recovery and 99, 159
    in strength vs. endurance training 122-123
    training volume and 81-84, 93
training plans. *See also* periodized training phases
    design tips for 170
    older runners 72-73t
    plyometrics 117t
    postmenopausal 61-63f
    strength training 125t, 155t
trans fat 196

U
urinary incontinence, menopausal 52-53
urine, as hydration indicator 199
USA Fit 88

V
vaginal dryness 52
vitamin C 204-205
vitamin D 58, 146, 162, 201-202
vitamin E 204-205
volume effect on heart 123
volume of training
    in base building 93-98, 94f
    bone mineral density and 150
    injury risk and 158-159, 169-170
    for older runners 74
    speed training and 114
    training adaptations and 81-84, 93

$\dot{V}O_2$max
    aging and 66, 70-71
    measuring 107-108
    menstrual cycle and 108
    performance factors and 8-9
    sex differences in 18-19, 22
    training volume and 83
$\dot{V}O_2$max test 102, 107-108
$\dot{V}O_2$max training
    interval training for 108-109
    menstrual cycle and 112
    pace for 109
    in periodized plan 134-135, 136t
    workouts 109-112, 111f

W
walking lunges 175
wall sits 174
weight gain 33, 39
weight loss
    body composition and 17, 143
    caloric intake and 188
    training volume and 82, 83
Wolff's law 162

Z
Zatopek, Emil 86

About the Authors

Jason Karp, PhD, is an exercise physiologist, a running and fitness expert, and the 2011 IDEA Personal Trainer of the Year. He offers science-based coaching to runners of all levels and consulting to coaches through his company, RunCoachJason.com. He is in demand as a presenter at numerous coaching, fitness, and academic conferences, including U.S. Track & Field and Cross Country Coaches Association, American College of Sports Medicine, American Society of Exercise Physiologists, and IDEA World Fitness Convention. Karp is also a prolific writer, with four books and more than 200 articles published in magazines, including *Runner's World, Running Times, Shape, Oxygen, Self,* and *Ultra-Fit.*

Karp has enjoyed success coaching at high school, college, and club levels. He has taught USA Track & Field's highest level of coaching certification and was an instructor at the USATF/U.S. Olympic Committee's Emerging Elite Coaches Camp at the U.S. Olympic Training Center. The founder and coach of REVO$_2$LT Running Team and a competitive runner himself, Dr. Karp is a USA Track & Field-certified coach and is sponsored by PowerBar as a member of PowerBar Team Elite.

Karp received his PhD in exercise physiology with a physiology minor from Indiana University in 2007, his master's degree in kinesiology from the University of Calgary in 1997, and his bachelor's degree in exercise and sport science with an English minor from Pennsylvania State University in 1995. Dr. Karp has taught exercise physiology and biomechanics at several universities and taught in the fitness certificate program at the University of California at Berkeley. He is currently an adjunct faculty member at Miramar College in San Diego, where he teaches applied exercise physiology.

Carolyn Smith, MD, is a family prac-

tice and sports medicine physician who serves as director of the student health service at Marquette University and the head medical team physician for the department of intercollegiate athletics. She also maintains her teaching interests in her role as medical director for the athletic training education program.

Smith is a versatile runner with a career that has spanned more than three decades. After a postcollegiate career running shorter distances, Smith embraced ultrarunning in 2002 and has enjoyed success in distances ranging from the 50-mile run to the 24-hour run. She is a former 24-hour and 100K national champion. She has had the privilege of representing the United States on two 24-hour national teams (2005, 2007) and is a 100K national team member (2004, 2007, 2008, 2009, 2010, 2011, 2012).

She is a national age-group record holder. In 2009, she held the fastest time in the world for the 50-mile ultramarathon and was ranked No. 1 in that event in the United States. In 2011 she set a national age-group record for the 12-hour run, finishing first among all participants in the FANS 12-hour ultramarathon in Minnesota, running 83 miles in 12 hours—more than 12 miles ahead of the second place finisher. She represented the United States for the seventh time in the 100-Kilometer World Championship, which was held in Italy in 2012. In 2012 the U.S. women's team won the gold medal, an accomplishment Smith was also a part of in 2009.

In addition to a medical degree from the University of Illinois, Smith holds a master's degree from Northern Illinois University and a bachelor's degree from the University of Wisconsin, both in exercise physiology. Following faculty positions with the St. Michael Hospital Residency Program in Milwaukee and the Medical College of Wisconsin, Smith joined the Marquette University student health service in 2002.